大学商务英语综合教程 1 学生用书

第二版
SECOND EDITION

主编
杨翠萍
蔡莉

江小娣 陈洁倩 吴朋
朱青 孔燕平 薛初晴 编
刘鸣放

清华大学出版社
北京

内 容 简 介

本教程选材涵盖当今国际经济贸易和商务的重要领域,时效性强、典型性高、语言地道。

教程板块设计突出国际商务知识的传授与英语技能提高的结合,注重培养学生的实际应用能力。每个单元重点讨论、分析一个商务专题,由"导入活动""阅读活动""商务实践"和"专业扩展"四部分组成。各部分内容的设计与编写坚持了操作性与挑战性并重的原则,以保持学生的学习热情和自觉实践的积极性。其中的"商务实践"板块围绕单元主题,参照各种真实的商务交际情景,为学生设计了灵活多样的商务英语口头与书面交际的任务,是本教程的一大特色。本教程配套精美教学课件,为教师课堂教学提供帮助。课件下载路径:ftp://ftp.tup.tsinghua.edu.cn。

本教程适合大学商务英语专业的学生及准备参加BEC(Business English Certificates)等商务英语考试的人员使用。

版权所有,侵权必究。举报:010-62782989,beiqinquan@tup.tsinghua.edu.cn。

图书在版编目(CIP)数据

大学商务英语综合教程学生用书.1/杨翠萍,蔡莉主编.—2版.—北京:清华大学出版社,2016(2024.9重印)
ISBN 978-7-302-44451-0

Ⅰ.①大… Ⅱ.①杨… ②蔡… Ⅲ.①商务–英语–高等学校–教材 Ⅳ.①H31

中国版本图书馆CIP数据核字(2016)第169632号

责任编辑:蔡心奕
封面设计:平 原
责任校对:王凤芝
责任印制:沈 露

出版发行:清华大学出版社
网 址:https://www.tup.com.cn,https://www.wqxuetang.com
地 址:北京清华大学学研大厦A座   邮编:100084
社 总 机:010-83470000   邮购:010-62786544
投稿与读者服务:010-62776969,c-service@tup.tsinghua.edu.cn
质量反馈:010-62772015,zhiliang@tup.tsinghua.edu.cn

印 装 者:涿州市般润文化传播有限公司
经 销:全国新华书店
开 本:185mm×260mm   印张:18.75   字数:365千字
版 次:2010年10月第1版 2016年8月第2版   印次:2024年9月第8次印刷
定 价:79.00元

产品编号:065958-03

第二版前言 Preface

《大学商务英语综合教程》（第2版）是一套依据现代外语教育对教材意义及功能的要求，结合应用语言学专门用途英语的最新研究成果设计和编写的、融英语语言知识及技能和国际商务知识及技能于一体的复合型英语教材。

本教材既可供高校英语专业或商务英语专业的本、专科学生使用，也可供国际经济贸易、金融、财会、工商管理等专业的学生作为复合型专业英语教材使用，还可作为大学英语选修课教材及相关行业的培训教材。

本教材的编写宗旨是：遵循现代外语教学理念和应用语言学专门用途英语的教学原则；充分考虑学习者在经济、贸易、金融、管理等方面的专业需求，力求以人为本，将英语技能的培养和专业知识的学习有机地结合起来，满足学生在专业和英语两方面的需求；提高学生的商务英语交际能力；拓宽学生的知识领域，全面提高学生的综合素质。

本教材是一套培养复合型、应用型人才的语言实践课教材，其设计和编写完全是从提高学生的综合语言应用能力出发，针对中国学生在商务英语方面的薄弱环节和实际需要，做到了有的放矢。教材的主要特点体现在以下几个方面：

一、选材新颖，内容丰富。本教材在选材上注重内容的知识性、趣味性、可思性、时效性和前瞻性，同时也注重语言的规范性和致用性。教材中专业知识覆盖面广，涉及了商务活动的各个方面，如市场竞争、营销策略、经营风险、企业管理、财税管理、商业文化、电子商务、国际化等。所用材料全部摘自国外主要经济、金融、管理等方面近年来的报刊、专业书籍以及因特网上的最新信息。而且，许多资料，如商务文件、信函、广告、产品说明书等都是来自某些企业、公司或公共场所的全真语料，旨在为学习者创造一个真实、生动的交际环境，有效地激发他们的学习欲望，使他们能自觉地提高自己用英语进行商务活动的能力。

二、以任务为路径，以交际为目的。本教材注重吸收国外商务英语教学及研究领域的成果，努力实现理论和实践的有机统一。教材遵循任务型编写原则，强调教学过程中的互动性，突出对学生交际能力的培养，通过灵活多样的商务活动情景或场合，为学习者设计了形式各异的交际任务，如双人讨论、小组讨论、角色扮演、情景模拟等，鼓励学生在完成任务的过程中发挥主动性，积极合作，将课堂所学用于实践，并将自己生活中的经历和观点融入交际活动中，以实现学以致用，提高交际能力的目的。

　　三、内容设计严谨，综合应用性强。本教材的每个单元由"导入活动（Lead-in）""阅读活动（Reading）""商务实践（Business Practice）"和"专业扩展（Relevant Extension）"四部分组成。各部分内容的设计与编写坚持了操作性与挑战性并重的原则，以保持学生的学习热情和自觉实践的积极性。

1. **导入活动** 以各种贴近学生生活、易于学生交流、与单元主题相关的内容为素材，设计了双人讨论和小组讨论等互动练习，旨在引发学生思考，激发他们对本单元内容的学习欲望。

2. **阅读活动** 主要围绕一篇与单元主题相关的文章进行。文章的长度适中，难易度由浅入深，其中的生词、习语、专有名词和有关表达等均有中英文注释，以帮助学生提高阅读效率。本教材注重提高学生分析问题的能力。每篇文章后面除了针对文中的观点、要点以及具体细节的理解设计讨论问题之外，还要求学生对文章的篇章结构和文体风格等进行分析、归纳，使他们在了解商务英语语言特色的基础上，明白文章形式与内容之间的关系，懂得观点的逻辑组织和清楚表达的重要性，从而对提高其写作能力提供一定的帮助。针对文章中重要的词或词组所设计的练习都以商务、经济等方面的内容为素材，而且形式多种多样，尽量避免重复，从而引发学生的新奇感，令其自觉参与活动。此外，这部分还设计了英汉互译练习，以增强学生的翻译技能，并提高其活学活用的能力。

3. **商务实践** 是本教材的重要特色。这部分围绕单元主题，参照各种真实的商务交际情景，为学习者设计了灵活多样的口头与书面交际的任务。在口头任务设计中，不仅注重培养学生的自主学习能力，同时还强调了研究性学习与合作性学习的重要性。多数活动要求学生以小组为单位，根据提示与指导，通过因特网和图书馆等途径获取有关资料，在小组研究与合作的基础上，规划实施各个步骤，最终实现交际目标。为了丰富输出内容和规范口语表达，这部分还给出了相关信息提示和常用表达范式。结合单元主题或口语练习，该板块还设计了关于各种商务应用文的写作练习，其中包括公司介绍、产品说明书、插页广告、备忘录、公司业务通信以及常见的贸易信函等，同时，提供了某些公司真实而优秀的商务文件作为范例，并对其构架及主要内容或表述方式进行了分析，以便于学生进行实践性写作练习。

4. **专业扩展** 是本教材的另一个重要特色。为了进一步满足学生对专业知识的需求，这部分根据单元主题设计了相关专业术语的巩固性练习和专业阅读练习。

鉴于学生在高年级还需分门别类、系统地学习专业课程，此处的练习避免过深过专，旨在使学生学习一些常用的专业术语，掌握一定的专业基础知识，提高他们在专业英语方面的阅读能力。另外，考虑到不少学生日后可能会参加 BEC（Business English Certificates）等商务英语考试，此处的练习从内容到形式都兼顾了这类考试的要求。所以，本教材也可以为学习者通过 BEC 或 TOEIC（托业）等国际商务英语考试提供很大的帮助。

四、学生配套用书各单元包括主题简介、课文相关信息注解、课文难句解释、常用词或词组学习、商务实践活动补充信息、课文参考译文，为教师的课堂教学实践和学习者的自主学习提供了有力的帮助和极大的方便。

五、本教程配套精美教学课件*，为教师课堂教学提供帮助。

《大学商务英语综合教程》（第二版）的编写立足本国，博采众长，力求新颖。教材宜采用糅合中外多种教学法之长的折中主义（eclecticism）教学法。教程每册由 10 个单元组成。建议每 6 个课时完成一个单元。但使用时，各校可根据情况灵活处理。

《大学商务英语综合教程》（第二版）为上海市教委第五期重点学科(外国语言学及应用语言学)资助项目（项目编号：A-3102-06-000），主要由上海对外经贸大学主持编写，邀请复旦大学、上海外国语大学、上海师范大学等院校多名具有丰富的商务英语教学经验的教师参与，由大家共同努力完成。此外，本教程还邀请国内商务英语教学领域的资深专家、上海对外经贸大学副校长叶兴国教授和美国达科他州立大学英语学院教授 John Nelson 博士对书稿进行了审阅。从教材编写体系的形成到文字内容的修改及润色，他们都提出了许多宝贵的建议，并给予热情的指导和帮助。清华大学出版社对此教程的编写提供了大力的支持。在此，我们教材编写组对所有关心、支持和帮助过该教材编写工作的领导、专家、教授以及有关同志一并表示衷心的感谢。

本教材从内容到形式有许多大胆的尝试，但由于编者的水平所限，书中难免有不妥或疏漏之处。欢迎外语界专家、同仁以及本教材的所有使用者批评指正。

编　者
2016 年 6 月

---

* 与本教程配套的教学课件，可以从清华大学出版社的资源库中免费下载。请访问 ftp://ftp.tup.tsinghua.edu.cn/，进入"外语分社"目录下，选择所需的课件。

Unit 1 Companies 1

Lead-in 2
Reading: **Wal-Mart: From Folk Hero to Corporate Monster** 3
Business Practice 11
Relevant Extension 15

Unit 2 Products 23

Lead-in 24
Reading: **The Product Life Circle** 25
Business Practice 36
Relevant Extension 43

Unit 3 Marketing 51

Lead-in 52
Reading: **What Is Marketing Anyway?** 53
Business Practice 62
Relevant Extension 70

Unit 4 Advertisements 75

Lead-in 76
Reading: **Advertising of, by, and for the People** 76
Business Practice 87
Relevant Extension 92

Unit 5 Sales 97

- Lead-in 98
- Reading: **A Sales Formula That's Pure Magic** 99
- Business Practice 110
- Relevant Extension 115

Unit 6 Consumers 121

- Lead-in 122
- Reading: **Power at Last** 122
- Business Practice 133
- Relevant Extension 136

Unit 7 Brands 143

- Lead-in 144
- Reading: **What, Exactly, Is a Brand?** 145
- Business Practice 155
- Relevant Extension 162

Unit 8 Business Leadership 169

- Lead-in 170
- Reading: **When It's Time to Think Again** 171
- Business Practice 181
- Relevant Extension 188

目 录

Unit 9　Teamwork 195

　　Lead-in... 196
　　Reading: **Executives Must Pull Together like Rowers
　　　　　　in the Boat Race**... 198
　　Business Practice... 208
　　Relevant Extension 214

Unit 10　Innovations 223

　　Lead-in... 224
　　Reading: **Businesses Must Learn to Let Go** 226
　　Business Practice... 236
　　Relevant Extension 243

　　附录 1　Glossary 253
　　附录 2　Phrases & Expressions 263
　　附录 3　Activity File 267

VII

UNIT 1
Companies

1. Look at the following logos of some renowned companies, and discuss the questions with your partner.

1) What company does each logo represent? What type of company does each of them belong to? (e.g. multinational corporation, private limited company, holding company, etc.)
2) Can you add to each type more companies with which you are familiar?
3) Besides the above, what other types of companies do you know?
4) What type of company would you like to work for? Why?

2. Work in groups. Try to name the leading companies of the following business sectors, and discuss about the competitive edges of these companies.

Business sectors	Leading companies	Competitive edges
Telecommunications		
Ratailing		
Banking		
Transport		

UNIT 1 Companies

续表

Business sectors	Leading companies	Competitive edges
Vehicle manufacturing		
Information technology		
Food and drink		
Tourism		

Preview: How did a seller of cheap goods become the mightiest global corporation? The growth of Wal-Mart goes something like this: in 1979 it racked up a billion dollars in sales. By 1993 it did that much business in a week; by 2001 it could do it in a day.

It's an amazing tale — one that drove Wal-Mart from rural Arkansas, where it was founded, to the top of the Fortune 500. Sam Walton, Wal-Mart's founder, pushed sales growth skillfully while squeezing costs with sophisticated information technology. He encouraged employees to sell better. Wal-Mart is the largest corporation in the world, but what has really changed in corporate America since 1955 are the important five small words: "How may we help you?"

Wal-Mart[1]: From Folk Hero to Corporate Monster

By Mallen Baker

[1] Few companies attract as much emotion as Wal-Mart. In a short time it has become the biggest and the most successful of its kind, **striding** across the world as a feared giant, the symbol of all that **epitomizes** the uncaring corporation. It has achieved this **unprecedented** success by **single-mindedly** and skillfully pursuing the lowest prices.

[2] Many trace the birth of discount retailing to 1962, the first year of operation for Kmart[2], Target[3] and Wal-Mart. But by that time, Sam Walton's[4] tiny chain of variety

---

1 Wal-Mart / ˈwɔːl mɑːt / 沃尔玛,世界知名的美国零售业连锁集团
2 Kmart / kˈmɑːt / 凯马特公司,美国零售业企业,现代超市型零售业的鼻祖
3 Target / ˈtɑːɡɪt / 塔格特公司,美国零售业企业,凯马特公司的主要竞争对手
4 Sam Walton / ˈsæm ˈwɔːltən / 山姆·沃尔顿,沃尔玛的创始人

stores in Arkansas[1] and Kansas[2] was already facing competition from regional discount chains. Sam traveled the country to study this **radical**, new retailing concept and was convinced it was the wave of the future. He and his wife, Helen, put up 95 percent of the money for the first Wal-Mart store in Rogers[3], Arkansas, borrowing heavily on Sam's vision that the American consumer was shifting to a different type of general store.

[3] As a man with few **pretensions**, Sam Walton sought to become successful in retail by cutting out **middlemen** and selling goods to the public at the lowest possible prices. Walton's early stores were **phenomenally** successful because there was a huge market of relatively poorer people in the out-of-town communities in the United States who **embraced** the opportunity to own the clothes and other goods that would otherwise have been out of their reach.

[4] In the early days, it was a real **underdog** story. The established retailers did their best to **undermine** and punish the upstart who challenged what had become a comfortable, closed shop. But Sam Walton, the **eccentric** who even once had become a billionaire still **hauled** his gun dogs about in his **beaten-up** truck, was **indefatigable** in locating people who would sell to him at rock bottom prices.

[5] The Wal-Mart approach didn't seem to be predicated on simply making the biggest profit. Clarence Leis[4] noted in Walton's **autobiography**: "Sam wouldn't let us **hedge** on a price at all. Say the list price was $1.98 but we had only paid 50 cents. Initially I would say 'Well, it's originally $1.98, so why don't we sell it for $1.25?'" And he'd say. 'No. We paid 50 cents for it. Mark it up 30 percent, and that's it. No matter what you pay for it, if we get a great deal, pass it on to the customer.'" Uncomfortable though it may be for many anti-corporate warriors, such an approach is considered by many customers to represent the front line of social responsibility.

[6] In addition, the success of Wal-Mart lies in an understanding of what consumers want from a retailer. "The secret of successful retailing is to give your customers what they want," Sam wrote in his autobiography. "And really, if you think about it from the point of view of the customer, you want everything: a wide **assortment** of good quality **merchandise**; the lowest possible prices; guaranteed satisfaction with what you buy; friendly, knowledgeable service; convenient hours; free parking; a pleasant shopping experience. You love it when you visit a store that somehow **exceeds** your expectations,

---

1 Arkansas /ˈɑːk(ə)nsɔː/ 阿肯色州（美国）
2 Kansas /ˈkænzəs/ 堪萨斯州（美国）
3 Rogers /ˈrəudʒəz/ 罗杰斯城，美国阿肯色州北部一城市，是畜牧区和旅游区的加工中心
4 Clarence Leis /ˈklærənsˈleis/ 克拉伦斯·雷斯，沃尔玛一行政官员

and you hate it when a store **inconveniences** you, or gives you a hard time, or pretends you're invisible."

[7] While other discounters such as Kmart quickly expanded across the country in the 1960s, Sam was able to raise the funds to build only 15 Wal-Mart stores. Wal-Mart got the **boost** it needed in 1970, when its stock was offered for the first time on the New York Stock Exchange[1]. The public offering created the capital infusion that grew the company to 276 stores by the end of the decade. By focusing on customer expectations, Wal-Mart was growing rapidly in 11 states.

[8] In the 1980s, Wal-Mart became one of the most successful retailers in America. Sales grew to $26 billion by 1989, compared to $1 billion in 1980. Employment increased **tenfold**. At the end of the decade there were nearly 1,400 stores. Wal-Mart Stores, Inc.[2] branched out into warehouse clubs with the first SAM'S Club[3] in 1983. The first **supercenter**, featuring a complete grocery department along with the 36 departments of general merchandise, opened in 1988.

[9] Today, Sam's gamble is a global company with more than 1.8 million **associates** worldwide and nearly 6,500 stores and wholesale clubs across 15 countries. Wal-Mart has become a textbook example of managing rapid growth without losing sight of a company's basic values. In Wal-Mart's case, the basic value was, and is, customer service.

(748 words)
From *Business Respect*

New Words

stride / straɪd /
v. walk with long steps; pass over in one step 大步跨过

epitomize / ɪˈpɪtəmaɪz /
v. contain or express in brief the whole of; be a perfect example of 成为……的缩影；集中体现

unprecedented / ʌnˈpresɪdəntɪd /
a. that has not previously occurred 前所未有的；空前的

single-mindedly / ˌsɪŋglˈmaɪndɪdlɪ /
ad. wholeheartedly, with one's heart and soul 专心致志地

radical / ˈrædɪkl /
a. advanced in opinions and policies 激进的

pretension / prɪˈtenʃn /
n. the unwarranted claim of great merit or importance 自负，自命不凡

middleman / ˈmɪdlmæn /
n. a trader who handles a commodity between its producer and its customer 中间商

---

1 New York Stock Exchange 纽约证券交易所
2 Wal-Mart Stores, Inc. 沃尔玛百货有限公司
3 SAM'S Club 山姆会员店，美国沃尔玛百货有限公司的一个分支机构

phenomenally / fəˈnɒmɪnəlɪ /
ad. remarkably; extraordinarily 非凡地；非常地

embrace / ɪmˈbreɪs /
v. make use of; take advantage of (an opportunity); accept an idea, a proposal, a set of beliefs, etc., especially when it is done with enthusiasm 抓住（机会）；欣然接受

underdog / ˈʌndədɒɡ /
n. a person in the process of being losing or defeated in a fight or a contest; a person who is in a state of inferiority or subjection 竞争失败者；处于劣势者

undermine / ˌʌndəˈmaɪn /
v. weaken gradually; ruin 逐渐削弱；破坏，损坏

eccentric / ɪkˈsentrɪk /
a. (of a person, behavior) habitually unusual; odd（人、行为等）古怪的；偏执的

haul / hɔːl /
v. pull or draw with force 用力拖或拉

beaten-up
a. shabby; damaged by overuse; worn out 年久失修的；残破的，破旧的

indefatigable / ˌɪndɪˈfætɪɡəbl /
a. unable to be tired out; untiring 不倦的；不屈不挠的

autobiography / ˌɔːtəbaɪˈɒɡrəfɪ /
n. the writing of one's own history; a story of a person's life written by himself or herself 自传

hedge / hedʒ /
v. minimize or protect against the loss by counterbalancing one transaction, such as a bet, against another 做两面买卖以防损失；两面下注

assortment / əˈsɔːtmənt /
n. collection of different things of one class or of several classes 属于一类或数类的各色物品之集合

merchandise / ˈmɜːtʃəndaɪz /
n. goods bought or sold 商品；货品

exceed / ɪkˈsiːd /
v. pass beyond 超出，超越

inconvenience / ˌɪnkənˈviːnɪəns /
v. cause difficulty, discomfort, unfitness, etc. 使感到不便；感到困难

boost / buːst /
n. a push; a promotion 上升，提高
v. increase; raise; stir up enthusiasm for, promote vigorously 增加；拔高；增强；激起……的热情；强有力地宣传

tenfold / ˈtenfəʊld /
n. ten times 十倍

supercenter / ˌsuːpəˈsentə /
n. a very large discount department store that also sells a complete line of grocery merchandise 超级中心；集规模较大的商场和小副食品商店为一体的、为顾客提供一站式消费服务的商场

associate / əˈsəʊʃɪeɪt /
n. person who has been joined with others in business undertaking; partner 共同经商者，合伙人

Phrases & Expressions

folk hero
someone that people in a particular place admire because of something special they have done 民间英雄

corporate monster
a corporation that conducts strongly unfavorable and avaricious business practices, and sometimes intends to force many small businesses to go defunct, and is usually anti-union or anti-competitive 企业巨头

variety stores
shops selling many kinds of small items 小百货商店；杂货店

UNIT 1 Companies

put up
   provide (money) as backing for an enterprise 提供（资金）

cut out
   defeat; eliminate (a rival in competition)（在竞争中）击败对手；排挤对方

closed shop
   a workshop or other establishments where only members of a trade union may be employed（根据工会与资方协议）只雇用某一工会会员的商店

gun dog
   a dog trained to retrieve for a gamekeeper or the members of a shoot 猎犬

rock bottom price
   the lowest possible price 最低价格

predicated on
   based on 使基于

pass... on to
   hand or give sth. (to sb. else), esp. after receiving or using it oneself 将某物传、交给（某人）

anti-corporate warriors
   反公司强硬派

front line
   the most important, advanced or responsible position 最重要的、最前面的或责任最大的位置

lie in
   depend on; rest or centre in 在于

capital infusion
   the pouring of accumulated wealth 资金注入

branch out
   (of business, firm, etc.) expand in a new direction, open new departments or lines of activities （指公司、业务等方面）向新的方向发展，扩充范围

lose sight of
   overlook sth.; fail to consider sth. 忽略或未考虑某事

wholesale club
   a retail store that sells a limited assortment of merchandise to customers who are members of the club 批发式会员店

warehouse club
   a giant store that sells merchandise in bulk at low prices, and in which customers must buy a membership in order to shop 仓储式零售商店，大型零售商店

Exercises

Comprehension

1. Answer the following questions with your partner.

   1) How did Wal-Mart achieve its unprecedented success?

2) When did discount retailing come into being?

3) What challenge did Sam Walton's chain of variety stores face in 1962?

4) What kind of strategy was adopted in Walton's early stores?

5) According to Sam, what is the secret of successful retailing?

6) How do customers feel about the Wal-Mart approach?

7) What happened to Wal-Mart in 1970?

8) What was the prominent feature of the first Supercenter?

9) How big is Wal-Mart today?

10) What is the basic strategy of Wal-Mart?

2. This passage can be divided into three parts. Work with your partner to complete the outline. Part of it has been done for you.

Parts	Main ideas
Part I (Para. 1)	Introduction: _____
Part II (Paras. 2-6)	Factors determing the success of Wal-Mart: _____
	1) _____
	2) _____
Part III (Paras. 7-9)	_____

Critical Thinking

Work in group to discuss the following questions.

1) The writer refers in the title to Wal-Mart as a "corporate monster". How do you understand it? What points and evidence might you provide to support your understanding?

2) Recently Wal-Mart has embarked upon an environmental effort, building more environmentally friendly stores and encouraging the use of energy-efficient light bulbs. How do these efforts fit with the corporate strategy described in the reading?

UNIT 1 Companies

Vocabulary

1. Use the words given below to write sentences with *company* or a paragraph concerning *company*.

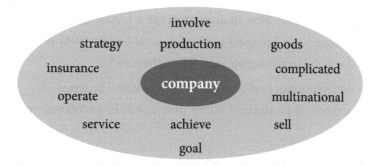

2. Fill in the blanks with the proper forms of the words or phrases given in the box.

assortment	borrow on	guarantee	pursue	radical	pass...on to
convince	epitomize	gamble	put up	stride	undermine

1) Automation isn't a(n) _____ of customer satisfaction, even if it does improve productivity.

2) The company is planning to _____ a considerable sum of money for an important sales campaign to promote their latest product.

3) In contrast to many relatively cheap fashion clothes, young people are generally _____ products with global brands when it comes to jeans.

4) We have a natural tendency to _____ blame _____ other people for failures, rather than attributing the poor performance to external and contextual factors.

5) No matter how we call it, the service economy, the information age, or the knowledge society, a new era that _____ a fundamental change in the way we work, is upon us.

6) After having studied a large number of organizations and leaders, John Gardner was _____ that there were some qualities or attributes that did appear to mean that a leader in one situation could lead in another.

7) Global markets offer greater opportunity for people to _____ forward into more and larger markets around the world.

8) Global disapproval of US foreign policy has become so intense that it is spilling over and _____ the image of US brands and culture.

9) Don't _____ things that you don't believe in and that you yourself are not good at.

10) This plaza deals in famous-brand Chinese and foreign products in great _____ and gives good services.

11) They had financed their company in a most honest and simple way; and they were desperately opposed to the financial banditti whose purpose was to transform the telephone business into a cheat and a _____.

12) The new economic reality should be investigated in terms of _____ shifts in the mode of production rather than a shift in sectoral composition of the economy.

3. Rewrite the following italicized parts by using the appropriate words or expressions from the text.

1) Microsoft has never *paid little attention* to the notion that if you give people the right tools, they will do new and exciting things.

2) Successful strategies *are based on* a thorough understanding of the capabilities of the business relative to the competition and the strategies, objectives, and intentions of the competitors.

3) Nike tells young people everywhere to surpass themselves, to *go beyond* the confines of their race and culture.

4) The pizza ad in the newspaper indicates that you can buy all kinds of the advertised pizza *at reduced prices*.

5) Business keeps moving faster and you'd better make *untiring* efforts to keep your strategy in line with changes in the business and its environment.

6) The friendly transaction reflects just how much the balance of power has *moved* from makers of consumer goods to giant discount retailers in recent years.

7) Wal-Mart, in fact, is the first service company to rise to the top of the *Fortune 500*, which *has never occurred before* in America.

8) We're already on the way to *expand* into an economy that is full of new participants: agents, objects, and machines, as well as several billion more humans.

Translation

1. Translate the following sentences into Chinese.

   1) In a short time Wal-Mart has become the biggest and the most successful

of its kind, striding across the world as a feared giant, the symbol of all that epitomizes the uncaring corporation.

2) It has achieved this unprecedented success by single-mindedly and skillfully pursuing the lowest prices.

3) As a man with few pretensions, Sam Walton sought to become successful in retail by cutting out middlemen and selling goods to the public at the lowest possible prices.

4) Walton's early stores were phenomenally successful because there was a huge market of relatively poorer people in the out-of-town communities in the United States who embraced the opportunity to own the clothes and other goods that would otherwise have been out of their reach.

2. **Put the following sentences into English, using the words and phrases given in the brackets.**

   1) 企业的主要功能在于迎合社会需求，生产物品，提供服务，从而创造社会价值，同时通过不断地为社会提供就业岗位为企业主和股东们创造利润。（lie in, merchandise, value, offering）

   2) 今天，企业界逐渐形成了一个基本观念，那就是，如果企业要不断获得成功，就不能完全依靠短期内追求最大利润，而是要靠其市场导向的、负责任的行为。（pursue）

   3) 一个公司必须认识到，要获得持续长久的发展，就要改变经营管理模式，加快经济增长，提高竞争能力；同时要致力于保护环境，承担社会责任，包括保护消费者的利益。（convinced, embrace, boost, shifting, focus on）

Company Presentation

Making an impressive company presentation to the potential customers can contribute a lot to the successful promotion of the company's products or services. Work in group of four. Suppose you are representatives of different companies, meeting at an international trade fair. You need to introduce your company in order to promote your products. Turn to page 267. The steps are as follows.

1) Each of you choose a role card and read the given information.
2) Prepare an introduction for a presentation about yourself and the company you work for.
3) Make your presentation to your group members, trying to answer any questions they ask. Your presentation should include at least the following points:

- *name of company;*
- *headquarters;*
- *business activities;*
- *main markets;*
- *competitive edges;*
- *others...*

Presentation Tips

The company presentation is one of the important ways that your company values and brand are communicated. Before you start putting together your slides, think about what your audience want to hear and not what you want to tell them. Do they really care about the arcane detail of your company structure? They may be more interested in understanding about how your unique proposition could directly benefit them. Always think about the key things you want your audience to remember. Here are a few tips.

◆ Greet the audience and tell them who you are. Good presentations follow this formula:

- tell the audience what you are going to tell them;
- then tell it to them;
- at the end tell them what you have told them.

◆ Keep to the time allowed. If you can, keep it short. It's better to under-run than over-run.

◆ Stick to the plan for the presentation. Don't be tempted to digress.

◆ Unless explicitly told not to, leave time for discussion and allow clarification of points.

UNIT 1 Companies

Language Hints

Greeting
- Good morning / afternoon, I'm ...
- Hello, everyone. Nice to see you.
- ...

Outlining
- I'll first tell you some basic information about our company.
- Then, I'll talk about the business activities and main markets of our company.
- Last of all, I want to present you our future plans.
- ...

Add new information
- Well, here are some statistics.
- Now, let's look at some additional figures.
- Let me tell you how we stand out internationally.
- Do you know what our strengths are?
- ...

Ending
- At last, I'd like you to know about our next plan.
- Finally, I have a few words about our new products.
- Thanks for listening to my talk.
- ...

Company Profile

As a representative of your company, you need to present a favorable first-sight impression on the minds of your company's potential customers and clients. Therefore, an attractive and well-written profile is indispensable because it can help to enhance your company's public image. A company profile usually includes the following:

- a general introduction, i.e., the company's brief history, its business field, its position in the trade, etc.;
- the company's present situation, including its assets, producing capabilities, performances, etc.;
- corporate culture, such as the company's working philosophy, expertise and so on.

The above items are optional according to the actual conditions of individual companies.

The tone of writing should be confident, sincere and polite. Do not exaggerate. The style is rather formal.

Study the following sample, and write a 150-word profile for one of the companies in the above oral exercise. Add anything necessary.

Sample

Bank of China

Brilliant history

Established in 1912, Bank of China is the oldest bank in China. It has been ranked one of the world's top banks in terms of core capital by The Banker. For over 100 years, Bank of China has played an important role in promoting China's economic and social progress through its active involvement in the country's international trade and financial activities.

Wide range of services

Bank of China is the first and the only Chinese bank that has presence in all major continents. At present the bank offers a wide range of financial services, including sales and investment financing, fund management and insurance. The bank provides services through its global networks of over 560 overseas offices in 25 countries and regions. In Hong Kong and Macao, Bank of China is one of the local note-issuing banks.

Our mission

With its proud 100-year history, Bank of China will continue to build on what has already been achieved to date, and leap forward with renewed energy to create an even greater organization in the future.

Benefits for customers

With our customers we want to create growth. To do this we can

- connect industry and technology know-how with the financial markets,
- offer new financial products and solutions, which we develop together with our customers, and
- give fast and friendly support.

> Company profiles are often found in publicity material.

> Tell the company's brief history.

> Tell what the company does.

> Make the customer see why the company is the best.

> Write in a tone of being confident, sincere and polite.

> Use the bullet points to highlight the main points.

UNIT 1 Companies

Business Expressions

1. Match the expressions in the box with the definitions below and translate them into Chinese.

joint stock company	general partnership
sole proprietor	public limited company
offshore company	listed company
limited liability company	holding company
conglomerate	investment company
multinational company	subsidiary company
joint venture	parent company
trust company	blue-chip company

   1) a type of business partnership in which the capital is formed by the individual contributions of a group of shareholders

   _____   _____

   2) a legal form of business company offering limited liability to its owners, which is similar to a corporation, and is often a more flexible form of ownership, especially suitable for smaller companies with a limited number of owners

   _____   _____

   3) a type of business entity which legally has no separate existence from its owner

   _____   _____

   4) an association of persons or an unincorporated company, which is formed by two or more persons, created by agreement, proof of existence and estoppel, and whose owners are all liable for legal actions and debts the company may face personally

   _____   _____

   5) a type of limited company whose shares may be offered for sale to the public

6) a company that owns part, all, or a majority of other companies' outstanding stock

7) a company that owns enough voting stock in another firm to control management and operations by influencing or electing its board of directors

8) an entity formed between two or more parties to undertake economic activity together

9) organization which acts as a fiduciary, trustee or agent for individuals and businesses in the administration of trust funds, estates and custodial arrangements

10) an entity that is controlled by another entity

11) a large business organization consisting of several different companies that have joined together

12) a company which does business in many countries

13) a company that has securities listed on the Stock Exchange

14) a company incorporated in a country where there is little government control and /or low tax rates

15) a company renowned for the quality and wide acceptance of its products or services, and for its ability to make money and pay dividends

16) a financial institution that sells shares to individuals and invests in securities issued by other companies

UNIT 1 Companies

2. Complete the following sentences with the words or expressions in the box.

ownership	restructuring
share capital	private limited company
overseas-funded enterprise	board of directors
civilian-run company	amalgamation
takeover	fold up
wholesale	transnational company
shareholders	retail

1) If a company sells directly to public, it is a(n) _____ business.
2) A(n) _____ business sells goods in bulk to other companies.
3) _____ only lose what they invested if the company goes bankrupt.
4) Unlike a public limited company, a(n) _____ is restricted from selling shares to the public.
5) A(n) _____ has global operations in many different countries.
6) Companies can be funded by _____, money raised from investors who bought shares.
7) Companies can be owned by shareholders who elect a(n) _____ to make business decisions and set company policy.
8) A company is bought by another company in a(n) _____, which can be friendly or hostile.
9) Funding influences the type of _____.
10) An ordinary _____ is a merger of at least two companies into a single entity.
11) _____ is often done as part of a bankruptcy or of a takeover by another firm, particularly a leveraged buyout by a private equity firm.
12) Governments at all levels shall treat _____ equally with state-owned enterprises in recommending enterprises to be listed and issue corporate bonds.
13) As the most active and earliest _____ engaged in the China's rural education, Coca-Cola company has set up 52 Coca-Cola Hope-Project Primary

17

Schools and built 100 Hope-Project Libraries with its donations in China's 26 provinces.

14) Several large banks in America and Europe _____ during the recent economic crisis.

3. **Fill in the gaps of the following passage with the words or expressions in the box. Change the form where necessary.**

sole trader	personal funds	Non-limited companies
Annual Returns	financial information	the public
finance	national defense	legal requirement
property	Limited companies	stock exchange
shareholders	public service	liability

　　It is important to distinguish between public and private sector organizations, as they will have very different characteristics and objectives.

　　The public sector organizations are 1) _____ by the state and they do not operate in order to make a profit but to provide a 2) _____. Examples of public sector organizations are schools, hospitals, libraries, police and the 3) _____. The private sector organizations operate in order to make a profit and are split into two categories: non-limited companies and limited companies.

　　4) _____ can be set up with relatively few formalities. It can be either a 5) _____ or partnership and the owner(s) will be personally liable for all of the debts if the business fails. There is no 6) _____ for non-limited companies to make any of their 7) _____ public.

　　8) _____ can be either privately owned when they are referred to as Limited (often abbreviated to Ltd) or publicly owned(Plc). Some Plc's can sell shares to members of the public on the 9) _____, unlike Ltd's that cannot. The 10) _____ for both Ltd's and Plc is limited. This means that if the company fails, the liability of the company's 11) _____ is limited to the value of the shares and not their 12) _____. All Limited companies are legally required to submit Company Accounts and 13) _____ every year. This information is available to 14) _____. A limited company has similar rights to a person; for example' it can buy assets, own 15) _____ and it can sue or be sued independently of its directors.

UNIT **1** Companies

Specialized Reading

1. Forms of businesses can be different in ownership, management and structure. Read the following passage about forms of business and choose the correct statement from A-F to fill each gap marked 1)-5). One statement is extra.

> A. A corporation provides the owner with limited liability.
> B. In fact, the largest 500 corporations account for about 80 percent of the total receipts of all U.S. businesses.
> C. Corporations' limited liability makes it easier for them to attract investment capital.
> D. A large percent of most corporations' stock is controlled by financial institutions.
> E. Proceeds from the sale of that stock make up what is called the equity capital of a company.
> F. In corporations, ownership is separated from control of the firm.

The three primary forms of business are sole proprietorships, partnerships, and corporations. Of the 25 million businesses in the United States, approximately 72 percent are sole proprietorships, 8 percent are partnerships, and 20 percent are corporations. In terms of total receipts, however, we get a quite different picture, with corporations far surpassing all other business forms. 1) _____.

Sole proprietorships, businesses that have only one owner, are the easiest to start and have the fewest bureaucratic hassles. Partnerships, businesses with two or more owners, create possibilities for sharing the burden, but they also create unlimited liabilities for each of the partners. Corporations, businesses that are treated as a person and are legally owned by their stockholders who are not liable for actions of the corporate "person", are the largest form of business when measured in terms of receipts. 2) _____. When a corporation is formed, it issues stock (certificates of ownership in a company) which is sold or given to individuals. 3) _____.

Corporations were developed as institutions to make it easier for company owners to be separated from company management. 4) _____. The stockholder's liability is limited to the amount that stockholder has invested in the company. With the other two forms of business, owners can lose everything they possess even if they have only a small amount invested in the company, but in a corporation the owners can lose only what they have invested in that corporation. If you've invested $100, you can lose only $100. In the other kinds of business, even if you've invested only $100, you could lose everything; the business's losses must be covered by the individual owners. 5) _____. Corporations pay taxes, but they also offer their individual owners ways of legally avoiding taxes.

2. **Read another passage and do the multiple-choice exercises.**

When a corporation is formed, it issues stock, which is sold or given to individuals. Ownership of stock entitles you to vote in the election of a corporation's directors, so in theory holders of stock control the company. In practice, however, in most large corporations, ownership is separated from control of the firm. Most stockholders have little input into the decisions a corporation makes. Instead, corporations are often controlled by their managers, who often run them for their own benefit as well as for the owners'. The reason is that the owners' control of management is limited.

A large percent of most corporations' stock is not even controlled by the owners; instead, it is controlled by financial institutions such as mutual funds (financial institutions that invest individuals' money for them) and by pension funds (financial institutions that hold people's money for them until it is to be paid out to them upon their retirement). Thus, ownership of corporations is another step removed from individuals. Studies have shown that 80 percent of the largest 200 corporations in the United States are essentially controlled by managers and have little effective stockholder control.

Why is the question of who controls a firm important? Because economic theory assumes the goal of business owners is to maximize profits, which would be true of corporations if stockholders made the decisions. Managers don't have the same incentives to maximize profits that owners do. There's pressure on managers to maximize profits, but that pressure can often be weak or ineffective. An example of how firms deal with this problem involves stock options. Many companies give their managers stock options — rights to buy stock at a low price — to encourage them to worry about the price of their company's stock. But these stock options dilute the value of company ownership and decrease profits per share and can give managers an incentive to overstate profits through accounting gimmicks, as happened at Enron, Xerox, and a number of other firms.

1) Some most powerful American corporations are primarily controlled by _____.

A. owners　　　　　　　　　B. stockholders

C. managers   D. mutual funds

2) Why can't the holders of the stock control the company?

　　A. Because they are separated from the managers.

　　B. Because they have a little input in making decisions.

　　C. Because they are limited in the control of management.

　　D. Because they are limited to the ownership of the company.

3) Which of the following statements is true of ownership of corporations?

　　A. Ownership is controlled by managers.

　　B. Ownership is separated from control of the company.

　　C. Ownership is removed from the stockholders.

　　D. Ownership is controlled by financial institutions.

4) What is used to encourage managers to maximize profits?

　　A. Stock option.   B. The right to own stock.

　　C. Controlling power.   D. Effective stockholder control.

5) Which of the following is NOT the disadvantage of stock option?

　　A. Dilution of the company value.

　　B. Profit decrease per share.

　　C. Profit overstatement through accounting tricks.

　　D. Stock purchase at a high price.

6) Which of the following is the best title of the passage?

　　A. Who Controls Corporation?

　　B. When Should the Stock Be Issued?

　　C. Importance of Financial Institutions

　　D. Stockholders and Managers

3. **Discuss the following questions with your group members.**

1) What are the advantages and disadvantages of the above-mentioned three forms of business?

2) What kind of company would you like to have if you could own one? Why?

UNIT 2
Products

1. Look at the following advertisement pictures, and discuss the questions below with your partner.

1) Are the products in the pictures famous in your country? How do you know them and what do you think of them?

2) Have you ever tried or bought the products? Tell about your personal experience of the products.

3) Besides these products, can you list any others which are famous in your country? And tell why they are popular with customers.

2. Work in groups for the following questions.

1) What are products?

2) What are the factors you should consider before you buy a product? Choose a luxury item you might buy, and rank the following factors from 1 to 5. Here, 1 is of the utmost importance, while 5 of the least importance. Now choose a device that would provide safety for your family. Don't forget to give reasons to support the ranking you have done.

Price (affordable?) ☐

Brand ☐

Appearance (color, shape, size, etc.) ☐

Function ☐

Warranty ☐

UNIT **2** Products

Quality	☐
Delivery	☐
After-sales services	☐
Complimentary gift	☐
…	☐

3) Match the words in the box to the corresponding meanings given below. Then arrange the 8 steps in a logical order to show the life cycle of a new product.

| manufacture | design | launch | test |
| discontinue | distribute | modify | promote |

a. change in order to improve   _____

b. build or make   _____

c. stop making   _____

d. introduce to the market   _____

e. try something to see how it works   _____

f. make a plan or drawing   _____

g. supply to shops, companies, customers   _____

h. increase sales by advertising, etc.   _____

The logical order:

  f   ___ ___ ___ ___ ___ ___ ___

Preview: In marketing, the term "product" is often used as a general word to identify solutions a marketer provides to its target market. Following this approach, we can classify products into these three categories: goods, services and ideas. A new product progresses through a sequence of stages from introduction to growth, maturity, and decline. This sequence is known as the product life cycle and is associated with changes in the marketing situation, thus impacting the marketing strategy and the marketing mix.

The Product Life Circle

By Sarah White

[1] The word "product" **covers** a lot more than the obvious **tangible**, physical articles available for sale. A product can be a service, like dry-cleaning or management consulting. A product can also be a concept you would like an audience to believe. You might be selling support for a person, place, event, organization, or idea.

[2] Your "product" will most likely be a combination of tangible items, services, and beliefs. That is why I like to use the word **offering**. What you offer customers will almost certainly contain elements of each. A haircut is a product, but it results from the service of cutting hair. A political candidate is in many ways a product, promising to **function** in a way that solves problems for you if you elect the candidate to office. Non-profit agencies sell feelings, asking us to support activities that make us feel good about doing good. Each of these examples represents a **discreet** "offering" someone is asking an audience to buy or buy into.

[3] As a marketer, you must understand something about the life cycle of your products. If one product is **slipping** in popularity, you need to have something else in the pipeline. How do you develop new products? Are there **innovations** you can bring to current products, to make them "new and improved"?

[4] The basic product life cycle goes like this: you introduce a product. If it's halfway successful, it passes from introduction into a growth **phase**. Eventually it reaches **maturity**, which is then followed by a nearly inevitable stage of decline. Products not only go through this cycle, but whole product **categories** do as well. Think about wine coolers, a classic marketing flash in the pan. The category was created by wine manufacturers, looking for an alternative to beer to offer young drinkers. The first products were created by Seagrams[1] and Gallo[2], names of **long-standing** with deep pockets to draw on and mature products elsewhere in their **families**.

[5] Once the big boys had used their muscle to introduce the concept of sweet, fruity, slightly alcoholic drinks, other upstarts came on the scene. But the crowd they appealed to, the 20-something drinkers, are **notoriously fickle** consumers. Wine coolers lost their **fizz** after only a couple of years on the market. At the bitter end of the category's life cycle, Coors[3] introduced Zima[4], a "clear beer". Sales were disappointing.

---

1 Seagrams / ˈsiːɡræms / 施格兰公司，美国酿酒公司
2 Gallo / ˈɡæləu / 嘉露公司，美国最大的葡萄酒酿造公司
3 Coors / ˈkɔːs / 美国康盛啤酒有限公司
4 Zima / ˈzɪmɑ / 瑞玛，康盛啤酒有限公司生产的清麦芽啤酒

To **invigorate** the **languishing** brand, Busch[1] added a **sibling brew**, now **amber** in color, called "Zima Gold". Are we back to beer yet?

[6] Your **strategy** as a company might involve being a market leader bringing new products on line early. Or you might prefer the more **conservative** "me-too" position, entering markets when they are more nearly mature. With the right price/value combination you can make money even on products that are in a declining phase. What's important is this: You should have products spread over several phases of the curve, to avoid **uneven** peaks and valleys in your sales and profits.

[7] When is a decline not a decline? Not every **drop** in sales indicates the end of your product's life cycle. Sometimes poor sales are indications of other problems, like **mix-ups** in the distribution channels, or activities of competitors. If a temporary **down-slide** in sales occurs, treat it as a warning sign, not a death knell.

[8] Never forget our First Rule of Marketing: People don't buy products, they buy solutions to problems. If you can create a product offering that continually evolves, solving customer needs as those needs evolve, you will have a successful long-term product strategy.

(603 words)
From *English World*

New Words

cover / ˈkʌvə /
v. include or deal with something 包括；涉及

tangible / ˈtændʒəbl /
a. that can be clearly seen to exist; that you can touch and feel 有形的；实际的；可触摸的

offering / ˈɒfərɪŋ /
n. the act of making an offer; something that is produced for other people to use, watch, enjoy etc. 提供；用品；供消遣的产品

function / ˈfʌŋkʃən /
v. serve; work in the correct way; operate 行使职责；工作；运转

discreet / dɪˈskriːt /
a. done or said in a careful way so that you do not offend, upset, or embarrass people（言行）谨慎的，慎重的

slip / slɪp /
v. become worse or lower than before 下降，下跌；变差，变坏

innovation / ˌɪnəʊˈveɪʃən /
n. a new idea; way of doing something, etc. that has been introduced or discovered 新思想；新方法

phase / feɪz /
n. a part of a process of development or growth 阶段；时期

maturity / məˈtjʊərɪti /
n. the state of being fully grown or developed 成熟；成熟期

---

1 Busch / ˈbʊʃ /   安海斯-布希公司，美国啤酒酿造公司

category /ˈkætɪɡəri/
n. a group of people or things that all have the same particular qualities 种类，类别

long-standing
a. that has existed or lasted for a long time 存在已久的，悠久的

family /ˈfæmɪli/
n. a group of products or product models made by the same manufacturer or producer 由同一生产商生产的具有共同性质和特征的一组东西

notoriously /nəʊˈtɔːrɪəsli/
ad. in a way that is famous 著名地，众所周知地

fickle /ˈfɪkl/
a. (of a person) often changing their mind in an unreasonable way so that you cannot rely on them 反复无常的

fizz /fɪz/
n. the bubbles of gas in some kinds of drinks or the sound that they make 充气饮料的气泡或其嘶嘶声

invigorate /ɪnˈvɪɡəreɪt/
v. make a situation, an organization, etc. efficient and successful 使蒸蒸日上；使兴旺发达

languish /ˈlæŋɡwɪʃ/
v. become weaker or less successful 变得衰弱无力，失去活力；凋萎

sibling /ˈsɪblɪŋ/
n. a brother or sister 兄弟；姐妹；同胞；同属

brew /bruː/
n. a type of beer, especially one made in a particular place（尤指某地酿造的）啤酒

amber /ˈæmbə/
a. yellowish brown 琥珀色，黄褐色

strategy /ˈstrætɪdʒi/
n. a plan that is intended to achieve a particular purpose 策略，计策

conservative /kənˈsɜːvətɪv/
a. not liking changes or new ideas 保守的；谨慎的

uneven /ʌnˈiːvən/
a. not following a regular pattern; not having a regular size and shape 无规律的；不规则的

drop /drɒp/
n. a fall or reduction in the amount, level, or number of something 下降，下跌；减少

mix-up
n. a situation that is full of confusion, esp. because somebody has made a mistake 混乱，杂乱

down-slide
n. a fall in the amount of business; downturn 下跌，下降

Phrases & Expressions

buy into sth.
(informal) believe something, esp. an idea that many other people believe in〈口〉相信；接受

in the pipeline
in preparation but not yer ready〈口〉在进行中；在生产中；在处理中；在运输中；在讨论（或规划、准备）中；在酝酿中

life cycle
all the different levels of development that an animal or plant goes through during its life 盛衰周期；生命周期

go through
experience something 经受；经历

UNIT **2** Products

wine cooler
  a drink made with wine, fruit juice, ice and soda water 由葡萄酒、果汁、冰和苏打水调制成的冰镇果酒饮料

flash in the pan
  a sudden success that ends quickly and is unlikely to happen again 转瞬即逝且很难再现的成功

deep pocket
  a lot of money 富裕，殷实；财力雄厚

draw on/upon sth.
  use a supply of something that is available 利用；凭借

come on the scene
  appear on the stage 出场，上场

distribution channel
  way of giving things to a large group of people or delivering goods to companies, shops, etc. 分配或分销渠道

death knell
  a sign that something will soon stop existing or stop being used 丧钟；事物完结的信号

Exercises

Comprehension

1. **Mark the following statements ture (T) or false (F) according to the text. Discuss with your partner about the supporting points for each statement.**

    1) _____ Some ideas and feelings can be products since they function as offerings for an audience to buy.

    2) _____ Generally speaking, a product will go through a life cycle, starting with an introduction phase and ending with a maturity stage.

    3) _____ A successful long-term product should be one that can satisfy customers' changing needs.

    4) _____ As an alternative to beer, wine coolers were by no means popular with young consumers on the market.

    5) _____ Having several products spread at different stages of life cycle is a wiser strategy than having just one product.

    6) _____ Once products reach the decline stage, they should be eliminated because they become valueless to the company.

    7) _____ The most commonly seen product is in the pure form of tangible and physical article.

8) _____ Seagrams and Gallo were the first and the only two companies who manufactured sweet, fruity, slightly alcoholic drinks.

2. Go through the text carefully and then complete the outline below with the missing information from the text.

Parts	Main ideas
Part I (Paras. 1-2)	The definition of "_____" has been broadened. It can be something tangible, a _____, an _____ or a _____ of all the three.
Part II (Paras. ___)	It is important for marketers to know the _____ _____ of their products and how their products or product categories go through it.
Part III (Paras. ___)	The product life cycle theory should be correctly deployed into marketer's company and product _____.
Part IV (Para(s). ___)	A successful long-term product strategy is to create _____ _____ which continually _____ to solve customer needs as those needs change.

Critical Thinking

Work in group to discuss the following questions.

1) Based on what you have learned about the product life cycle from the text, tell how you understand the following graphs.

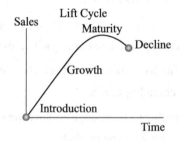

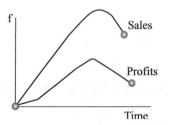

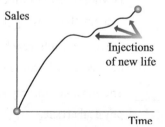

2) If you are considering entering an industry and making a product, knowing where the product is in its life cycle can provide valuable information of how to position your product in the market in terms of price, promotion and distribution. Products typically go through four stages during their lifetime. Each stage has its own characteristics and requires marketing strategies unique to the stage. Look at the following lists of characteristics and promotion strategies and then classify them under the corresponding stages: Introduction stage, Growth stage, Maturity stage and Decline stage.

Characteristics

- An emphasis is on product style rather than function.
- It is signaled by a long-run drop in sales.
- Sales grow at an increasing rate.
- Failure rate is high.
- Annual models of many products are on the market.
- Product modification are frequent.
- Sales volume has created economies of scale.
- Sales grow slowly.
- Skimming pricing.
- Profits reach their peak.
- Large companies may acquire small pioneering firms.
- Product lines are widened or extended.
- Falling demand forces many competitors out of the market.
- Profit is minimal or negative.
- The marketplace is approaching saturation.
- Sales continue to increase but at a decreasing rate.
- A few small specialty firms may still manufacture the product.
- Marginal competitors begin dropping out of the market.
- There is little competition.
- Many competitors enter the market.
- Marketing costs are high.
- Profits are healthy.
- Prices normally fall.

- Development costs have been recovered.
- Production costs are high.
- Stimulate trial.
- Product models are limited.
- Prices and profits begin to fall.

Promotion strategies

- Find new target markets for the product.
- Find new uses for the product.
- Differences between brands should be made.
- Dropping a product from the company's product line is the most drastic strategy.
- Add new ingredients.
- Develop new distribution channels.
- Gaining wider distribution is a key goal.
- Make a dramatic new guarantee.
- Informing about product benefits.
- Heavy promotions to both the dealers and consumers are required.
- Price the product below the market.
- Focusing on primary demand for the product category.
- Intensive personal selling to retailers and wholesalers is required.
- Developing product awareness.
- Company retains the product but reduces marketing support.
- There should be heavy brand advertising.
- Delete old ingredients.
- Promote more frequent use of the product by current customers.

Characteristics	Promotion strategies
Introduction stage	
Growth stage	

UNIT 2 Products

续表

Characteristics	Promotion strategies
Maturity stage	
Decline stage	

Vocabulary

1. Spell the equivalent words of the following definitions, and then use the correct form of these words to further complete the table.

    - *make changes; introduce new things*
    - *developed over a period of time to produce a strong, rich flavour*
    - *fall to a lower level; to become worse*
    - *make a situation, an organization, etc. efficient and successful*
    - *become weaker or fail to make progress*
    - *make beer*
    - *send goods to shops/stores and businesses so that they can be sold*
    - *become or make sth. weaker, lower or less*
    - *class or group of things in a complete system of grouping*
    - *the sound that is made by bubbles of gas in a liquid, or a sound similar to this*

	Verbs	Nouns	Adjectives
1)	i_____		
2)			m_____
3)	___p		
4)	_____ate		
5)	l_____		
6)	b___		×
7)	d_____		
8)	d___		×
9)		____ory	
10)		f___	

2. Use the words given below to write sentences with *product*.

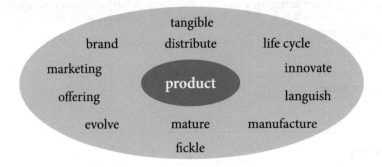

3. Choose the correct word and use its right form to complete each sentence.

   1) sell, sale

      A. We will offer our _____ agents and purchasers many kinds of services and benefits.

      B. The regional manager is not very enthusiastic about _____ our new photocopiers.

   2) classic, classical

      A. In the history of _____ music, there are almost uncountable famous musicians such as Beethoven, Mozart, Chopin, Brahms and Vivaldi.

      B. _____ product management activities relate to understanding markets, defining customer requirements, and conducting competitive assessments.

   3) label, brand

      A. Prior to the launch of a new product, the company's Public Affairs Department requested a risk assessment for the product, the developed _____, as well as the marketing and communication strategy.

      B. Manufacturers put _____ on product packages so that customers know what they contain.

   4) appeal, attract

      A. Hypermarkets _____ to customers with their comprehensive product selection and low prices when compared with supermarkets and convenience stores while having the drawbacks of crowdedness and lengthy payment waiting time.

      B. Our attorneys work with our clients to design compensation and benefit packages that _____ and retain essential talent.

5) long-standing, long-term

   A. Google Inc. and Clear Channel Communications Inc. announced a _____ agreement Sunday that will allow the Internet search leader to place advertising for its online customers on more than 675 Clear Channel radio stations.

   B. There is a _____ conflict of view between the general manager and the chairman of the board of directors.

6) create, innovate

   A. A qualified manufacturing engineer should have the ability to _____ product design and production processes to reduce costs while improving product quality and value.

   B. This year, Guangdong will take more measures to _____ equal and more job opportunities for disabled people.

7) involve, cover

   A. The candidate's qualification must _____ high proficiency in both English and Mandarin.

   B. In America, hundreds of thousands of bylaws in the legal system almost _____ everything which happens daily.

8) family, category

   A. A qualified product manager should analyze market trends and requirements to define clear product specifications for a product _____ which is positioned to have competitive advantage and gain high market share.

   B. This company offers high-quality products in the 5 product _____ of toys, electronic and electrical products, household gadgets, paper products and stationery.

Translation

1. **Translate the following sentences into Chinese.**

   1) Not only products but also whole product categories go through a basic life cycle which contains four stages: introduction, growth, maturity and decline.

   2) The category of wine coolers, a classic marketing flash in the pan, was created by wine manufacturers, looking for an alternative to beer to offer young

drinkers.

3) The first products of wine coolers were created by Seagrams and Gallo, names of long-standing with deep pockets to draw on and mature products elsewhere in their families.

2. Put the following sentences into English, using the words and phrases given in the brackets.

1) 产品不仅仅指有形的东西，它也可以是一种服务、一种观念或者是这三者的综合体。（tangible, combination）

2) 从投入市场到撤出市场，产品的生命周期一般都会经历引进阶段、成长阶段、成熟阶段和衰退阶段四个时期。（life cycle, go through）

3) 企业应根据产品的不同生命周期，制定相应的产品策略，以拥有处于生命周期不同阶段的不同产品，避免因产品人气下滑失去活力导致的销售和利润上的大起大落。（spread, uneven peaks and valleys, languish, slip）

4) 营销学的核心思想认为，实际上，产品要解决的是客户不断发展的需求和问题，因此只有那些使自己的产品能不断满足客户需求的企业，才能在市场竞争中长久地处于不败之地。（evolve, long-term）

Product Presentation

As a sales representative, you often need to introduce your products and create public interest in buying the products by presenting them to prospective customers and answering their questions. Now work in group of four and do the following steps.

1) Each group chooses one of the following products and read the given information on page 270, or you may choose any other products you want.

2) Prepare a presentation for the product through discussion.

3) Make your product presentation to the whole class, trying to answer their questions. Your product presentation should include at least the following points:

UNIT **2** Products

- *name of the product;*
- *functions of the product;*
- *appearance of the product (color, size and dimensions, shape, etc.);*
- *features/selling points of the product;*
- *price of the product;*
- *others...*

Product A

Swatch Mise & Cow Watch

Product B

EcoPure Reverse Osmosis Drinking Water System

Product C

Freeplay Energy Kito LED Self-Powered Flashlight

Product D

Omron HEM-650 Wrist Blood Pressure Monitor

Notes of Product Presentation

- Introduction: Introduce yourself, and the point of the product presentation.
- Agenda: It is optional, but provides you with an opportunity to tell your audience what you are going to cover in your presentation.
- Company information: Giving company information is a way to establish credibility and to make the audience feel comfortable with your company.

- Positioning: Successful products have a unique technology or positioning that sets them apart from other products on the market. Introduce this aspect of your product up front to let your audience know how your product is different and why they should listen to the rest of your presentation.

- Product description: Clearly describe your product in terms that your audience can understand. Present the features, benefits and details of the products.

- Examples/successes: At this point in the presentation your audience should be familiar with your product and know why it is different and better. Show them home use examples of how your product is being used and how customers have benefited from the product.

- Closing argument: Summarize your product presentation, reiterate the point of the presentation, and interact with your audience.

Language Hints

Introducing the product
- Morning everybody. Today we're going to talk about our latest product ...
- Look at our new product, please!
- Here is our new product ...
- ...

Describing the product
- Before looking at its selling point, I'd like to describe it briefly.
- As you can see, the differences are size, weight, and, of course, cost.
- It comes in several versions.
- It measures just ...cm square.
- It's made of steel / wood / plastic...
- The total weight is only... grammes.
- The standard version will retail at $ ...
- ...

Telling the product's uses
- It is used in construction plant jobsite.
- It's ideal for cleaning the big house.
- It is specially designed for...
- It is available for ...
- ...

Stating selling points
- It takes great pride in its history of providing reliable, innovative products.
- It is doing whatever it can to provide all of its customers and partners the absolute best product possible.
- It is designed with the newest technology.
- It has several special features...
- It has a special power-saving design.

- It can be operated easily...
- ...

Dealing with questions
- If you have any questions, I'll be happy to answer them as we go along.
- Feel free to ask any questions.
- Does anyone have any questions?
- ...

Product Instruction

As a staff of the product department of your company, you need to design an attractive and well-written product instruction. A product instruction usually includes:

- name of the product;
- specification or ingredients of the product;
- functions, effects or results of the product;
- how to install the product;
- how to use the product.

The above items are optional according to different products.

Key tips for well-written instructions are as follows:

- Approach it with logic and common sense;
- Don't assume any prior knowledge on reader's part;
- Start right at the beginning of the process;
- Use simple, plain language in short sentences;
- Use "active voice," not "passive voice";
- Keep each step separate, no matter how simple you think it is;
- If you use illustrations, make sure they're clear and uncomplicated.
- Make sure your instructions are written for your audience, not your organization.

Study the following sample instruction on Caltrate®600+D, then do the exercise according to the direction.

Caltrate® 600+D

Caltrate® 600+D contains 600 mg calcium plus 400 IU of vitamin D per tablet. No leading brand has more calcium per tablet than Caltrate® to help fight bone loss and maintain a healthy colon. And each Caltrate® 600+D tablet now contains double vitamin D for calcium absorption.

Caltrate® 600+D is ideal for adults over the age of 65 who are particularly susceptible to vitamin D deficiency. It may also benefit those who do not consume adequate amounts of dairy products since most vitamin D is gotten from consuming fortified milk and cereal products.

Supplement Facts

Amount Per Serving	% Daily Value
Vitamin D 400 IU	100%
Calcium 600mg	60%

Osteoporosis affects middle-aged and older persons, especially those with a family history of fragile bones in later years.

A healthy diet that includes calcium along with a lifetime of regular exercise builds and maintains good bone health, and may reduce the risk of osteoporosis later in life.

While adequate calcium intake is important, daily intakes above 2, 000mg are not likely to provide any additional benefit.

Ingredients

Calcium Carbonate, Starch. Contains < 2% of: Acacia, Cholecalciferol (Vit. D3), Croscarmellose Sodium, dl-Alpha Tocopherol, FD&C Yellow No. 6

UNIT 2 Products

Aluminum Lake, Magnesium Stearate, Medium-Chain Triglycerides, Polyethylene Glycol, Polyvinyl Alcohol, Sucrose, Talc, Titanium Dioxide, Tricalcium Phosphate.

Suggested Use — usage of the product

Take one tablet twice daily with food or as directed by your physician. Not formulated for use in children.

As with any supplement, if you are pregnant, nursing, or taking medication, consult your doctor before use.

Keep out of Reach of Children. — cautions of the product

Store at room temperature. Keep bottle tightly closed. Bottle sealed with printed foil under cap. Do Not Use if foil is torn.

Marketed by: Wyeth Consumer Healthcare Madison, NJ07940 Madison, NJ 07940 Made in USA

Exercise:

The instructions below tell people how to operate a Sliding Bicycle, but they are not in the right order. Rearrange them and put them under appropriate headings. Write the introductory paragraph with the words or expressions given in the box. Add anything if necessary.

Sliding Bicycle	thank	light weight	attention	high quality
special	convenient	anywhere	read	product
shipment	attract	carefully	make	purchase
properly	before	use	attract	operate
illustration	so as to	aluminum alloy	please	safely

Instructions:

- If children operate the product, they must be accompanied by adults.
- Open the lever B and extend the handle pole. Lock the lever B after clicking it into place.
- Do not ride the product when you are in poor health or bad spirit.

- Make sure all the levers are locked before using it.
- The step brake is only an auxiliary part.
  Sometimes it may not brake the bicycle immed-iately.
- Use the product safely after reading the following "Note" and "Dangers".
- Insert the grip into handle pole. When it clicks, it's ok.
- Do not ride the bicycle among the crowds, on a sliding road or a steep slope, etc.
- Open the lever A in the bottom of the handle pole and pull the handle pole to set its position, and then fix it with regulation button.
- Disassemble the product in the reverse order of the assembly sequence.
- Do not ride the bicycle in dangerous corners or at high speed.
- Obey traffic regulations and do not ride the bicycle on main public roads.
- Be careful not to let your fingers get squeezed when assembling and disassembling it.
- Check carefully to lock all levers before riding the bicycle. Operating it with loose levers can cause an accident.

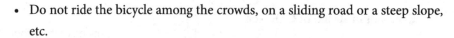

Sliding Bicycle
Operation Instruction

_____
_____
_____
_____

Attention: The design of the appearance, the cover of the illustration and others will be different due to the change improvement of product.

Assembly:

  1) _____

UNIT 2 Products

> 2) _____
> 3) _____
> Usage:
>   1) _____
>   2) _____
>   3) _____
> Note:
>   1) _____
>   2) _____
>   3) _____
>   4) _____
> Dangers:
>   1) _____
>   2) _____
>   3) _____
>   4) _____
> **Confirmation:** Our company has no responsibility for personal damage caused by improper operation.

Business Expressions

1. Complete the following sentences with the expressions in the box and change the form if necessary.

specialty goods	shopping goods	convenience goods
waste product	end product	potential product

| quick-selling product | by-product | high-end product |
| like product | seasonal product | gross domestic product |

1) _____ are ordinary, typical goods including food, newspapers, drugstore products and the like, whose using requires no knowledge.

2) _____ are those that more time is spent selecting, for example, a certain type of mystery book, furniture and clothes and so on.

3) The price of _____ is extremely high, which include: works of art, real estate, jewelry and the like.

4) The _____ is very popular with customers and it is easily out of stock.

5) The competition between _____ can be very intense since they are alike in many aspects.

6) _____ refers to extended guarantee, transport, installments package of insurance.

7) The price of the _____ will change in accordance with the passage of time and can be cheap when it is in season.

8) The final product of a manufacturing process is called _____.

9) Coke（焦炭）is a _____ obtained in the manufacture of coal gas.

10) To protect the environment, it is important to dispose of the _____.

11) As to the rich consumers, the executive has attached great importance to developing _____.

12) The booming IT sector has accounted for 12 percent of the city's total _____.

2. Give the English equivalents of the Chinese expressions in the table below.

Chinese	English
1) 王牌产品	
2) 尖端产品	
3) 名优产品	
4) 畅销商品	
5) 拳头产品	
6) 批量经营产品	

续表

Chinese	English
7) 冒牌货	
8) 劣质产品	
9) 土特产品	
10) 成品	
11) 日用品	
12) 消费品	
13) 家用产品	
14) 紧缺商品	
15) 产品规格	
16) 产品鉴定	
17) 产品性能	

3. Complete the following passage with the given expressions.

product's functionality	product marketing	product management
product value	product life cycle	particular product

Product management is an organizational function within a company dealing with the product planning or 1) _____ of a product or products at all stages of the 2) _____. Product Management is also a collective term used to describe the broad sum of diverse activities performed in the interest of delivering a 3) _____ to market.

From a practical perspective, product management is an occupational domain which holds two professional disciplines: product planning and product marketing. This is because the 4) _____ is created for the user via product planning efforts, and 5) _____ is presented to the buyer via product marketing activities.

Product planning and product marketing are very different but due to the collaborative nature of these two disciplines, some companies erroneously perceive them as being one discipline, which they call 6) _____. Done carefully, it is very possible to functionally divide the product management domain into product planning and product marketing, yet retain the required synergy between the two disciplines.

Specialized Reading

1. Products can be classified into several types. The following are three major types. Read them and judge whether the given statements are T (True) or F (False).

> **Convenience goods**
>
> Convenience goods are inexpensive frequent purchases, and there is little effort needed to purchase them. Examples may include fast food and confectionery products. Convenience products are split into staples, such as milk, eggs and emergency products which are purchased when the need arises, for example, umbrellas. They are purchased on a regular basis for a relatively low price. The distributional network is fairly dense. The intensive distribution facilitates shopping because you can buy the goods you need without effort, at any place and at any time (convenient location of outlets). Promotion makes the core of marketing policy. It is important to make customers aware of the particular brand. On this account two different means are used, namely push and pull strategies. A "push" strategy makes use of a company's sales force and trade promotion activities to create consumer demand for a product. The producer promotes the product to wholesalers, the wholesalers promote it to retailers, and the retailers promote it to consumers. A "pull" selling strategy requires high spending on advertising and consumer promotion to build up consumer demand for a product. If the strategy is successful, consumers will ask their retailers for the product, the retailers will ask the wholesalers, and the wholesalers will ask the producers. Though attached to certain brands, customers are apt to buy substitutes.

> **Shopping goods**
>
> Shopping goods are usually high risk products where consumers like to shop around to find the best features and price for that product. Examples include buying fridges, freezers or washing machines. The decision to buy shopping goods is not immediate but is a result of thorough information processing of available brands. Our choice is determined by economic as well as by socio-cultural factors such as: prestige, influence of other people. The distribution is less intensive than in the case of casual goods. The outlets are located mainly in places of high circulation of customers. Promotion strategies: push and pull.

> **Speciality goods**
>
> Speciality goods are the products that are purchased infrequently. They are bought extremely seldom, sometimes even once in a lifetime. The consumers will conduct extensive research to make sure that their purchase decision is right, because specialty goods are expensive and infrequent purchases. The organization will support the product with an extensive warranty package. Examples include watches and diamonds. There are usually little or no substitutes for these products. The focus of specialty goods is on the brand. What counts is the uniqueness and originality of the product. Thus, it entails an extremely high price. The product is supposed to satisfy our most sophisticated need: the feeling of prestige. Customers are loyal towards the brand they appreciate and do not accept substitutes. The decision concerning the purchase takes time. Promotion is based on pull strategy.

1) _____ To promote convenience goods, push and pull strategies can be used.
2) _____ Customers who buy convenience goods can hardly accept substitutes.
3) _____ One feature of convenience goods is that they are available at any place and at any time.
4) _____ To buy shopping goods is a considered decision.
5) _____ The distribution of shopping goods is as intensive as that of convenience goods.
6) _____ Whether to buy shopping goods is mainly based on one's economic situation.
7) _____ Consumers choose specialty goods for the uniqueness and originality.
8) _____ Compared with convenience goods and shopping goods, the price of specialty goods is much higher.
9) _____ Selling techniques of different goods are similar.
10) _____ Customers of specialty goods have higher brand loyalty.

2. The following are some important elements concerning the manufacture and marketing of the products. Read them carefully and answer the questions after them.

Elements of Product Marketing

Business models

The concept of product vs. product in competitive marketing is dying. It's slowly becoming business model vs. business model. Business model innovation can make the competition's product superiority irrelevant. Business model innovation allows a marketer to change the game instead of competing on a level playing field.

Customer focus

Many companies today have a customer focus(or customer orientation). This implies that the company focuses its activities and products on consumer demands. Generally there are three ways of doing this, i.e., the customer-driven approach, the sense of identifying market changes and the product innovation approach.

In the consumer-driven approach, consumer wants are the drivers of all strategic marketing decisions. No strategy is pursued until it passes the test of consumer research. Every aspect of a market offering, including the nature of the product itself, is driven by the needs of potential consumers. The starting point is always the consumer. The rationale for this approach is that there is no point spending R&D funds developing products that people will not buy. History attests to many products that were commercial failures in spite of being technological breakthroughs.

Resources

Companies with a greater number of resources than their competitors will have an easier time competing in the marketplace. Resources include financial(cash and cash reserves), physical (plant and equipment), human (knowledge and skill), legal (trademarks and patents), organizational(structure, competencies, and policies), and informational (knowledge of consumers and competitors). Small companies usually have a harder time competing with larger corporations because of their disadvantage in resource allocation.

Relationships

Success in business, as in life, is based on the relationships you have with people. Marketers must aggressively build relationships with consumers, customers, distributors, partners and even competitors if they want to have success in today's competitive marketplace. There are four types of relationships, i.e., win-win, win-lose, lose-lose and lose-win.

1) What is the change in the current competitive marketing?
2) What makes the competition's product superiority irrelevant?
3) How many ways are mentioned to focus products on consumer needs?

4) What do business resources refer to?
5) How many types of relationships are discussed in business models?
6) Give your comments on business models, resources and relationships that are discussed above.

UNIT 3
Marketing

1. Discuss the following questions with your partner.

   1) What are roles of marketing? What parts of it might you find the most appealing? What is appealing about them?

   2) How many ways do you know to promote a product? Try to make a list of them. Which of the ways seem to be the most effective?

   3) Think of some products you bought under the influence of the marketing mix (the four Ps: product, price, promotion, and place). Tell which of the four Ps was a decisive factor when you bought the product. Remember to give the reasons and justify your answers.

2. The following pictures may associate us with some well-known companies and products. Look at them and discuss the questions with your group members.

   1) What competition are they each facing now?

   2) Try to tell how they are marketing their products to cope with the competition?

   3) Take one of them as an example. Try to tell how marketing relates to the success of a modern business.

UNIT **3** Marketing

Preview: Marketing is an ongoing process of planning and executing the marketing mix (Product, Price, Place, Promotion often referred to as the 4 Ps) for products, services or ideas to create exchange between individuals and organizations. Good marketing must be able to create a "proposition" or set of benefits for the end customer that delivers value through products or services. In this passage, the author not only explains the marketing mix through Kalika's marketing activities — providing a suitable product, choosing a right place, attracting potential customers, and satisfying the customers' needs, but also points out that a marketing manager should take all the four basic elements into consideration when formulating a marketing strategy and try to build a trust in potential customers.

What Is Marketing Anyway?

By Sarah White

[1] Marketing is the process of creating a product, then planning and carrying out the **pricing, promotion**, and **placement** of that product by stimulating buying exchanges in which both buyer and seller **profit** in some way. Got that? Of course not, it's simply too big an idea to **swallow** whole. Instead, let's look at the parts. An example will help.

[2] Kalika is new to this country. She's turned to **entrepreneurship** to create a job opportunity. She owns a **lemonade stand**, or more precisely a juice cart. She **tows** a **cabin** on wheels down to the local university campus every day and serves juice and peanut butter and banana sandwiches to students.

[3] How is Kalika engaged in marketing? First, she's selected a family of products she knows something about and believes that students want. Second, she's arrived at a price for those products, based on the costs for her materials, her cart, and the value she puts on her time. She **promotes** her **wares** with brightly colored signs and menu boards around the cart. If she were a little more **sophisticated**, she might create promotional strategies like buy-one-get-one-free **coupons**, multiple-purchase discount cards, or business-card **drawings**.

[4] She begins the act of placing her product by **maneuvering** her cart into position in the morning. With that **ungainly** drive, she brings the factory to the store to the customer. Kalika does more than just place her product in front of her customers: she is a one-woman distribution channel. Kalika the factory worker cuts fruit, then **blends** to order with skill and speed. Kalika the **distributor** sees to it that raw materials are on

hand, and supplies like **silverware** and cups are also at the ready. Kalika the sales agent discusses menu **options** with **prospects**, helping them decide what sizes and **flavors** will satisfy their appetite and thirst. She even provides support after the sale — mostly filling requests for more ice or a napkin. That's Kalika's marketing activity.

[5] What was the last part of that marketing definition? "...stimulating buying exchanges in which both buyer and seller profit in some way." If both aren't profiting, one or the other will hesitate before repeating the experience.

[6] Kalika and her customers both feel happy with the buying exchange at the juice stand. Her customers satisfy their hunger or thirst. Kalika satisfies her profit objectives, going home with lighter fruit baskets and a heavier cash drawer. Both parties of the exchange look forward to repeating the experience soon and often.

[7] I bring up Kalika and her juice cart to introduce you to one of the most **fundamental** ways to understand marketing. There are a number of activities involved. To get a handle on them, we break down the activities into the "Four Ps". These are Product, Price, Promotion, and Place(or distribution). As a manager of marketing activity, you need to study each area and **formulate** a strategy for your situation.

[8] In the meantime, let's move on to another important marketing fundamental: What, and why, do people buy?

[9] Your audience, or target market, is the universe of potential customers for your products or service. I use the word "audience" more, and there's a reason. It reminds me that life is like theater. As a marketer, you're like an actor trying to please and entertain. You need your audience to believe in who you are and what you're offering. You'll also hear this group of people called customers, **clients**, prospects, or a market segment. You want those people to know about you.

[10] Product to a marketer is an umbrella **unfurled** to cover not just tangible products but also services and even ideas. Most marketing involves promoting a combination of products and services, for example, a **photocopier**(product) and its extended **maintenance** contract (service). Services can include the selling of products too. Think about how your hairdresser sells you shampoo, or how attending a movie might also include purchasing **refreshments**. Product is what you offer that has value to your audience.

(680 words)
From *English World*

UNIT 3 Marketing

New Words

price / praɪs /
v. fix, ask about, the price of sth.; mark (goods) with a price 定价；标价

promotion / prə'məʊʃn /
n. encouragement of the sale by publicity, etc. 促销

placement / 'pleɪsmənt /
n. the act of placing or putting in place; the act of locating or positioning 布置；定位；销售渠道

profit / 'prɒfɪt /
v. obtain a financial advantage or benefit, especially from an investment 获益，得到好处

swallow / 'swɒləʊ /
v. accept, believe without question; cause or allow sth. to pass down the throat 接受，毫无疑问地接受；吞，咽

entrepreneurship / ˌentrəprə'nɜːʃɪp /
n. the activity of running business 创办企业

lemonade / ˌleməˈneɪd /
n. a drink made of fresh lemon with sugar and water added 柠檬汁

stand / stænd /
n. a small often outdoor shop or place for showing things 摊子，摊位

tow / təʊ /
v. pull along with a rope or chain 拖，拉

cabin / 'kæbɪn /
n. a piece of wooden furniture 木橱，木柜

promote / prə'məʊt /
v. bring (goods) to public notices in order to increase sales 宣传；推销；促销

wares / weəs /
n. articles for sale 货品；商品

sophisticated / sə'fɪstɪkeɪtɪd /
a. having or showing a knowledge of social life and behaviors 通世故的；老练的

coupon / 'kuːpɒn /
n. a ticket that shows the right of the holder to receive some payment, service, etc. 优待券

drawing / 'drɔːɪŋ /
n. an occasion when something is decided or won in a chance way by drawing lots 抽签

maneuver / mə'nuːvə /
v. perform or cause to perform a movement or a series of moves requiring skill and care 移动

ungainly / ʌn'geɪnli /
a. not graceful; awkward in movement 难看的，笨手笨脚的

blend / blend /
v. mix 混合；掺杂

distributor / dɪs'trɪbjʊtə /
n. an agent who supplies goods to shops and other businesses 经销商；分销商

silverware / 'sɪlvəweə /
n. knives and other cutting instruments 刀具；餐刀

option / 'ɒpʃən /
n. sth. chosen or offered for choice; choice 可选择之物；选择

prospect / 'prɒspekt /
n. a potential customer, client, or purchaser 可能的顾客、委托人或购买者

flavor / 'fleɪvə /
n. taste; quality that only the tongue can experience 味；味道

fundamental / ˌfʌndə'mentl /
a. being at the base from which all else develops 基本的；根本的
n. a basic rule or principle; an essential part 基本规律；根本法则；基本原理

formulate / 'fɔːmjʊleɪt /
v. create or devise methodically (a strategy or a proposal) 设计；规划

client / 'klaɪənt /
n. a customer or patron 顾客，客户或主顾

unfurl / ʌn'fɜːl /
v. make or become spread out from a rolled or folded state 展开；拉开

photocopier / 'fəʊtəʊˌkɒpɪə(r) /
n. a machine that makes copies of documents, etc. by photographing them 影印机，复印机

maintenance / 'meɪntənəns /
n. the work of keeping something in proper condition; upkeep 养护；维修

refreshments / rɪ'freʃmənts /
n. a snack or light meal and drinks 点心；快餐，方便饮食

Phrases & Expressions

carry out
do as required or specified; fulfill; conduct 实行；完成；进行

turn to
begin work; work 开始工作；着手

be engaged in
make oneself busy in; spend one's time in 从事；忙于……

arrive at
decide on or find sth., especially after discussion and thought 作出（决议等）；得出（结论等）

put on
add to... 增加，添加

see to it that
ensure 务必做到；保证

on hand
be available 现有；在手头

at the ready
available to be used immediately 随时可用，即刻使用

sales agent
person empowered to represent another company and manage sales affairs for it 销售代理

bring up
raise a matter for discussion or consideration 提出；引出

get/have a handle on
understand or know about sth./sb. especially so that you can deal with it or them later 弄懂，理解，搞明白

break down... into
separate into different kinds or divide into types 划分；分门别类

target market
the market segment or group of customers that a company has decided to serve, and at which it consequently aims at its marketing activities 目标市场

market segment
the geographic, demographic or other customer classification targeted by an organization for the purchase and use of its products and services 市场细分

Exercises

Comprehension

1. Answer the following questions with your partner.

   1) What are the main elements in marketing a product?

   2) According to Kalika's story, what should an entrepreneur do to guarantee a

UNIT **3** Marketing

successful marketing?

3) What roles does Kalika play when she is marketing her products?

4) How can customers and sellers both benefit from marketing activities?

5) What other ways can Kalika promote her products if she is an experienced seller?

6) How does a marketing manager formulate a suitable marketing strategy for his /her company?

7) Why does the author describe the marketer as an actor, the customers as audience?

8) How does the author look at a product?

2. The text can be roughly divided into three parts. Now put down the paragraph numbers of each part and then give its main idea. The last one has been done for you.

Parts	Paragraphs	Main ideas
Part I	Para. 1	
Part II	Paras. _____	
Part III	Paras. _____ -10	Fundamental elements of marketing

Critical Thinking

Work in group to discuss the following questions.

1) How does the simple example of Kalika's business compare to a more complex product, such as the strategies needed for marketing a bicycle, a telephone, or even a set of dishes?

2) In the example, Kalika is not apparently taking advantage of modern technologies to market her products. How might computers, telephones, cameras, and other technological devices be used to enhance her business?

3) Kalika's business relies entirely upon her. What weaknesses or dangers are there in having such a business? For example, how might her business be affected if she suddenly developed a skin problem? How do larger businesses shield themselves from such weaknesses?

Vocabulary

1. **Tick the word which is the odd one out in each group.**

    1) executive   director   manager   customer
    2) promotion   distribution   description   placement
    3) market share   market segment   target market   supermarket
    4) wares   commodities   purchases   commerce
    5) photocopier   hairdresser   distributor   producer
    6) stand   vender   station   kiosk
    7) silverwares   napkin   table manners   tableware
    8) invoice   receipt   menu   coupon
    9) logo   board   slogan   brand
    10) maintenance   assistance   service   consultation

2. **Rewrite some part in each sentence below with the word or phrase from the box, trying to keep the original meaning.**

    | stimulate | get a handle on | promotion | carry out | extend |
    | formulate | potential | sophisticated | at the ready | coupon |

    1) When some multinational companies cannot fully understand the local customers' needs, they tend to invite a good consultant into their decision-making.

    _____

    2) Usually a businessman who has life experiences and thus forms a good judgment about socially important things can deal with the customers' complaints in sweet and honeyed words.

    _____

    3) The company will showcase the latest product introductions, innovations, and service to the attendees from all over the world to intensify its overseas advertising campaign.

    _____

    4) The holiday scheme aims to boost domestic demand, encourage consumption, and restructure the economy.

    _____

UNIT **3** Marketing

5) E-commerce is the way of conducting business communication and making transactions through computer networks.

   _____

6) How to establish good relationships with prospective customers is a crucial skill for a salesperson.

   _____

7) In order to attract young people, the bookstore has added digital reading to their traditional bookselling.

   _____

8) A qualified secretary should be careful enough to make all the necessary documents available for immediate use just before the board meeting.

   _____

9) The sales manager, district manager and sales representative must learn to develop plans and strategies that are effective in achieving business objectives.

   _____

10) The company promised that those who bought the newly-advertised product could get a printed note for paying at a 10% discount.

   _____

3. **Complete the following dialogues by making sentences with the given phrases.**

   1) carry out

   A. Why did Bill suddenly drop out from that university? It meant he gave up a promising future.

   _____

   B. What will the manager do if his marketing strategy turns out to be improper in local market?

   _____

   2) turn to

   A. How did Bob kill the leisure time after he resigned from executive management of the company?

   _____

   B. What will this 100-year-old shop do when facing fierce competition home and abroad?

___

3) be engaged in

A. Can we meet this Saturday? I heard that all the staff in your Department are busy with market development.

___

B. I haven't seen John these days. Is he very busy recently?

___

4) arrive at

A. Did the board meeting get any result after the heated discussion?

___

B. What did the shareholders learn from the company's annual report?

___

5) put on

A. Why did the company raise the price of their product?

___

B. What did Bill say as for calculating the cost of marketing?

___

6) on hand

A. Why do you bring cash with you rather than a credit card when you travel?

___

B. What kind of partner can be considered trustworthy?

___

7) bring up

A. Why did the director look so angry after the board meeting? Did his proposal on reform meet challenge?

___

B. Are there any chances for ordinary employees to put forward their suggestions in your company?

___

8) break down (into)

UNIT 3 Marketing

A. Is your boss satisfied with the annual report made by John?

_____

B. What can we do with the Logistics Department? It has too many staff and is difficult to manage.

_____

Translation

1. **Translate the following sentences into Chinese.**

   1) Marketing is the process of creating a product, then planning and carrying out the pricing, promotion, and placement of that product by stimulating buying exchanges in which both buyer and seller profit in some way.

   2) Your audience, or target market, is the universe of potential customers for your products or service.

   3) As a marketer, you're like an actor trying to please and entertain because you need your audience to believe in who you are and what you're offering.

   4) This group of people can also be called customers, clients, prospects, or a market segment.

2. **Put the following sentences into English, using the words and phrases given in the brackets.**

   1) 创业者必须建立一支专业的市场营销团队，这支团队，凭借良好的市场营销知识，负责提出合适的营销策略。（entrepreneurship, bring up, marketing strategy）

   2) 只有制定合适的营销策略，他们才能促进产品或服务的销售，但是执行营销策略并不简单。（formulate, promote, carry out）

   3) 市场销售人员，就像演员一样，应该使消费者感兴趣并能激发他们的购买欲望。（entertain, potential, stimulate）

   4) 在市场营销中，销售代表应该取得顾客的信任，并与顾客保持良好的关系，以使顾客信任他们所销售的产品。（sales representative, offer）

Business Practice

SWOT Analysis

It is useful to complete an analysis that takes into account not only your own business, but your competitors' activities and current industry happenings as well when conducting strategic planning for any company. A SWOT is one such analysis. Work in groups of five. Suppose you are staff of the marketing department, discussing a marketing plan of a certain product in a meeting. What you focus on is the SWOT analysis of the product.

1) (Turn to page 273). Each group chooses a product with 5 cards including executive summary and SWOT analysis.

2) Each student in a group gets one card, reads the card respectively and then teaches it to your group.

3) Summarize the information on your cards, and share it with the whole class, trying to answer any questions. Your summary should include at least the following points:

- *name of the product;*
- *its strengths;*
- *its weaknesses;*
- *its opportunities;*
- *its threats;*
- *others...*

A Basic SWOT Analysis

SWOT stands for strengths, weaknesses, opportunities, and threats. You can develop the basic analysis in a brainstorming session. To begin the analysis, create a four-cell grid or four lists, one for each component: strengths, weaknesses, opportunities, and threats. Then, begin filling in the lists.

- Strengths: Think about what your company does well. Some questions to help you get started are: What makes you stand out from your competitors? What advantages do you have over other businesses?

- Weaknesses: List the areas that are a struggle for your company. Some questions to help you get started are: What do your customers complain about? What are the unmet needs of your sales force?

- Opportunities: Traditionally, a SWOT looks only at the external environment for opportunities. You'd better look externally for areas your competitors are not fully covering, then go a step further and think how to match these to your internal strengths. Try to uncover areas where your strengths are not being fully utilized. Are there emerging trends that fit with your company's strengths? Is there a product/service area that others have not yet covered?

- Threats: As with opportunities, threats in a traditional SWOT analysis are considered an external force. By looking both inside and outside of your company for things that could damage your business, however, you may be better able to see the big picture. Some questions to get you started: Are your competitors becoming stronger? Are there emerging trends that amplify one of your weaknesses? Do you see other external threats to your company's success? Internally, do you have financial, development, or other problems?

Language Hints

Direct questions
- What sort of survey do you carry out?
- Are you happy with the service?
- What do you think of the program?
- Do you always ...?
- ...

Indirect questions
- Could I ask you what you think of ...?
- Do you mind if I ask you ...?
- Could I start by asking you ...?
- Can I now move on to ask you some questions about..?
- ...

Statement questions
- I suppose you do ...?
- So you like the idea of ...?
- So you say ..., is that right?
- ...

Direct answers
- No, I ...

- Yes, I do.
- ...

Confirming
- That's right.
- I suppose so ...
- ...

Contradicting
- No, actually I don't.

- I didn't say that.
- ...

Time to think
- Let me think ...
- Well ...
- ...

Executive Summary

An executive summary is an overview. The purpose of an executive summary is to summarize the key points of a document for its readers, saving them time and preparing them for the upcoming content. In business, the most common use of an executive summary is as part of a business plan. The purpose of the executive summary of the business plan is to provide your readers with an overview of the business plan. Think of it as an introduction to your business. Therefore, your business plan's executive summary will include summaries of:

- a description of your company, including your products and/or services;
- your mission statement;
- your business's management;
- the market and your customer;
- marketing and sales;
- your competition;
- your business's operations;
- financial projections and plans.

The executive summary will end with a summary statement, a "last kick at the can" sentence or two designed to persuade the readers of your business plan that your business is a winner.

Dos and Don'ts of Executive Summary:

- Be persuasive.
- Don't be demonstrative (don't focus on features).
- Keep a strong, enthusiastic, and proactive language.

- Try to avoid passive-voice sentences.
- Write simple, short sentences intended to be read by an executive.
- Keep your executive summary short.
- Don't provide unnecessary, technical details, and remember that an executive should be able to read it.
- Avoid excessive jargon, and write the definition first.
- Correct spelling, punctuation, style, and grammar errors.

Study the following sample first, and then do the exercise according to the direction.

Sample

Pet Grandma
Executive Summary

Pet Grandma offers on-site pet sitting services for dogs and cats, providing the personal loving pet care that the owners themselves would provide if they were there. Our clients are dog and cat owners who choose to leave their pets at home when they travel or who want their pets to have company when their owners are at work. *(Company, products and services)*

Pet Grandma offers a variety of pet care services from day visits through 24 hour care over a period of weeks — all in the pet's home environment.

Across Canada the pet care business has seen an explosion of growth over the last three years. West Vancouver is an affluent area with a high pet density. Our market research has shown that 9 out of 10 pet owners polled in West Vancouver would prefer to have their pets cared for in their own homes when they travel *(Market and customer)* rather than be kenneled and 6 out of 10 would consider having a pet sitter provide company for their dog when they were at work.

While there are currently eight businesses offering pet sitting in West Vancouver, only three of these offer on-site pet care and none offers "pet visit" services for working pet owners. [Competition]

Pet Grandma's marketing strategy is to emphasize the quality of pet care we provide ("a Grandma for your pet!") and the availability of our services. Dog owners who work, for instance, will come home to find happy, friendly companions who have already been exercised and walked rather than demanding whiny animals. [Marketing and sales/mission statement]

All pet services will be provided by staff trained in animal care. On start up we will have six trained staff to provide pet services and expect to hire four more this year once financing is secured. To begin with, co-owner Pat Simpson will be scheduling appointments and coordinating services, but we plan to hire a full-time receptionist this year as well. [Business's operations]

The management of Pet Grandma consists of co-owners Pat Simpson and Terry Estelle. Pat has extensive experience in animal care while Terry has worked in sales and marketing for 15 years. Both partners will be taking hands-on management roles in the company. In addition, we have assembled a board of advisors to provide management expertise. The advisors are: Juliette LeCroix, partner at LeCroix Accounting, Carey Boniface, veterinarian and partner at Little Tree Animal Care Clinic, John Toms, president of Toms Communications Ltd. [Business's management]

Based on the size of our market and our defined market area, our sales projections for the first year are $340,000. The salary for each of the co-owners will be [Financial projections and plans]

> $40,000.
>
> We are seeking an operating line of $150,000 to finance our first year growth. Together, the co-owners have invested $62,000 to meet working capital requirements.
>
> Already we have service commitments from over 40 clients and plan to aggressively build our client base through newspaper, local television and direct mail advertising. The loving on-site professional care that Pet Grandma will provide is sure to appeal to cat and dog owners throughout the West Vancouver area.

Exercise:

Suppose you are working in the management of **Studio67** and are asked to present an executive summary to the bank from which your company is to borrow some start-up funds. Through discussing with your staff, you have got some data and ideas in terms of **Service, Customers, and Management** (listed below). Some parts of the summary are already done for you. Continue to write it up with the given information. You need to reorganize the information to make it more logical and readable.

Service

- have great food in a social environment
- a large repertoire of ethnic ingredients and recipes
- recognize the trend in restaurant industry
- provide a diverse, unusual menu
- the majority of purchases from chef's recommendations
- offer a trendy, fun place
- emphasize healthy dishes
- demand for healthy cuisine

Customers

- target market segmented into four distinct groups
- the first group of lonely rich, 400,000 people
- the second group of young happy customers growing at an annual rate of 8% with 150,000 potential customers
- the third group of rich hippies, naturally desire organic foods as well as ethnic cuisine
- the last group of dieting women, number 350,000 in the Portland area, particularly interested in the menu's healthy offerings

Management

- assemble a strong management team
- the general manager, with extensive management experience of organizations ranging from six to 45 people
- manager of the finance and accounting, with invaluable financial control skills in keeping Studio67 on track and profitable
- the chef, with over 12 years of experience, responsible for the back-end production of the venture
- achieve financial success through strict financial controls
- ensure success by offering a high-quality service and extremely clean, non-greasy food
- plan to raise menu rates as the restaurant gets more and more crowded
- charge a premium for the feeling of being in the "in crowd"

Studio67 Executive Summary

◆ **Company**

Studio67 is a new medium-sized restaurant located in a neighborhood of Portland, Oregon. Studio67's emphasis will be on organic and creative ethnic food. An emphasis on organic ingredients is based on Studio67's dedication to sustainable development.

◆ **Service**

- **Customers**

- **Management**

- **Financial projections**

The market and financial analyses indicate that with a start-up expenditure of $141,000, Studio67 can generate $350,000 in sales by year one, $500,000 in sales by the end of year two and produce net profits of 7.5% on sales by the end of year three. Profitability will be reached by year two.

- **Mission**

Studio67 is a great place to eat, combining an intriguing atmosphere with excellent, interesting food that is also very good for the people who eat there. We want fair profit for the owners, and a rewarding place to work for the employees.

Business Expressions

1. Match the expressions in the box with the definitions below.

market leader	persuasion process	market share
target market	market penetration	promotional mix
market niche	market segmentation	focus group interview
distribution channel	direct marketing	referral premium

1) a group of individuals who collectively, are intended recipients of an advertiser's message

   _____

2) a premium offered to customers for helping sell a product or service to a friend or acquaintance

   _____

3) the amount that a company sells of its products or services compared with other companies selling the same things

   _____

4) the company that sells the largest quantity of a particular kind of product

   _____

5) using several different types of communication to support marketing goals which include advertising, personal selling, publicity, and sales promotions

   _____

6) the process used by advertising to influence audience or prospect attitudes, especially purchase intent and product perception by appealing to reason or emotion

   _____

7) a research method that brings together a small group of consumers to discuss the product or advertising, under the guidance of a trained interviewer

   _____

UNIT 3 Marketing

8) sending a promotional message directly to consumers, rather than via a mass medium, including methods such as direct mail and telemarketing

   _____

9) an opportunity to sell a product or service to a particular group of people who have similar needs, interests

   _____

10) a system or method that you use to supply goods to shops and companies for them to sell

    _____

11) a marketing technique that targets a group of customers with specific characteristics

    _____

12) increasing market share of an existing product, or promoting a new product, through strategies such as bundling, extensive advertising, lower prices, or volume discounts

    _____

2. **Complete the following sentences with the business expressions in the box and change the form if necessary.**

market activity	market demand	overseas market	market supply
market economy	potential market	market value	market place
sluggish market	corner the market	saturate the market	market incentive

1) It was because of the _____ that the development of the digital home in China experienced an "ice age". However, the terminator of the ice age comes earlier than imagined.

2) No one can _____, since the Forex market is so vast and has so many participants that no single entity, not even a central bank, can control the market price for an extended period of time.

3) For small towns with dwindling population and small local community, putting a mega store would just _____ and squeeze out all the small competitors.

4) As the oil prices drop down in international market, private enterprises in China, constrained by domestic quotas for oil use, try to seek more oil

resources from _____.

5) Despite this supposed _____, governments still have to fund research with grants and tax breaks.

6) Because of adequate source of the second-hand cars and people's reception of the second-hand cars, there is a large _____ for second-hand cars in China.

7) Companies must be able to compete in the _____.

8) To buy a car at $ 500 is far below its current _____.

9) Legal _____ include taking some type of paid job or working for oneself, directing supplying products or services to customers.

10) In the _____ based on private property, individuals decide how, what and for whom to produce.

11) Sound economic growth must be based on strong _____ and good economic returns.

12) As with market demand, _____ is determined by adding all quantities supplied at a given price.

Specialized Reading

1. In marketing, someone has summarized the general sets of activities as 4Ps while someone else has expanded them into 7Ps. Read the following passage and choose the most suitable sentence from A–G to complete the passage.

> A. This fourth P has also sometimes been called *Place*.
> B. This is done by providing physical evidence, such as case study, testimonials or demonstrations.
> C. This refers to the process of setting a price for a product, including discounts.
> D. His typology has become so universally recognized that his four activity sets, the Four Ps, have passed into the language.
> E. Even so, having made this important caveat, the 4 Ps offer a memorable and quite workable guide to the major categories of marketing activity, as well as a framework within which these can be used.
> F. As a result of this, they must be appropriately trained, well motivated and the right type of person.
> G. Industrial products, services, high value consumer products require adjustments to this model.

UNIT 3 Marketing

In popular usage, "marketing" is the promotion of products, especially advertising and branding. However, in professional usage the term has a wider meaning which recognizes that marketing is customer centered. Products are often developed to meet the desires of groups of customers or even, in some cases, for specific customers. E. Jerome McCarthy[1] divided marketing into four general sets of activities. 1) _____ The four Ps are:

- Product: The product aspects of marketing deal with the specifications of the actual good or service, and how it relates to the end-user's needs and wants. The scope of a product generally includes supporting elements such as warranties, guarantees, and support.

- Pricing: 2) _____ The price need not be monetary — it can simply be what is exchanged for the product or service, e.g. time, or attention.

- Promotion: This includes advertising, sales promotion, publicity, and personal selling, and refers to the various methods of promoting the product, brand, or company.

- Placement refers to how the product gets to the customer; for example, point of sale placement or retailing. 3) _____ It refers to the channel by which a product or service is sold (e.g. online vs. retail), in which geographic region or industry, to which segment (young adults, families, business people), etc.

These four elements are often referred to as the marketing mix. A marketer can use these variables to craft a marketing plan. The four Ps model is most useful when marketing low value consumer products. 4) _____ Services marketing must account for the unique nature of services. Industrial or B2B marketing must account for the long term contractual agreements that are typical in supply chain transactions. Relationship marketing attempts to do this by looking at marketing from a long term relationship perspective rather than individual transactions.

As a counter to this, Morgan[2], in *Riding the Waves of Change*, adds "Perhaps the most significant criticism of the 4Ps approach, which you should be aware of, is that it unconsciously emphasizes the inside-out view (looking from the company outwards),

---

1 E. Jerome McCarthy is a professor at Michigan State University, USA, and an internationally known marketing consultant.
2 Gareth Morgan is CEO of Gareth Morgan Investments portfolio manager, and chairman of and a consultant to economics consultancy Infometrics Ltd which he founded in 1982. He is also a well-known columnist, television debater, a sought-after conference speaker, and writer. His books include *Images of Organization, Riding the Waves of Change,* and *Imaginization: New Ways of Seeing, Organizing, and Managing.*

whereas the essence of marketing should be the outside-in approach." 5) _____

As well as the standard four Ps (Product, Pricing, Promotion and Place), services marketing calls upon an extra three, totaling seven and known together as the extended marketing mix. These are:

● People: Any person coming into contact with customers can have an impact on overall satisfaction. Whether as part of a supporting service to a product or involved in a total service, people are particularly important because, in the customer's eyes, they are generally inseparable from the total service. 6) _____ Fellow customers are also sometimes referred to under "people", as they too can affect the customer's service experience (e.g., at a sporting event).

● Process: This is the process involved in providing a service and the behavior of people, which can be crucial to customer satisfaction.

● Physical evidence: Unlike a product, a service cannot be experienced before it is delivered, which makes it intangible. This, therefore, means that potential customers could perceive greater risk when deciding whether to use a service. To reduce the feeling of risk, thus improving the chance for success, it is often vital to offer potential customers the chance to see what a service would be like. 7) _____

2. **Discuss the following questions with your group members.**

   1) "PHILOSOPHY" is regarded by someone as the potential 8th P of marketing. How do you understand it?

   2) In India, there are 4As, which referred to

      ● Acceptability of the product or services;

      ● Affordability of the product or services;

      ● Awareness of the product and services;

      ● Availability of the product and services.

   Compare and comment on 4Ps and 4As.

UNIT 4
Advertisements

1. Discuss the following questions with your partner.

   1) When are you least likely to experience advertisements? How aware are you of advertising in your daily life?

   2) If you worked in the advertising department of a sportswear company, *Adidas*, for instance, what kind of advertising would you exercise? Why?

   3) Can you think of any types of offensive advertisement? What are they? Why do you think they are offensive?

   4) Look at your clothes and the items you have with you. How are you currently advertising?

2. Work in groups. Discuss whether or not you agree with the following statements.

   1) Good advertising can make people want things they don't need.

   2) Advertising usually has a bad influence on children.

   3) Using film stars in advertising is always eye-catching.

   4) Without proper advertising, it's impossible to succeed in launching new products.

   5) Advertising increases the cost of a product.

Preview: Advertising is a form of communication that typically attempts to persuade potential customers to purchase or to consume more of a particular brand of product or service. The following passage is concerned with advertising that becomes democratized. Today, involving "ourselves" in the course of making advertisement is a new and popular idea in the profession of advertising. One typical example is an Audi marketing campaign that encouraged people to weave a complicated serialized mystery of a stolen car, and some 500,000 people tracked the story by following online clues. It sets a good example of "democratized advertisement". Other examples cited in the text illustrate the central idea of letting the public play in the ad game is what some call brand democratization.

Advertising of, by, and for the People

*Getting consumers to create ads saves a ton of money — and builds **buzz.***

By David Kiley

[1] Donovan Unks, a 28-year-old **biotech** researcher at Stanford University[1], spent valuable minutes every day for three months to follow an Audi[2] marketing campaign. The ads for the new A3 **hatchback**, appearing in magazines and on TV, **billboards**, and the Internet, **wove** a complicated serialized mystery of a stolen car. Some 500,000 people, according to Audi, tracked the story by following online clues. But Unks and his friend Laura Burstein didn't just play the game. They were **drafted** to be characters in the **plot** by ad agency McKinney & Silver (HAVS) in Durham,[3] N.C.[4], after they answered an **encrypted** ad that only solvers of **binary** code could read in *The Hollywood Reporter*. In their Audi roles, the two drove all night to a music festival, **crashed** a party, were **blogged** about by fans of the story, and **webcast** worldwide on the final night of the drama at the Viceroy Hotel[5] in Santa Monica[6], Calif.[7], on June 30.

[2] That's the kind of marketing **punch** that companies such as Nike[8], Cingular Wireless[9], General Motors(GM)[10], Samsung[11], and others are seeking by drawing consumers into the ad-making process. Instead of **cajoling** consumers into passively absorbing ads, the idea now is to get the public to create and participate in them. In a time when consumers can **scrub** advertising from their **laptops** and distribute ad-free amateur radio shows online, marketers are giving away some control over their ads. Their hope is that the public will accept them as entertainment rather than advertising. The most successful have found it a way to **spark** buzz and get creative ads on the cheap.

---

1 Stanford University / ˈstænfəd - / 美国斯坦福大学
2 Audi / ˈɔːdɪ / 德国奥迪汽车制造公司；奥迪汽车
3 Durham / ˈdʌrəm / 达勒姆，美国北卡罗来纳州中北部城市
4 N.C. North Carolina / nɔː ˌkærəˈlaɪnə / 美国北卡罗来纳州
5 Viceroy Hotel / ˈvaɪsrɒɪ - / 美国维斯罗利酒店
6 Santa Monica / ˈsæntə ˈmɒnɪkə / 圣莫尼卡，美国加利福尼亚南部城市
7 Calif. California / ˌkælɪˈfɔːnjə / 美国加利福尼亚州
8 Nike / ˈnaɪkiː / 美国耐克体育用品公司；耐克牌（运动衫、运动鞋等）
9 Cingular Wireless / ˈsɪŋɡjʊlə ˈwaɪəlɪs / 美国辛谷拉移动运营公司
10 General Motors (GM) / ˈdʒenərəl ˈməʊtəz / 美国通用汽车公司
11 Samsung / ˈsæmsʌŋ / 三星电子公司，是韩国最大的企业集团

[3] Audi spent $5 million-plus to run "The Art of The **Heist**" game. The carmaker thinks few online gamers will actually buy an A3. The real goal is to generate buzz among the 25-to-35-year-old, upper-income males Audi targets, says Lee Newman, group account director at McKinney & Silver. "If they see Audi as **inclusive** and **innovative**, we hope they won't turn our messages off," says Newman. During the three-month campaign, hits to Audi's website were up 140% from last year, with the heaviest traffic coming from the "Heist" game sites. Dealers got 10,000 sales leads and handled some 3,500 test drives.

[4] The idea of letting the public play in the ad game is what some call brand **democratization**. When Sausalito[1] (Calif.) agency Butler, Shine, Stern & Partners[2] **pitched** Nike's $10 million Converse[3] account, agency co-creative director John Butler persuaded Converse executives to **outsource** ads to fans. Butler **solicited** 60-second films from anyone with an idea and a camera. After the initial seven films about Converse went up on the Net, more films flooded in. "Our customers tend to be creative, and we've given them the biggest canvas we have to express themselves — our advertising," says Converse's global marketing chief, Erick Soderstrom.

[5] **Enlisting** consumers as ad creators isn't enough for some to see beyond the sales pitch. Even Laura Burstein, who **co-starred** in Audi's ad game, admits: "I had fun but felt slightly uncomfortable being used as free advertising." And McKinney's own report to Audi contained Web postings **decrying** the game as mere **hucksterism**. Still, with many consumers freely mixing their own music and editing their own videos, it's **naive** to think they'll sit attentively while sales pitches wash over them. Those attracted to playing at advertising are called "Generation C" by some marketing experts. "The 'C' is for creative, and they're part of the **tsunami** of consumer-generated 'content' on the Web," says Trendwatching.com[4] director Reinier Evers.

[6] One of the most **intriguing** tools for letting consumers create ads is the cell phone, but unlike with telemarketing, consumers place the call. This fall, Samsung will link users to interactive billboards in Hollywood and Manhattan's Times Square[5], possibly allowing them to put text messages up for thousands to see. Sharon Lee

---

1 Sausalito /ˌsɔːsəˈliːtəu/ 索萨利托，美国加利福尼亚州西部城市

2 Butler, Shine, Stern & Partners /ˈbʌtlə ʃaɪn stɜːn ənd ˈpɑːtnəz/ 美国一广告代理公司

3 Converse /kənˈvɜːs/ 美国匡威公司；匡威牌（运动鞋）

4 Trendwatching.com 荷兰消费者趋势观察公司网址

5 Manhattan's Times Square /mænˈhætən --/ 曼哈顿时代广场

UNIT 4 Advertisements

Ricketts, a 19-year-old student from Corpus Christi[1], Tex.[2], recently stood before the 22-story Times Square Nike billboard fingering her phone. By means of a **toll-free** phone link to the board, she was using her phone to **customize sneakers** she was ordering online in front of 1,000 or so **onlookers**. "This is way cool. Look what I just did. I just controlled that whole board," she **marveled**. And to think she only set out to buy a pair of sneakers.

(741 words)
From *Business Week*

New Words

buzz / bʌz /
n. a strong feeling of excitement, pleasure, or success speculative or excited talk or attention relating especially to a new or forthcoming product or event 兴奋之感；喜悦心情；成就感；好奇或兴奋的谈论或关注

biotech / ˌbaɪəʊˈtek /
n. (*inf*) biotechnology 生物科技

hatchback / ˈhætʃˌbæk /
n. an automobile having a sloping back with a hatch that opens upward 舱盖式汽车

billboard / ˈbɪlbɔːd /
n. a panel for the display of advertisements in public places, such as alongside highways or on the sides of buildings 大幅广告牌

weave / wiːv /
v. put facts, events, details, etc. together to make a story or a closely connected whole （把……）编成，编造（故事等）

draft / drɑːft /
v. choose people and send them somewhere for a special task 选派；抽调

plot / plɒt /
n. the series of events which form the story of a novel, play, film, etc. 故事情节；布局

encrypted / ɪnˈkrɪptɪd /
a. having been put into code or cipher 设成密码或暗码的

binary / ˈbaɪnərɪ /
a. of or relating to a system of numeration 二进制的

crash / kræʃ /
v. (*inf*) join or enter (a party, for example) without invitation 不请自来；不经邀请进入（如宴会）；闯入

blog / blɒg /
v. write commentary on the net 在网络上写日志或发表评论

webcast / ˈwebkɑːst /
v. broadcast an event on the Internet, at the time the event happens 网络广播

punch / pʌntʃ /
n. force and effectiveness 力量；有效（影响）

cajole / kəˈdʒəʊl /
v. (into) make sb. to do sth. by talking to them and being very nice to them; wheedle 劝诱；哄骗；诈骗

scrub / skrʌb /
v. remove (dirt or unwanted) 擦掉；消除

laptop / ˈlæpˌtɒp /
n. a microcomputer small enough to use on

---

1 Corpus Christi / ˈkɔːpəs ˈkrɪstɪ / 珀斯克里斯蒂，美国得克萨斯州城市
2 Tex. Texas / ˈteksəs / 美国得克萨斯州

one's lap 便携式电脑

spark / spɑːk /
v. cause sth. to start or develop, especially suddenly 引发；触发

heist / haɪst /
n. an act of stealing sth. valuable from a shop, store or bank; robbery; burglary 抢劫；盗窃

inclusive / ɪnˈkluːsɪv /
a. taking a great deal or everything within its scope; comprehensive 包罗万象的；综合性的

innovative / ˈɪnəˌveɪtɪv /
a. marked by new ideas; original 革新的，创新的

democratization / dɪˌmɒkrətaɪˈzeɪʃn /
n. the action of making something democratic 民主化

pitch / pɪtʃ /
v. try to persuade sb. to buy sth., to give you sth., or to make a business deal with you 推销；争取支持（或生意等）

outsource / ˈaʊtˌsɔːs /
v. arrange for sb. outside a company to do work or provide goods for that company 交外办理；外购

solicit / səˈlɪsɪt /
v. ask for sth., such as money, support or information; try to get sth. or persuade sb. to do sth. 索求；请求……给予（援助、钱或信息）；征求；筹集

enlist / ɪnˈlɪst /
v. persuade sb. to help you or to join you in doing sth. 争取，谋取（帮助、支持或参与）

co-star / ˈkəʊˌstɑː /
v. appear as one of the main actors with sb. in a play or film 与其他明星联合主演

decry / dɪˈkraɪ /
v. condemn openly 公开谴责

hucksterism / ˈhʌkstərɪzəm /
n. the action of selling things in a way that is too forceful and not honest 大吹大擂（或强行）推销商品的言论或做法

naive / nɑːˈiːv /
a. lacking critical ability or analytical insight; not subtle or learned 天真的；幼稚的

tsunami / tsjuːˈnɑːmɪ /
n. a very large ocean wave caused by an underwater earthquake or volcanic eruption 海啸

intriguing / ɪnˈtriːgɪŋ /
a. interesting; fascinating 引起兴趣的；有诱惑力的

toll-free / ˈtəʊlˈfriː /
a. without having to pay 免费的

customize / ˈkʌstəmaɪz /
v. make or alter to individual or personal specifications 定做；按照客户具体要求制作或改制；用户化

sneaker / ˈsniːkə(r) /
n. a sports shoe usually made of canvas and having soft rubber soles 帆布胶底运动鞋

onlooker / ˈɒnlʊkə(r) /
n. one that looks on; a spectator 旁观者；观众

marvel / ˈmɑːvəl /
v. be very surprised or impressed by sth. 感到惊奇；大为赞叹

Phrases & Expressions

a ton of
a lot of, a large quantity of 大量的

marketing campaign
an organized and coordinated effort to promote the sale of a certain product or group of products in accordance with a particular theme, using multiple forms of media 营销活动

UNIT **4** Advertisements

serialized mystery
the mystery or marvel that is written or published in serial form 连载广告（故事）

participate in
take part in sth. 参加某事

give away
give sth. free of charge 免费送出某物；赠送

get/buy sth. on the cheap
get or buy sth. cheaply 便宜地得到或买到某物

turn... off
cease paying attention to 不注意

wash over
flow powerfully over; surge over 涌进（某人的）脑子里；突然袭来

place the call
make a call 打电话

sales pitch
what salespersons say in order to persuade someone to buy sth. from them 推销员的游说；商品宣传

put... up
make a display 显示，展示

set out
start doing sth. or making plans to do sth. in order to achieve a particular result 开始；打算；规划

Exercises

Comprehension

1. Mark the following statements true (T) or false (F) or not mentioned (NM) in the passage. Discuss with your partner about the supporting points for each statement.

   1) _____ Donovan Unks and his friend spent three months making advertisements for A3.

   2) _____ Donovan Unks and his friend in their roles of the games drove to join a party where a music festival was being held.

   3) _____ Consumers were passive consumers of advertisements in the past, but now they have a say in how to make advertisements and which ones to see.

   4) _____ Advertising today is much more an entertainment than a commercial

81

activity.

5) _____ The carmaker thinks that their "Heist games" will definitely attract many online gamers to buy their cars.

6) _____ John Butler suggested to Converse executives that fans could make advertisements.

7) _____ According to the article, we can conclude that people who play in the ad games are comfortable participating in the creation of free advertising and find the activity rewarding.

8) _____ Cell phone is a good tool to be used in creating ads because a company can call the consumers to promote their products.

9) _____ Sharon Lee Ricketts succeeded in ordering online a pair of Nike sneakers in front of the public by using the phone.

10) _____ The passage suggests that advertising should involve the public more throughout the making process.

2. **Match the headings with their equivalent numbered paragraphs, and compare your answers with your partner's.**

   Para. 1   A. Nike's success in its "brand democratization" suggested by John Butler

   Para. 2   B. Nike's employment of cell phone to involve consumers in advertising

   Para. 3   C. Two common people playing roles in a serialized "Heist" story online for the advertising of Audi

   Para. 4   D. The goal of the A3 advertisement and the success achieved by the "Heist" game online

   Para. 5   E. Different opinions of consumers and executives

   Para. 6   F. More companies getting the public to create and participate in their advertisements

Critical Thinking

Work in group to discuss the following questions.

1) Allowing consumers to participate in advertising is a recent phenomenon, at least in actually creating advertisements. But how is wearing a shirt with a logo on it similar? Does carrying a bag or cup with a logo on it also qualify as advertising? What would you have to do to stop advertising for products that you own?

UNIT 4 Advertisements

2) General Motors recently launched a contest to see which member of the public could craft the best commercial for the Chevy Tahoe, a new sport utility vehicle. Hundreds of people used the Internet to circulate thousands of videos that charged GM with contributing to global warming, protested the war in Iraq or just demeaned the Tahoe's quality. Some videos also contained profanity or sexually explicit messages. The offer of prizes did not stop many people from creating ads that criticized the company and the product. How do you feel about such a contest? Is it worthwhile? How can marketers discourage people from creating negative advertisements?

Vocabulary

1. Fill in the blanks with the proper forms of the words and phrases given below.

punch	innovative	by means of	outsource	decry
give away	solicit	wash over	marvel	enlist

   1) The company's slogan is "to develop the first-rate business _____ scientific and technical innovation".

   2) One of the responsibilities of companies is to improve their business performance to _____ more manpower into the business to reduce unemployment of the nation.

   3) Anyone who _____ this as a waste of money should consider how much has been spent repairing motorways in the last 25 years.

   4) Increasingly, Converse clients are seeking to _____ the management of their facilities.

   5) More than 500 workers—and perhaps 1,000 or more—are in the process of being told by the company that their services are no longer needed. As the layoffs _____ the company, emotions run high.

   6) The company is striving to offer customers with the products which are cheaper, more _____ and more reliable than those of their competitors.

   7) The fast development of the company _____ its competitive rivals, and they all wondered the reasons.

   8) The electronic company is slowly losing its _____, but its sales still remain at a high level.

   9) The company is to call on potential customers to develop new business or maintain regular contacts with existing customers to _____ business.

10) Today, many companies often _____ publicity products to promote their sales volume as well as to give customers an opportunity to sample their new products.

2. There is a wrongly used word in each of the following sentences. Choose a proper word or phrase from the box to replace it.

| a ton of | scrub | plot | cajole | intriguing | crash |
| passive | absorb | inclusive | co-star | put up | outsource |

1) One of the negative effects of advertisement is to sometimes force customers into buying many things they don't need.

2) Before making an advertisement, the advertising company usually has an appealing scheme that guarantees the success of the advertising.

3) Within a month, the advertising company has received plenty of letters and packages from the public responding to the enlisting of the company on newspaper.

4) The professional advertising people often work out a charming idea to create a successful advertisement.

5) Faced with the huge cost of launching new aircraft, Airbus needs two things: more commercial partners to share the risk; and the chance to allot production to low-cost countries.

6) They made it clear that they would only take pessimistic measures in emergency circumstances.

7) This "democratized" advertisement enabled the public to coordinate with the famous film actress.

8) Our one-stop incorporated financial PR services have earned wide market recognition.

9) The twin sisters sometimes smashed the weekend party of their friends when they couldn't find other entertainments.

10) The first step of valuing the advertisements from the public is to refuse those that don't seem much appealing at the first sight.

UNIT 4 Advertisements

3. Link each word on the left with a noun on the right to make partnerships. Then complete the sentences below using the partnerships. You may have to make some changes to fit the grammar of the sentences.

A	B
marketing	pitch
serialized	tool
sales	campaign
intriguing	mystery
encrypted	festival
music	letter
amateur	phone
toll-free	shoes
interactive	play
customize	process

1) The treaty on tobacco control states that tobacco products have to be banned advertising and _____ in the member countries as far as their national constitutions permit.

2) NIKE has made a _____ of sales in recent years, especially on classic style of sportswear shoes.

3) The advertising company usually turns to a(n) _____, computer or DV (digital video), for instance, to take advantage of customers' creation.

4) Successful sales or service industry professional must learn through extensive in-depth probing what type of buyer he is dealing with and then create a custom-tailored _____ based specifically on the answers he receives from his probing.

5) After failing to restructure the company and improve the work efficiency, the administrator received a(n) _____ from the headquarters.

6) Through encouraging customers to engage in _____ in advertisement production, ADIDAS reached a considerable sales height.

7) If you want to know more details about the product, please call our nationwide _____ number.

8) It is a custom in this country to have a New Year _____ on the first day of a year.

9) With the aid of high-technology development, customers now can involve in the _____ of advertisement production.

10) Double Star, China's own sportswear brand, has been trying to _____ to compete with international brands.

Translation

1. Translate the following sentences into Chinese.

   1) That's the kind of marketing punch that companies such as Nike, Cingular Wireless, General Motors (GM), Samsung, and others are seeking by drawing consumers into the ad-making process.

   2) Instead of cajoling consumers into passively absorbing ads, the idea now is to get the public to create and participate in them.

   3) In a time when consumers can scrub advertising from their laptops and distribute ad-free amateur radio shows online, marketers are giving away some control over their ads.

   4) With the hope of making the public accept them as entertainment rather than advertising, the most successful have found it a way to spark buzz and get creative ads on the cheap.

2. Put the following sentences into English, using the words and phrases given in the brackets.

   1) 现在的广告公司经常采用在报纸、广播、电视及互联网上招募群众广告的方式推销产品。（pitch，by means of，enlist）

   2) 这不仅使广告制作成为互动的过程，而且还向顾客提供了免费成为明星的机会。（interactive，toll-free）

   3) 通常公众会提交大量由自己设计制作的广告，有些甚至还寄来自拍自演的录像带。（tsunami，video tape）

   4) 这种广告民主化的过程往往能使人们对新的产品耳熟能详，从而使推销产品取得预期的效果。（democratization，punch）

UNIT 4 Advertisements

Creating an Advertisement

Nowadays, instead of cajoling consumers into passively absorbing ads, some companies are trying to get consumers to create ads or participate in the ad-making process. Work in groups. Suppose you are the customers of different companies, participating in their campaign of creating an advertisement.

1) Each group choose a product on page 280 and read the given information.

2) Create a new advertisement based on the given information. You may also design a new advertisement of any other products. You can design the advertisement by discussing the following points:

- *the features of the product;*
- *the unique selling points;*
- *the target audience;*
- *the proper media (TV, radio, newspaper, internet, etc.);*
- *others...*

3) Prepare a TV commercial for your products. Imagine you yourselves are the actors or actresses of the advertisement and act it to the whole class. After showing your advertisements to the whole class, try to answer any questions they ask, especially the questions based on the above discussion points.

Effective Advertising Campaign Tips

The goal of advertising is to cost-effectively reach a large audience and attract customers. If done correctly, advertising can enhance the success of your business. Here are some advertising tips to pay attention to:

- Go after your target audience. An advertising campaign should be geared to your niche market.
- Highlight your competitive advantage. One of the keys to all advertising is to accentuate the pros of your company, those factors that give you your competitive edge.

- Establish an image. There are plenty of products that you recognize by their packaging or logo. Image counts when it comes to advertising and promoting your business.

- You have to spend money to make money. There are ways to save money, but typically advertising is not the place to cut corners. Successful advertising may cost some money, but that is because it works.

- Advertise in the right places. Your favorite magazine, radio station, or even television program might not be a favorite of your audience. Know what they read, watch, and listen to, and advertise in media that reaches your target market.

- Diversify. Do not want to put all of your eggs in one basket. Spread your advertising dollars around.

- Don't try to be everything to everyone. No product or service will appeal to everyone. Therefore, find your market and be everything you can be to that audience.

- Test your ads in advance. If you have the time or money to invest in focus groups, you should test your ads on other people. Do they understand and accept the message that you are trying to convey? There are other less-expensive ways to test your ads as well: questionnaires, for example.

- Monitor your ads. It is very easy to ask new customers or clients where they heard about you. It is advantageous to know which ads generate business.

Language Hints

Inquiring about a product
- What size (shape, color) is it?
- What's it made of?
- What does it look like?
- What's it used for?
- How does it work?
- Is it guaranteed?
- ...

Asking for clarification
- Sorry, but I don't really see why you have to ...
- Sorry, can you say that again, please?

UNIT **4** Advertisements

- Excuse me. I'm not very clear about ...
- ...

Interruption
- Excuse me, can I ask a question?
- Can I interrupt again?
- Can I just clarify one point?
- ...

Checking understanding
- Ok so far?

- Are you with me?
- Is that clear?
- Do you see what I mean?
- ...

Encouragement
- Of course, go ahead.
- Sure.
- Certainly.
- ...

Sales Leaflets

Leaflets are a type of open letter or postcard, designed to be handed out to people, either by hand, by post, inserted in local newspapers for distribution, left in venues, shops, restaurants, cafes, libraries... ANYWHERE where they will catch a person's eye.

A leaflet usually includes four parts: title, text, contact and date. The following is a list of common writing tips for leaflet drafting:

- Bear in mind the intended audience and expected effect.
- Use clear and concise language with a sincere, friendly and reader-oriented tone.
- Use words, phrases and incomplete sentences instead of full sentences.
- Use figures instead of words to make numbers more impressive.
- Use heading titles that can get a message across to people who only read the "big print".
- Use stirring slogans or quotations and set in bold for emphasis.
- Proof the text to correct errors.

Study the following sample, and then design a leaflet yourself based on the given information. Or you may design your own leaflet on what you like. Add anything necessary. Use illustrations, slogans or quotations to make your leaflets more attractive.

Exercises:

1. You work for Crosby's Fruit & Vegetables, which has just opened another chain-store in a newly built residential area. To publicize your store and your services, you have to adapt the following information to a written leaflet to put it in a local newspaper.

   Name of the shop: Crosby's Fruit & Vegetables
   Address: 615 Chorley Old Road, Bolton

Tel: 840548

Open time: 9:00 am-5:30 pm, Monday to Friday

Range of business: grade 1 fruit and vegetables; wide range of fresh fish; stockists of creams, eggs, cooked meat and cheeses as well as authentic Italian pasta and sauces.

Others: free delivery, order now for Christmas

2. You are working for an advertising agency. Christmas is approaching. To seize the golden opportunity of the selling season earlier, a client of yours comes to your office, asking you to design a new leaflet for the businesses he is carrying on. He supplies you with the information as follows.

Name of the shop: GlobeTrekker — Outdoor Shops

Address: 25 High Street, Heritage Close (opposite: Clock Tower), Albans Al3 4EH

Tel/Fax: 01727 835777

Open time: 9:00 am - 5:30 pm, Monday to Saturday; 11:00 am - 5:00 pm, Sunday

Stock the leading brands in: Waterproof jackets, fleeces, walking boots, rucksacks, sleeping bags, walking poles, travel equipment.

Great Christmas gifts in store: leathermen tools, Swiss army knives, Maglite torches, walking socks, Leki walking poles, hats and gloves, G.P.S systems.

Coupon: 15% retail prices with this leaflet, valid to 24/ 12 /2009

Others: good value, quality service, guaranteed to keep buyers warm and dry this winter; specialists in outdoor clothing, footwear and equipment

Relevant Extension

Business Expressions

1. Match the terms on the left to their meanings on the right.

Terms	Meanings
1) billboards	a. give money to a sports event, theatre, institution, etc., especially in exchange for the right to advertise
2) brochure	b. a piece of paper advertising something or giving information on a par ticular subject
3) sponsor	c. hoarding
4) leaflet	d. legible words in the sky from the smoke trails of aircraft, usu. to adver tise sth.
5) poster	e. booklet or pamphlet advertising sth.
6) slogan	f. poster
7) flier	g. a short phrase that is easy to remember and is used in advertisements
8) bill	h. a large printed notice, picture, or photograph, used to advertise some thing
9) sky-writing	i. small advertising leaflet that is widely distributed

2. Match words from each box to make word partnerships, for example, *consumer promotion*. Then translate the word partnerships into Chinese.

press	neon	shop
~~consumer~~	sales	radio
peak	window	in-store
publicity	target	market
media	opinion	

time	~~promotion~~	incentive
poll	display	campaign
coverage	group	signs
commercial	streamer	demo
release	hype	

UNIT **4** Advertisements

Word partnerships	Chinese equivalents
1) consumer promotion	_____
2) _____	_____
3) _____	_____
4) _____	_____
5) _____	_____
6) _____	_____
7) _____	_____
8) _____	_____
9) _____	_____
10) _____	_____
11) _____	_____
12) _____	_____
13) _____	_____
14) _____	_____

3. Complete the following sentences with the proper expressions in the box and change the form if necessary.

advertising campaign	word-of-mouth advertising	advertising sign
advertising rate	advertising dealer	advertising effect
advertising budget	mural advertising	classified advertisement
mass advertising	advertising slot	advertising client

1) If you want to sell your product, why not launch a national _____?

2) The huge eye-catching _____ on the narrow wall, created by trendsetting graffiti artists, forms a sharp contrast.

3) People wishing to buy or sell something can place _____ in a newspaper.

4) _____ are, more often than not, individuals and corporations in hope of increasing the demand for their products or services.

5) The cigarette-smoking actor proves to have some negative _____ on kids.

6) To promote the new service, the firm's _____ is growing swiftly.

93

7) Experienced consumers care much about commercials, ads, banners and other fancy wording and imagery, so there are more relevant ways to replace _____.

8) _____ can be the very best advertising for a home-based business, because it is free, sincere, believable, and unsolicited.

9) If the _____ charges fees, you then spend the next several years advertising their dealership free of charge with your moving billboard.

10) Publisher reserves the right to revise _____ with 30 days notice.

11) The _____ of coca-cola is a household symbol with huge potential value.

12) Additionally, Google could simply create a new ad unit that rests at the very top of the page, preserving all existing _____.

Specialized Reading

1. Read the following passage and write a brief heading for each paragraph.

_____

1) Advertising is paid, one-way communication through a medium in which the sponsor is identified and the message is controlled. Variations include publicity, public relations, product placements, sponsorship, underwriting, and sales promotion. Every major medium is used to deliver these messages, including: television, radio, movies, magazines, newspapers, the Internet, and billboards. Advertisements can also be seen on the seats of grocery carts, on the walls of an airport walkway, on the sides of buses, heard in telephone-hold messages and in-store PA systems[1]. Advertisements are usually placed anywhere an audience can easily and/or frequently access visuals and /or audio, especially on clothing.

_____

2) Advertising clients are predominantly, but not exclusively, for-profit corporations seeking to increase demand for their products or services. Some organizations that frequently spend large sums of money on advertising but do not strictly sell a product or service to the general public include: political parties, interest groups, religion-supporting organizations, and militaries looking for new recruits. Additionally, some non-profit organizations are not typical advertising

---

1 PA system is an electronic amplification system used as a communication system in public.

UNIT 4 Advertisements

clients and rely upon free channels, such as public service announcements. For instance, a well-known exception to the use of commercial advertisements is Krispy Kreme[1] doughnuts which relies on word-of-mouth.

3) The advertising industry is large and growing. In the United States alone, spending on advertising reached $144.32 billion, reported TNS Media Intelligence[2]. That same year, according to a report titled Global Entertainment and Media Outlook: 2006-2010 issued by global accounting firm PricewaterhouseCoopers, worldwide advertising spending was $385 billion. The accounting firm's report projected worldwide advertisement spending to exceed half-a-trillion dollars by 2010.

4) While advertising can be seen as necessary for economic growth, it is not without social costs. Unsolicited commercial email and other forms of spam have become so prevalent as to have become a major nuisance to users of these services, as well as being a financial burden on internet service providers. Advertising is increasingly invading public spaces, such as schools, which some critics argue is a form of child exploitation. One scholar has argued that advertising is a toxic by-product of industrial society which may bring about the end of life on earth.

2. **Read a short report on advertising below and discuss the questions with your partner.**

The advertising market is highly competitive, and the ads are expensive. A 30-second advertising slot on a typical prime-time television show costs over $60,000. The price goes up to $2 million during the Super Bowl in America.

Companies know that people don't like advertising and often try to avoid it. A remote in the hands of a man means that three programs can be watched at once although stations often run the commercials simultaneously to stop this, but firms recognize that much of their advertising is "clicked" away.

Because advertising budgets are often directly related to sales, the demand for advertising fluctuates significantly. Thus, when the economy slows down,

---

1 Krispy Kreme is a chain of doughnut stores. Its parent company is Krispy Kreme Doughnuts, Inc. based in Winston-Salem, North Carolina.
2 TNS Media Intelligence is the leading provider of strategic advertising intelligence to advertisers, advertising agencies and media properties.

the demand for advertising also slows down. In 2001, that's precisely what happened. The U.S. economy began to slow, and companies cut advertising budgets significantly. The advertising market fell into its worst decline since World War II, with advertising cutting their demand by 10 percent.

1) Why are most of the ads usually expensive?
2) Why don't many people like advertising on television?
3) How is advertising influenced by the economic trend?

UNIT 5
Sales

1. Discuss the following questions with your partner.

   1) Have you ever replied to a sales pitch and bought the promoted products? Consider especially times when you have bought items you didn't really want or need. Have you ever been tempted and yet refused? Tell your partner about an incident in which you either refused a good sales pitch or bought a product after a sales pitch, and discuss what influenced your decisions.

   2) Shoppers attending sales should be especially cautious to be sure they get their money's worth. From your experience, what cautions can you offer shoppers?

   3) There are many methods which a company or salesperson uses to sell their products. Which methods work best on men? Which work well on women?

2. What separates successful salespeople from everyone else? Most successful salespeople, in virtually any industry, are thought to possess some common characteristics. Work first individually and then in groups to figure out at least five characteristics. Then rank the ones you have identified.

Characteristics of Successful Salespeople:

- _____
- _____
- _____
- _____
- _____
- _____
- _____
- _____
- _____
- _____

UNIT 5 Sales

Reading

Preview: Successful salespeople should be in possession of good plans and terrific execution. Just as sensible eating habits and exercise are the cornerstones of weight-loss program, implementing good sales plans is key to successful marketing. Salespeople should put a lot of effort into the sales strategy, but they do not need to overwork so that they run short of the time and energy needed to put plans into action. The salesperson should make use of the prospective customers' feedback to refine the plan. Once the plan does not work, modifications in time become necessary. To achieve success, salespeople should be able to target prime potential customers accurately, and they should be able to develop top-notch selling skills.

A Sales Formula That's Pure Magic

*There's no strategy for success that omits the two most vital **ingredients** of them all: sound planning and hard work.*

By Michelle Nichols

[1] It's January. Folks are surveying their **swollen silhouettes** after all the **overindulgence** of the holiday season, and late-night TV is responding with a fresh crop of those crazy weight-loss ads. My favorite claims that, if I call a 1-800 number and buy some magic pills, I'll be able to continue eating anything and everything I fancy while those **excess** pounds simply melt away as I sleep.

[2] Yes, it's ridiculous — but it's not just desperate dieters who put their misplaced faith in magic. Some salespeople also believe that customers will call them up and order — **abundantly** and at full price, no less — without the investment of any real thought and effort.

[3] Unfortunately, there are no **enchanted potions** that will make products sell themselves. The closest you can come is a simple, two-part **prescription**, one that could have a magic effect on the number of deals you close. The first ingredient is a good sales plan. The second, terrific **execution**. Just as sensible eating habits and exercise are the **cornerstones** of any successful weight-loss program, adopting and **implementing** a good sales plan is key to achieving sales goals.

[4] First, don't over-think and under-do. By all means put a lot of mental effort into your sales strategy, but don't devote so much that you run short of the time and energy needed to put it into action. Once you get out and start selling, the reactions of **prospective** customers will **refine** your basic plan. Either they'll buy, which means

the plan works, or they won't, which means **modifications** are in order. Until you've actually taken your act on the road, that vital customer feedback will always be the missing ingredient.

[5] The big question is how to develop both a good plan and a great execution? Let me **tackle** those elements one at a time.

[6] Start by analyzing your present selling plan. I remember reading a quote from Anthony M. Frank, who became the fifth person in six years to head the problem-**plagued** U. S. Postal Service[1]. "If it's neither snow nor rain nor heat nor gloom of night, what the devil is wrong with this place?" he asked. The same goes for selling. If your current plan isn't getting you to your monthly sales goals, you need a new one.

[7] My favorite definition of **insanity** is doing the same thing over and over again while continuing to expect a different result. If you keep using last year's selling strategy, you're going to repeat last year's results. If that's not what you want, go back to the drawing board.

[8] There are several **components** to a good plan, and one of the most important is the ability to accurately target prospects. Funnyman Bill Cosby[2] once said: "I don't know the key to success, but the key to failure is trying to please everybody." Believe me, the same goes for selling. If you want to fail, try selling to everyone you meet. A much better approach is to develop a hunter's **mentality** that recognizes the specific openings and opportunities likely to increase the chance of success. One way of doing this is to identify the buying characteristics of a **prime** customer and then identify others who share the same **profile**.

[9] Targeting your prime potential customers will also achieve better results when seeking **referrals**. Simply asking prospects and clients if they know anyone else who might need what you're selling is a vague approach that will almost always produce vague responses. If you can clearly describe the type of person you'd like to be introduced to, you'll get specific referrals — and more of them, too. Infamous **bandit** Willie Sutton[3] put it this way when asked why he kept robbing banks: "Because that's where the money is." As salespeople, when we target our customers, we should also go where the money is.

[10] Now, let's tackle execution. Successful selling takes plenty of hard work. There

---

1 U. S. Postal Service 美国邮政管理局
2 Bill Cosby / bɪlˈkɒzbɪ / 比尔·科斯比，美国滑稽剧演员
3 Willie Sutton / ˈwɪlɪ ˈsʌtn / 威利·萨顿，美国经济大萧条时期著名的银行抢劫犯

is simply no substitute for lots of calls and face time with qualified prospects. Successful execution includes more than hard work, however — it also demands **top-notch** selling skills, as Aristotle[1] knew. "The fool tells me his reasons," said the philosopher, "the wise man persuades me with my own." Can you say that you have **honed** your selling skills to a sharpness that sees your customers persuade themselves? If not, now is the time to review those skills and update them.

[11] If you improve your selling skills and make just one more sales call per day, it will multiply your results. Add **intense** desire to practiced presentations and you'll definitely have terrific execution. In his inspiring poem, *The Will to Win*, Berton Braley[2] describes the essential **mindset**:

If you'll simply go after that thing that you want,

*With all your **capacity**,*

*Strength and **sagacity**,*

*Faith, hope and confidence, **stern pertinacity**,*

*If neither cold poverty, **famished** and **gaunt**,*

Nor sickness nor pain

Of body or brain

Can turn you away from the thing that you want,

*If **dogged** and **grim** you **besiege** and **beset** it,*

You'll get it!

[12] No matter how you do with those New Year's resolutions to lose weight, the goal of increasing sales is one best achieved by planning first, then taking action. Don't put it off; start today, because there is a lot of hard work ahead. As *60 Minutes*' resident **curmudgeon** Andy Rooney[3] observed: "Patience is a virtue. Impatience is a virtue too." Happy selling!

(935 words)
From *Business Week*

---

1 Aristotle / ˈærɪstɒtl / 亚里士多德，古希腊哲学家
2 Berton Braley / ˈbɜːtn ˈbræli / 伯顿·布莱利，美国诗人
3 Andy Rooney / ˈændi ˈruːni / 安迪·鲁尼，美国记者、专栏作家

New Words

formula / ˈfɔːmjələ /
n. a method of doing or treating sth. that relies on an established, uncontroversial model or approach 公式；准则

ingredient / ɪnˈɡriːdjənt /
n. an element in a mixture or compound; a constituent（混合物的）组成部分；成分；要素

swollen / ˈswəʊlən /
a. expanded by or as if by internal pressure 肿起的；膨胀的

silhouette / ˌsɪluˈet /
n. the shape of a person's body or of an object （人的）体形；（事物的）形状

overindulgence / ˌəʊvərɪnˈdʌldʒəns /
n. excessive yielding to inclination, passion, desire or propensity in oneself or another 过度放纵

excess / ˈekses /
a. being more than that is usual, required, or permitted 过量的；超额的；多余的

abundantly / əˈbʌndəntlɪ /
ad. in large quantities 大量地

enchant / ɪnˈtʃɑːnt /
v. cast a spell over; to bewitch; to attract and delight 对……施行妖法，用妖术迷惑；使心醉；迷住

potion / ˈpəʊʃən /
n. a drink that contains medicine, poison, or something that is supposed to have magic powers（含药物、毒物或有魔力的）饮料

prescription / prɪsˈkrɪpʃən /
n. a plan or a suggestion for making sth. happen or for improving it 计划；建议；秘诀

execution / ˌeksɪˈkjuːʃən /
n. the act of doing a piece of work, performing a duty, or putting a plan into action 实行；执行；实施

cornerstone / ˈkɔːnəstəʊn /
n. the most important part of sth. that the rest depends on 最重要的部分；基础；柱石

implement / ˈɪmplɪment /
v. put into practical effect; carry out 履行；落实；实施；执行

prospective / prəˈspektɪv /
a. likely to become or be 预期的；未来的

refine / rɪˈfaɪn /
v. improve (sth.) by removing defects and attending to detail（去粗取精、一丝不苟）改良（某事物）

modification / ˌmɒdɪfɪˈkeɪʃən /
n. a small alteration, adjustment 变更；修正；改进

tackle / ˈtækl /
v. take on and wrestle with (an opponent or a problem, for example) 着手处理

plagued / pleɪɡd /
a. pestered or annoyed persistently or incessantly 受麻烦困扰的

insanity / ɪnˈsænətɪ /
n. very stupid actions that may cause you serious harm 十分愚蠢的行为；荒唐的行为

component / kəmˈpəʊnənt /
n. a constituent element, as of a system 成分；系统的组成要素

mentality / menˈtælətɪ /
n. the sum of a person's intellectual capabilities or endowment 思想；心理；心态

prime / praɪm /
a. most important; chief; fundamental 最重要的；主要的；基本的

profile / ˈprəʊfaɪl /
n. the general impression that sb./sth. gives to the public and the amount of attention they receive 印象；形象

referral / rɪˈfɜːrəl /
n. a person recommended to someone or for something, a sales lead 被推荐的人；销售线索

bandit / ˈbændɪt /
n. robber, esp. a member of a gang of armed robbers 土匪；强盗

top-notch / tɒpˈnɒtʃ /
a. first-class 顶级的

hone / həʊn /
v. develop and improve your skill at doing sth., especially when you are already very good at it 磨炼；训练；使……完美

intense / ɪnˈtens /
a. very strong（指感情等）强烈的，热烈的

mindset / ˈmaɪndset /
n. a set of attitudes or fixed ideas that sb. has and that are often difficult to change 观念模式；思想倾向或习惯

capacity / kəˈpæsətɪ /
n. ability to perform or produce, capability 能力；本领；能量

sagacity / səˈɡæsətɪ /
n. wisdom and good judgment 睿智；精明；精确的判断

stern / stɜːn /
a. uncompromising; strict; firm 严格的；苛刻的；坚定的

pertinacity / ˌpɜːtɪˈnæsətɪ /
n. the quality or state of being persistent 坚持，顽强，不屈不挠

famished / ˈfæmɪʃt /
a. very hungry 非常饥饿的

gaunt / ɡɔːnt /
a. (of a person) made exceptionally thin by hunger or illness; haggard（指人因饥饿或疾病）憔悴的；骨瘦如柴的

dogged / ˈdɒɡɪd /
a. determined; not giving up easily 顽强的，不屈不挠的

grim / ɡrɪm /
a. determined in spite of fear 坚定无畏的

besiege / bɪˈsiːdʒ /
v. surround (sb./ sth.) closely; crowd round 围住（某人／某事物）；团团围住

beset / bɪˈset /
v. surround (sb./ sth.) on all sides; trouble constantly 围绕（某人／某事物）；困扰

curmudgeon / kɜːˈmʌdʒən /
n. an ill-tempered person full of resentment and stubborn notions 脾气坏的人（尤指老人）；难以取悦的人

Phrases & Expressions

a crop of
 a group, quantity, or supply appearing at one time（同时涌现的）一批；一群；一系列

melt away
 disappear or vanish gradually as if by dissolving 融化；消失；消散

no less
 (often ironic) used to suggest that sth. is surprising or impressive（表示惊讶或钦佩）竟，居然

by all means
 of course, certainly 当然

run short of
 use up so that a supply becomes insufficient or scanty 用尽；使供给缺乏或不足

put... into action
 carry out 实行；实施

be in order
 be a suitable thing to do; be required or expected 妥当，适宜

go for sth. / sb.
 apply to sth./ sb. 适用于某事物（某人）

face time
time spent interacting in the presence of or in the same location as another or others 实时沟通时间

go after
seek to obtain 追求；设法得到

turn away from
stop supporting someone, or stop using or being interested in sth. 拒绝帮助某人；对……不再感兴趣

Exercises

Comprehension

1. Answer the following questions with your partner.

   1) Why does a weight-loss ad "appeal" so much to the author?

   2) Do you think the author really has faith in such weight-loss ads? Why or why not?

   3) What, according to the author, really works when one wants to lose some weight?

   4) What are the two essential elements the author thinks that will work wonders when it comes to successful sales?

   5) Is it true, according to the author, that salespeople should not execute their sales plans until they make sure that they are nearly perfect? Why or why not?

   6) Why does the author quote Anthony M. Frank?

   7) Explain Bill Cosby's idea that "the key to failure is trying to please everybody". Why is trying to please everybody a bad idea in sales?

   8) When it comes to execution, why does the author quote Willie Sutton?

   9) It is clever to persuade people to buy, but with their own reasons, not the salespeople's. Discuss this and illustrate the point with some examples.

   10) Suppose you were a salesperson. Which would be your stronger feature at this time in promoting products, selling skills or diligence? Why? How might you improve the other?

UNIT **5** Sales

2. The text can roughly be divided into three parts. Go through the text carefully and then complete the outline below with the missing information from the text.

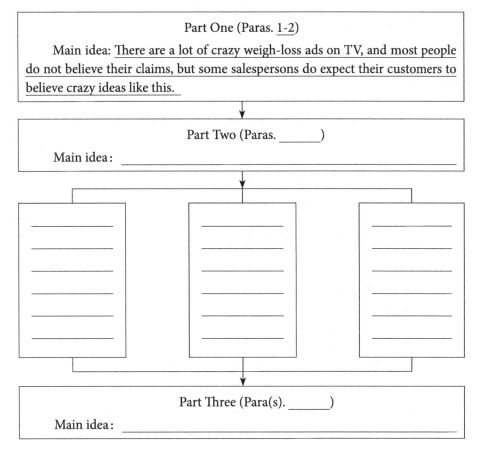

Critical Thinking

Work in group to discuss the following questions.

1) When salespeople first meet their prospects, they tend to immediately launch into a product presentation or "pitch". They extol the virtues of what they sell and tell the prospective buyers how good, fast, reliable, inexpensive or easy it is to use their product. They talk, talk, and talk, hoping they'll convince the buyer that their product or service is of value. How do you feel about this phenomenon? Is it right for salespeople to do so? Why or why not?

2) When making a sale, it is important to remember the AIDA marketing communication model. Do you know what the acronym AIDA stands for? Guess the answer from the clues given in the following model, and tell about how important it is for salespeople.

- get the customer's A _____;
- stimulate the customer's I _____;
- create the D _____ to buy;
- confirm the A _____ to be taken.

Vocabulary

1. Explain in English the underlined parts in the following sentences.

   1) *melt*

      A. The spring sun usually <u>melts the snow</u> by mid March.

      B. Her worry <u>melted away</u> when she read a newspaper report that indicated that the U.S. economy registered modest growth in the early summer, according to a nationwide survey.

      C. The meat was beautifully cooked by the French chef — it just <u>melted in your mouth</u>.

   2) *fancy*

      A. Do you <u>fancy a walk</u> after supper?

      B. I <u>fancy</u> that if that shop attempted a sales promotion, the shopkeeper would be likely to beat his rivals.

      C. The tourists stayed in a <u>fancy hotel</u> near Champs-Elysees.

   3) *order*

      A. Are you ready to <u>order</u>, or would you like to look at the menu for a little longer?

      B. Each <u>order</u> is for one week's pension in advance.

      C. The house had just been vacated and was in <u>good order</u>.

   4) *current*

      A. Mr. Lee started his <u>current job</u> as a salesman in 2006.

      B. She opened <u>a current account</u> with HSBC this morning.

      C. The EU is attempting <u>a current of</u> greater economic integration.

   5) *approach*

      A. As I <u>approached</u> the scientist, I got to know not only the man and the friend, but also the professional.

      B. We have been <u>approached</u> by a number of companies that are interested in our product.

C. We need a whole new <u>approach</u> to the job of landing a contract to supply components to an American computer manufacturer.

6) *prime*

   A. A doctor's <u>prime concern</u> is the well-being of the patient.

   B. This is a company <u>in its prime</u>.

   C. The money was intended to <u>prime the community care pump</u>.

2. **Rewrite the following sentences using the noun forms of verbs in the box. Do not change the meanings of the sentences.**

execute	adopt	enchant	prescribe	implement
modify	analyze	define	identify	review

   Example: We will promote this product by offering customers a free gift.

   Our promotion of this product will involve offering customers a free gift.

   1) The bank is going to execute a new team business plan and tactics to maximize return and minimize operational cost.

      _____.

   2) Unibrain has adopted business practices requiring enhanced quality control on design, production, and after-sales service and enters the twenty-first century with confidence and pride.

      _____.

   3) At the celebration the company enchanted its employees with the gift of extra bonuses.

      _____.

   4) Once the drug is approved for sale, doctors will be able to prescribe it for diabetes.

      _____.

   5) The changes to the national banking system will be implemented next year.

      _____.

   6) If you would like to add your business listing to our site, or need to modify an existing business listing, please complete and submit the following form.

      _____.

7) The researchers analyzed the purchases of 3,000 households.
   _____.

8) Using a variety of techniques to define optimal business processes allows you to discover new features needed in existing or to-be-built applications.
   _____.

9) A very critical step in IT deployment projects is to identify the business problem.
   _____.

10) Thompson, an investment adviser, sent out letters that ask that each company review its business ties to Japan.
    _____.

3. Complete each sentence with the correct form of the words in capital letters.

   1) OMIT

      Intentionally misleading someone by the _____ of pertinent information is just as bad as telling them an all-out lie.

   2) PROSPECTIVE

      If your _____ has recently bought or sold a business, use one of these sites to find a similar business for sale.

   3) OBSERVE

      Some enterprising, and certainly _____, locals decided to copy elements of the Starbucks brand and serve coffee themselves to their fellow countrymen.

   4) VIRTUE

      These statistics mean that a _____ marketing cycle is dramatically improving Apple's already robust business.

   5) FORMULA

      The establishment of a trade association shall be accompanied by the _____ of the constitution of the trade association.

   6) EXCESS

      This fall, one of the busiest times for business travel, British Airways is launching a promotion that guarantees to _____ your business class expectations.

   7) MULTIPLY

      The _____ entities are strategically funded to minimize vulnerable assets within the business form.

8) DIET

Getting advice from both a _____ and a physician at the same time helps in achieving weight loss, according to a report released recently.

9) INSANITY

Before you present your business model to the Board of Directors, make sure you do a _____ check and compare it against existing companies in your target sector.

10) REFERRAL

Some member companies will benefit from having access to a relevant industry _____ business process model that is being actively managed, maintained, and enhanced.

Translation

1. **Translate the following sentences into Chinese.**

    1) My favorite definition of insanity is doing the same thing over and over again while continuing to expect a different result.

    2) There are several components to a good plan, and one of the most important is the ability to accurately target prospects.

    3) Funnyman Bill Cosby once said: "I don't know the key to success, but the key to failure is trying to please everybody." Believe me, the same goes for selling. If you want to fail, try selling to everyone you meet.

    4) A much better approach is to develop a hunter's mentality that recognizes the specific openings and opportunities likely to increase the chance of success. One way of doing this is to identify the buying characteristics of a prime customer and then identify others who share the same profile.

2. **Put the following sentences into English, using the words and phrases given in the brackets.**

    1) 通常认为，成功的销售策略应包含两大重要因素：一是良好的营销计划，二是对计划的完美执行。（ingredients, execution.）

    2) 销售人员应充分利用潜在顾客的反馈来完善计划，如果发现计划行不通，要及时修改。他们可以用一切方法来促销其产品或服务。（prospective, feedback, refine, modification, by all means）

3) 促销就是说服潜在顾客购买某种产品或服务，主要促销手段有折扣券、免费礼品和会员卡等。（potential，coupon）

4) 如今会员卡成为一种重要促销手段，用以鼓励顾客成为某些零售店的忠实成员。（loyalty）

Telephone Selling

Telemarketing uses the telephone as a direct marketing medium through which a variety of sales and market research activities can be carried out. It can also be a key source of information on a company's prospective and current customer base, markets, inventory, distribution channels, advertising and promotional efforts. Now work with your partner, role-playing the following situations.

1) You work for China Highlights, a travel agency. A foreign university student, referred to you by one of your former customers, has come to China for a tour during the summer vacation. Read Card A(turn to page 282) and talk to the student on the phone, introducing and promoting your products or services.

2) Reverse your roles. You are a salesperson of China Ticket Online. Your partner is the manager of public relations of a company, who regularly contacts you to buy some tickets for the important clients or cooperators, or customers. Read Card B (turn to page 283) and talk to the manager on the phone, introducing and promoting your products or services.

3) You should include at least the following points:
   - *Find out the customer's needs;*
   - *Give related information of your products or services;*
   - *Help the customer choose a product or a service package;*
   - *Others...*

Telephone Selling Tips

Many people would agree that the best way to make a sale would be through a direct sale, say, from your shop, or on the Internet. Consequently, telemarketing is commonly overlooked, but in fact it is responsible for millions

UNIT 5 Sales

of sales each year and is currently being adopted by all businesses. The following are tips to help you sell successfully on the phone:

- Be focused before you start calling.
- The first few seconds are crucial.
- Keep it simple. Speak clearly in a polite and friendly tone of voice and not too fast.
- Be natural — use the right equipment.
- Don't go blank — use notes.
- Avoid insulting the customer.
- Give the customer a friend they can trust.
- Call at a convenient time.
- Finish the call in a positive, friendly way.

REMEMBER: You probably want an appointment from the phone, not to make the actual sale. Set a time for the FREE meeting. Most of the sales happen from a FREE session of some sort. Very rarely it is right from the call itself.

Language Hints

Making telephone sale calls
- Hello, is this (person's name)?
- This is (your name) from (company's name).
- This is a sales call. Do you want to hang up on me?
- That's a good question. Let me explain it in simple terms.
- I'm a/ We're a (type of product /service you offer) and we help people like you to ...
- Would you like a free estimate / consultation/ session / sample?
- ...

Sample questions
- Can you tell me about...
- Does it have any special features?
- Of course. What would you like to know?
- What are you selling?
- Sounds great.
- Tell me more about it.
- ...

Answering telephone sale calls
- Yes, speaking.
- Hang on a second/a minute.
- Would you like to hold?
- Hold the line, please.
- Sorry, but can we continue this later? My other line is ringing.
- Can I call back? Something has come up.
- Can I have your name and telephone number?
- I'll have to take your number and call you back.
- Sorry, I am afraid I am busy now.
- ...

A Memo

Memo

Memo, the short form for memorandum, is an informal written note of a transaction or proposed instrument sent by one person to another (or a group of people) between departments within a business or official agency or between agencies. It is a device very frequently used which provides a fast, efficient, and convenient way of exchanging information, stating policies, and asking questions.

Usually, memos are made up of two parts: memo head and body. The head of a memo needs to include information about the intended recipient, the sender, the subject matter and the date. Normally such information is placed under the sub-headings:

- To (the person who should get the memo)
- From (the person sending the memo)
- Subject (what it is about)
- Date (when the memo was written)

The word Memo is frequently the main heading so that it is clear before reading the memo what type of message it is. The usual positioning is:

```
                    Memo
To      _____
From    _____
Subject _____
Date    _____

(Body text)_____
```

The memo body is usually separated into paragraphs. Unlike business letters, memos don't need a salutation or a complimentary close.

As far as formality is concerned, a memo is something between a business letter and a note. It is important to follow the following rules while you are writing a memo:

- Be courteous;
- Be accurate;
- Be brief;

- Be clear;
- Avoid abruptness;
- Avoid over-politeness;
- Avoid unnecessary expressions.

Look at the following situations and write memos according to them. The memo for Situation 1 is given as a sample. Do Situation 2 and Situation 3 by yourself.

Situation 1

You work for Dunn's Wholesale Confectionery. The office manager is Miss Jane Treadgold. You come to work one morning and find the following note from her on your desk. Carry out her instructions.

> Write a memo under my name to all the company's representatives, informing them that the new supply of company-headed writing paper, and ballpens embossed with the company's name and address, which are to be given to customers, have arrived and will be available to the company reps from next Tuesday from the office. I need to know in writing by next Monday the quantities of these items each rep requires.

Sample memo

> | To | All representatives of Dunn's |
> | From | Jane Treadgold, Office Manager |
> | Subject | Order your headed paper and embossed ballpens |
> | Date | Sep. 8, 2008 |
>
> New supplies of the following will be available on Tuesday:
> - headed notepaper;
> - embossed advertising pens as gifts for customers.
>
> Order the amounts you need from me:
> - in writing;
> - by Monday.
>
> It will be very helpful if you keep to the dates set.

Situation 2

Mrs. Juanita Farrugia, Staff Training Officer at Uplands Bank, has invited you to help organize the Bank's training program more efficiently. She suggests that you write a memo to all staff outlining the way in which requests for training will be dealt with in future. She adds, "I have made some notes which may help you."

Mrs. Farrugia's notes:

> Staff — encouraged to seek additional training
> - attend courses/conferences
> - take examinations, etc.
>
> in addition to our own in-house staff training programme.
>
> Difficulties:
> - staff needing leave of absence at awkward times
> - costs to the Bank, etc.
>
> We shall TRY to agree to all requests.
>
> Apply early!
>
> Staff Training Officer will advise on choice of courses. If request is impossible, (too many away on any day, etc.), she will try to recommend an alternative.

Situation 3

You work for Tracer Limited, a firm that makes, sells and installs burglar alarm systems. The general manager is Mrs. Joan Pearce.

Just after a colleague of yours, Charles Thompson, has left to go home, Mrs. Pearce tells you that you will be needed for a few days at the Torquay Branch since two of their staff will be on a course at Exeter University. Mrs. Pearce asks you to write a memo to Charles Thompson asking him to do the important jobs you had planned for tomorrow and telling him to report directly to her to receive instructions for the following days.

Here is the entry in your forward planning diary:

> Wednesday   June 16, 2008
> - Phone Somerfield & Co. — 0121 751 9272 — quoted price includes VAT — earliest date for fitting — 20 July(checked with Fitting Department).

UNIT 5 Sales

> - Mrs. Marie Smith — Smith Gemstones — arriving 2 p.m. — interested in demonstration of CCTV.
> - Remind Harry Grainger to set it up and to be there!
> - TORQUAY (probably 5 days)! Memo to Charles Thompson!

Business Expressions

1. Translate the following sentences into Chinese, paying attention to the underlined expressions.

   1) They held a bring-and-buy sale last Saturday, raising money to help their classmate suffering from a kind of deadly disease.

   2) The jumble sale made $500 for cancer research.

   3) The sale of the car fell through when the buyer pulled out.

   4) Those newly built houses are on sale now, but there are not so many buyers as expected due to their extortionate prices.

   5) These goods are delivered to the supermarts and other outlets on a sale or return basis.

   6) An aggressive sales pitch from the company rep has made its product more competitive on the market.

   7) Rather than lose a sale, salesmen of the real estate company sometimes bring down the price.

   8) Instead of keeping such items in the warehouse collecting dust, we placed them all here for a clearance sale at cost prices.

   9) Car dealers are being urged to step up their sales drive on greener models after a survey underlined consumer ignorance of environmentally friendly vehicles.

   10) Gross sales are the sum of all sales during a time period. Net sales are gross sales minus sales returns, sales allowances, and sales discounts.

2. Look at the following expressions in the box and classify them under the proper headings.

sales force	sales presentation	sales potential	sales effort
massive sales	boost sales	overall sales	sales promotion
sales campaign	sales volume	sales patter	sales director
sales clerk	sales rep	sales team	sales performance
sales opportunity	unit sales	sales lead	sales staff
sales slump	closing-down sales	sales revenue	sales level

Headings	Relevant expressions
People:	
Activities/Process:	
Amount:	
Market:	

3. Complete the passage by filling in the missing words based on the given letters and the spaces for the missing letters.

1) M_ _ _ _ _ _ _ _places very important part in sales. If marketing department generates 2) p_ _ _ _ tial customers list, it can be beneficial for sales. The marketing department's goal is to bring people to the sales team using 3) p_ _ _ _ _ _ _ _ _ _ techniques such as advertising, sales promotion, publicity, and public relations. In most large corporations, the marketing department is structured in a similar fashion to the 4) s_ _ _ _ department and the managers of these teams must coordinate efforts in order to drive profits and business success. Driving more customers "through the door" gives the sales department a better chance by ratio of 5) s_ _ _ ing their product to the consumer.

UNIT **5** Sales

Organizations seldom profit from single 6) *pur_ _ _ _ _ _* made by first-time customers. Normally they rely on repeat business to generate the 7) *p_ _ _ _ _* that they need. However, there are some industries which have a business model based on one time only sales 8) *re_ _ _ _ _ _ship*. These tend to be the sale of very expensive, unusual household 9) *p_ _ _ _ _ _ _* such as houses and new and used cars. The economic reason for this behavior is that these items are usually unique. Consumers buy people not products. 10) *C_ _ _ _ _ _ _ _* will often pay more and accept less quality if they like and trust the sales person. A customer is buying a product because of that product's features and benefits along with their emotional attachment and feelings about the sales person and 11) *c_ _ _ _ _ _* credibility.

Specialized Reading

1. **The following is an analysis of some deceitful selling practices. Read carefully and judge the statements below it True (T) or False (F).**

   If your product appeals to the customer the first time they are likely to buy it again. So build a sales strategy that works and appeals to the customer to make the largest profit possible. But to some people, the purpose of selling is to help a customer realize his or her goals in an economic fashion. This assumption neglects the fact that buyer and seller may not have the same interests. Even if the selling organization recognizes that its sustainability depends on the maintenance of a healthy relationship with repeat customers, the salesperson does not necessarily share that goal. Many sales professionals are characterized by their short-term goals, desire quick returns on effort, and not the long-term building of relationships that the most successful sales people undertake. This dysfunctional behavior is encouraged by:
   - incentives of salespeople to increase their total number of sales, especially where retailers keep track of sales or offer commission-based salaries;
   - incentives from the manufacturers of products or the companies of service providers to salespeople to sell their products where other similar products offered by competitors are offered;
   - incentive to sell a customer a product that is in need of being cleared out, despite the fact that a customer may be better to wait for the new product.

   Salespersons recognize that a deceived customer is unlikely to buy a similar product for a long time, and so the salesperson has no incentive to offer any extra quality of service to encourage a long-term relationship. This behavior is generally true only of business-to-consumer sales.

1) _____ The author might agree that the purpose of selling is to help a customer realize their goals with money.

2) _____ The author doesn't think that the buyer and seller have the same interests.

3) _____ Many sellers tend to have the short-term goals.

4) _____ Sales people relying on commission are more likely to have short-term goals.

5) _____ The author mainly stresses the importance of having long-term relationships with customers.

6) _____ The short-term practices are in the best interest of customers.

7) _____ The most successful sales people undertake the long-term building of relationships.

8) _____ The short-term behavior is generally true only of business-to-consumer sales.

2. **Read the following sales strategies. Do the multiple-choice exercise and answer the given question.**

   How can a company improve its sales? One of the keys to more effective selling is for a company to first decide on its "sales strategy". In other words, what is the role of the sales person? Is the salesperson's job narrative, suggestive, or consultive?

   The "narrative" sales strategy depends on the salesperson moving quickly into a standard sales presentation. His or her pitch highlights the benefit for the customer of a particular product or service. This approach is most effective for customers whose buying motives are basically the same and is also well suited to companies who have a large number of prospects on which to call.

   The "suggestive" approach is tailored more for the individual customer. The salesperson must be in a position to offer alternative recommendations that meet a particular customer's needs. One key aspect of the suggestive approach is the need for the salesperson to engage the buyer in some sort of discussion. The salesperson can then use the information gleaned from the customer to suggest an appropriate product or service.

"We tell our salespeople to be like wine stewards," says Mindy Sahlawannee, a corporate sales trainer, "the wine steward first checks to see what food the customer has ordered and then opens by suggesting the wine that best complements the dish. Most companies who use a narrative strategy should be using a suggestive strategy. Just like you can't drink red wine with every dish, you can't have one sales recommendation to suit all consumers."

The final strategy demands that a company's sales staff act as "consultants" for the buyer. In this role, the salesperson must acquire a great deal of information about the customer. They do this through market research, surveys, and face-to-face discussions. Using this information, the salesperson makes a detailed presentation tailored specifically to a consumer's needs.

"Good sales consultant", says Alan Goldfarb, president of Ad Pro, Inc. in the United States, which publishes the weekly newspapers, seasonal magazines and specialty publications, "are the people who use a wide range of skills including probing, listening, analysis, and persuasiveness. The best sales consultant, however, are the ones who can think outside the box and use their creativity to present a product and close a sale. The other skills you can teach. Creativity is innate. It's something we look for in every employee we hire."

More and more sales teams are switching from a narrative or a suggestive approach to a more consultative strategy. As a result, corporations are looking more at intangibles such as creativity and analytical skills and less at educational background and technical skills.

1) The main difference between narrative sales and suggestive sales is that _____.

   A. the former stresses the benefits

   B. the former can satisfy individual's needs

   C. the latter involves a lot of discussion

   D. the latter has to prepare for unexpected information

2) Mindy compares salespeople to wine stewards because they both _____.

   A. have to close the sale

   B. offer customer-tailored service

   C. make a living by their persuasive skills

   D. have to offer recommendations constantly

3) The biggest challenge for a consultative salesperson is that it requires _____.

A. face-to-face discussion

B. precise presentation

C. a lot of research

D. appropriate technical skills

4) In Alan's opinion, creativity in salespeople is _____.

A. something that can not be acquired

B. something that can be made perfect through practice

C. the ability to "think outside the box"

D. the ability of eloquence

5) The passage mainly tells us _____.

A. the requirement of salespeople

B. the new trend in training salespeople

C. the importance of creativity in sales

D. different approaches to sales

6) What are the main strategies of the three Sales Approaches discussed in the passage?

Narrative sales: _____

Suggestive sales: _____

Consultative sales: _____

3. Discuss the following questions with your group members.

1) Are the three sales strategies, that is, narrative sales, suggestive sales, and consultative sales, inclusive? Why or why not?

2) What sales strategy is the most effective and demanding? Give your reasons.

UNIT 6
Consumers

1. Discuss the following questions with your partner.

   1) What do you mainly rely on to help you make purchasing decisions? Advertisements or word of mouth? Why?

   2) By and large, as a consumer, are you satisfied with the quality of products on the Chinese market? Why or why not?

   3) What role can the Internet play in helping consumers make informed purchasing decisions?

   4) Some car-buyers are highly knowledgeable about the cars they are interested in buying because they have visited the auto manufacturer's website and obtained the information about a model before going to the showroom. With so much information around, what role do auto salespeople play?

2. Suppose your group is working for a certain Consumers Association. Faced with a few of the following typical questions asked by consumers, you have to work out the answers through discussion.

   1) I am interested in purchasing goods over the Internet, but fear that if I pay in advance, the product may turn out to be shoddy upon arrival, or it may never arrive. What can I do to protect myself while shopping on the Internet?

   2) My mother bought a skincare product last week. Yesterday it was reported to contain certain toxins, and when I asked for a refund, the retailer simply said I should contact the manufacturer. Who is responsible in this case?

   3) I have just ordered a new stereo system over the Internet but have now seen it cheaper in a street shop. What would happen if I cancel the online order?

Preview: The high-sounding slogan "customer is king" has a century-long history. In the past, retailers only paid lip service to that lofty ideal; the consumer did not enjoy a high status in the eyes of the retailer because the former had only limited access to information, while the latter took advantage of their control of information. But since the very beginning of the Internet, power has shifted from the supplier to the consumer. The Internet allows people to compare prices more easily. The shift has created a new world of implications for the consumer and retailer both.

Power at Last

Armed with the Internet, the customer has finally got on top.

By Paul Markillie

[1] "When a customer enters my store, forget me. He is king," **decreed** John Wanamaker, who in 1876 turned an abandoned railway **depot** in Philadelphia[1] into one of the world's first department stores. This revolutionary concept changed the face of retailing and led to the development of advertising and marketing as we know it today.

[2] But **compelling** as that slogan was, in truth the shopper was cheated of the crown. Although manufacturing efficiency boosted the variety of goods and lowered prices, advertising provided most information about products. Through much of the past century, ads spoke to a captive audience **confined** to just a few radio or television channels or a limited number of publications. Now media choice has **exploded** too, and consumers select what they want from a far greater variety of sources — especially with a few clicks of a computer mouse. Thanks to the Internet, the consumer is finally seizing power.

[3] Consumer power has **profound implications** for companies, because it is changing the way the world shops. Many firms already claim to be "**customer-driven**" or "**consumer-centric**". Now their claims will be tested as never before. Trading on shoppers' ignorance will no longer be possible: people will know — and soon tell others, even those without the Internet — that prices in the next town are cheaper or that certain goods are inferior. The internet is working wonders in raising standards. Good and honest firms should benefit most.

[4] But it is also **intensifying** competition. Today, window shopping takes place online. People can compare products, prices and reputations. They can read what companies say about products in far greater detail, but also how that **tallies** with the opinions of others, and — most important of all — discover what previous buyers have to say. Newsgroups and websites constantly review products and services.

[5] This is changing the nature of consumer decisions. Until recently, consumers usually learned about a product and made their choice at the same time. People would often visit a department store or **dealership** to seek advice from a salesman, look at

---

1 Philadelphia /ˌfɪləˈdelfɪə, -fjə/ 费城，美国宾夕法尼亚州主要城市

his recommendations and then buy. Now, for many, each of these steps is separate. For instance, Ford[1] is finding that eight out of ten of its customers have already used the Internet to decide what car they want to buy — and what they are willing to pay — even before they arrive at a showroom.

[6] Of course, the amount of time people spend researching and checking prices tends to rise in proportion to the value of the product — and cars are expensive. But consumers are displaying similar behaviors when they purchase other things, such as digital cameras, mobile phones or fashionable clothes. And while supermarket shoppers may not research in this way all the individual items they drop into their trolley, many suppliers of the packaged goods sold in supermarkets are already **acutely** aware that their customers, too, are better informed than ever before about the value or health implications of the products they sell.

[7] Reaching these better-informed consumers with a marketing message is not easy, and not only because they are more **skeptical**. Many people now spend as much time surfing the web as they do with television, magazines or newspapers. The audience for advertising is **splintering** and its attention is harder to attract. On top of that, many people are arming themselves with technology to avoid marketing messages, such as pop-up ad-blockers for the Internet and personal video recorders that make it easy to **skip** TV commercials.

[8] Despite the flood of product and price information suddenly available, consumers are unlikely ever to become wholly **calculating**. Tastes and fashion will differ. Brands are likely to remain popular. But brand **loyalties** are weakening. A **slip** or delay can cost a firm **dearly** and hand the advantage to an **opportunistic rival**. This is how Apple's iPod **snatched** from Sony the market leadership in portable-music devices.

[9] Many firms do not yet seem aware of the revolutionary implications of newly **empowered** consumers. Too many companies relaxed after the bursting of the dotcom **bubble**, assuming that the online threat had faded. This was a mistake. It is true that the vast majority of people still go to shops for most purchases. Before doing that, however, most have used the Internet. More than 90% of people aged between 18 and 54 told America's Online Publishers Association[2] in a survey that they would turn to the Internet first for product information. The differences between the **virtual** and the **bricks-and-mortar** worlds do not worry consumers. But they should worry companies. Many consumers first **encounter** a firm through its website, and yet for too many firms, their online presence remains a low **priority**.

---

1 Ford /fɔːd/ 美国福特汽车公司
2 America's Online Publishers Association 美国网络出版商协会

UNIT **6** Consumers

[10] By contrast, some businesses have embraced the Internet wholeheartedly, and been rewarded for it. Dell[1] has **by-passed** retailers and used direct sales to become the world's leading supplier of personal computers. The web is also **transforming** the travel business, giving consumers the power to book flights, hotels and cars directly. And it has allowed hundreds of thousands of small businesses, from **mom-and-pop** stores to traders of **collectibles** on eBay[2], to reach a global market.

[11] The explosion of choice that followed the opening of Mr. Wanamaker's store is **minuscule** compared with the **cornucopia** already provided by the Internet. But the consumer's choice is about to become even greater. Internet search firms such as Google[3], Yahoo![4] and MSN[5] are now falling over each other to offer more **localised** services. These promise to open up a new goldmine in search advertising. And this facility is available not just on PCs at home or work, but on mobile phones. At a touch, consumers will be able to find a local store and then check the offers from nearby **outlets** even as they browse the **aisles**, or listen to a salesman. When that happens consumers will truly be kings, and only those firms ready and able to serve these new **monarchs** will survive.

(1,002 words)
From *The Economist*

New Words

decree / dɪˈkriː /
v. order 命令；规定

depot / ˈdepəʊ /
n. a warehouse or storehouse 仓库

compelling / kəmˈpelɪŋ /
a. interesting; attractive; persuasive; urgently requiring attention 激发兴趣的；引人注目的；强制性的

confine / kənˈfaɪn /
v. keep within limits 限制；使局限

explode / ɪkˈspləʊd /
v. increase rapidly in size, number or extent 激增；迅速扩大

profound / prəˈfaʊnd /
a. (of a state, quality, or emotion) very great or intense（状态、品质或情感）深刻的

implication / ˌɪmplɪˈkeɪʃən /
n. a possible effect or result of an action or decision 可能的影响（或作用、结果）

customer-driven / ˈkʌstəməˈdrɪvən /
a. focusing on customers' needs 以顾客为本的

consumer-centric / kənˈsjuːməˈsentrɪk /
a. consumer-centered 以消费者为中心的

intensify / ɪnˈtensɪfaɪ /
v. become greater in strength, amount, or degree 加强；增强

tally / ˈtælɪ /
v. agree, correspond or match 符合；吻合

---

1 Dell / del / 美国戴尔电脑公司
2 eBay / ˈiːbeɪ / 美国电子港湾公司
3 Google / ˈguːgl / 美国谷歌公司
4 Yahoo! / ˈjɑːhuː / 美国雅虎公司
5 MSN (Microsoft Network) 美国微软公司的因特网服务提供商

dealership /ˈdiːləʃɪp/
n. an authorized sales agency 商品特许经销商

acutely /əˈkjuːtlɪ/
ad. strongly; keenly 剧烈地

skeptical /ˈskeptɪkəl/
a. having doubts about sth. 表示怀疑的

splinter /ˈsplɪntə/
v. break into different parts 分裂

skip /skɪp/
v. pass over without notice or mention; omit 略过;跳过

calculating /ˈkælkjuleɪtɪŋ/
a. shrewd; crafty 审慎的;精明的

loyalty /ˈlɔɪəltɪ/
n. the quality of staying firm in one's friendship or support for sb. or sth. 忠诚, 忠心

slip /slɪp/
n. a small or unimportant mistake in judgment, policy, or procedure 疏忽;差错

dearly /ˈdɪəlɪ/
ad. at a high price; with much loss or suffering 昂贵地;惨重地

opportunistic /ˌɒpətjuːˈnɪstɪk/
a. taking advantage of opportunities as they arise with little regard to principle or consequences 机会主义的

rival /ˈraɪvl/
n. a person, business, or organization competing against another in the same area or for the same thing(s) 竞争对手;敌手

snatch /snætʃ/
v. quickly seize sth. in a rude or eager way — 把抓起(某物);夺得

empower /ɪmˈpaʊə/
v. give power to do sth.; make sb. stronger and more confident, esp. in controlling their life and claiming their rights 授权于;增强(人)的力量和信心(尤指使能够掌握自身命运及维护自身权利)

bubble /ˈbʌbl/
n. (fig.) a state that is unstable and unlikely to last〈喻〉泡沫

virtual /ˈvɜːtʃʊəl/
a. not physically existing but made by software to appear to do so【计算机】虚拟的

brick(s)-and-mortar /ˈbrɪk(s)ənˈmɔːtə/
a. located or serving consumers in a physical facility (as opposed to providing online services)(相对网络公司而言的)传统公司的;实体的;(企业)按传统模式(而非通过因特网)运营的

encounter /ɪnˈkaʊntə/
v. meet; confront 与……邂逅, 与……偶遇

priority /praɪˈɒrətɪ/
n. a thing that is regarded as more important than others 优先考虑的事

by-pass /ˈbaɪpɑːs/
v. avoid 越过;避开

transform /trænsˈfɔːm/
v. make a thorough or dramatic change in the form, appearance, or character 彻底改变, 使发生巨变, 使改观, 变革

mom-and-pop /ˈmɒmənˈpɒp/
a. (of a small shop) run by a married couple (小店)夫妻经营的

collectible /kəˈlektəbl/
n. (亦作 collectable) a rare or beautiful object that is valued very highly by collectors 收藏品

minuscule /ˈmɪnəskjuːl/
a. extremely small; tiny 非常小的;微不足道的

cornucopia /ˌkɔːnjuːˈkəʊpɪə/
n. an abundant supply of good things of a specified kind 丰富;充裕

localise /ˈləʊkəlaɪz/
v. (亦作 localize) make (sth.) local in character 使本土化;使具有地方特色

outlet /ˈaʊtlet/
n. a point from which goods are sold or distributed 商店, 门店

aisle /aɪl/
n. a passage between rows of shelves in a store or supermarket (商店、超市等的)过道

monarch /ˈmɒnək/
n. a person who rules a kingdom or empire as a king, queen, emperor, or empress 君主;国王;皇帝

UNIT **6** Consumers

Phrases & Expressions

cheat sb. (out) of sth.
prevent sb. from having sth., especially in a way that is not honest or fair（尤指用不诚实或不正当的手段）阻止某人得到某物

captive audience
audience with little or no freedom to go away and therefore easily persuaded to listen or watch 被动听众，被动观众（因无法轻易离开者而易受诱者）

thanks to
as a result of; due to 幸亏；由于

trade on sth.
make use of sth. for one's own advantage 利用某事物谋取私利

window shopping
the activity of looking at goods in shop/store windows usually without intending to buy anything 浏览商店橱窗

look at
think about, consider, or study sth. 考虑或研究某事物

in proportion to
与……成比例

on top of
in addition to 除……之外

pop-up ad-blocker
a computer program that prevents online advertisements from displaying 弹出广告拦截器

fall over each other
compete for attention 互相竞争；争先恐后

open up
make available to others 开发；开辟

Exercises

Comprehension

1. **Mark the following statements true (T) or false (F) or not mentioned (NM) according to the text. Discuss with your partner about the supporting points for each statement.**

   1) _____ From John Wanamaker's point of view, when customers entered his store, he should automatically disappear so that his existence would not be noticed.

   2) _____ John Wanamaker's idea revolutionized retailing and boosted advertising and marketing.

3) _____ When customers purchased goods in the past, they did not enjoy a high status and sellers could more easily take advantage of them.

4) _____ During much of the last century, the target audience of ads already had a large number of information channels, apart from TV, radio, newspapers, etc.

5) _____ Due to the Internet, the consumer is becoming more powerful than before in controlling their shopping experience.

6) _____ The advent of the internet can make commercial competition less fierce because much of the consumer's attention will be diverted from traditional bricks-and-mortar stores.

7) _____ The Internet is responsible for much of the information revolution hitting the retail industry.

8) _____ Some new-car buyers spend time researching their proposed purchases online before visiting a dealership.

9) _____ With the development of the market, consumers' loyalty to brands increases as the number of choices of goods available explodes.

10) _____ Worldwide many companies are now racing to meet the constantly changing demands of the internet-empowered consumers.

2. Identify which paragraph contains information that fits each phrase given below, and compare your answers with your partner's.

Paragraphs	Information
Para. __	Discussion on the research cost
Para. __	More intense competition
Para. __	Why the customer wasn't king
Para. __	What marketers can do
Para. __	How the customer was considered before
Para. __	How the internet changes the balance of power
Para. __	Different decision-making
Para. __	Problems with marketing to these informed consumers
Para. __	Companies' illusions about the online threat

UNIT **6** Consumers

Critical Thinking

Work in group to discuss the following questions.

1) By combining e-Commerce with social networking teambuying offers customers an innovative and money-saving shopping approach. Did you ever get anything through teambuying? If you did, share your experience with your group. How does teambuying or *Tuangou* manifest growing consumer power in China? Do you think *Tuangou* will exist generation for generation or it is just a temporary purchasing phenomenon? Why or why not?

2) What negative impact does the Internet have on consumers? As a consumer, do you have any unpleasant experience caused by the negative impacts of the Internet? If you do, what is it?

Vocabulary

1. Make two-word expressions connected with business by combining words from the two lists: A and B. Match each expression with the appropriate phrase. Use each word once. The first one has been done for you.

A	B
consumer	reality
competitive	bubble
department	loyalty
direct	leadership
dotcom	store
virtual	edge
brand	sales
market	power

1) unsolicited advertising material which is mailed and thrown away immediately by the people who receive it

   junk mail

2) a speculative bubble covering roughly 1995 — 2001 during which stock markets in Western nations saw their value increase rapidly from growth in the new Internet sector and related fields

   _____

3) customer's ability to understand, control and potentially change the market place

   _____

4) the advantage that a business has over its competitors

   _____

5) an environment which is produced by a computer and seems very like reality to the person experiencing it

   _____

6) a large shop which sells many different kinds of goods

   _____

7) a consumer's repeated buying of a product or service or other positive behaviors such as word of mouth advocacy

   _____

8) the marketing of products or services to consumers through sales tactics including presentations, demonstrations, and phone calls without using a "middle man" such as retail outlets, distributors or brokers

   _____

9) the status of a business which commands a large share of the market and achieves public recognition

   _____

2. **Fill in the blanks with the proper forms of the words and phrases given below.**

| tally with | work wonders | implication | priority | encounter |
| minuscule | fall over each other | localise | in proportion to | cornucopia |

1) Under the new incentive package, the employees of the company are paid _____ the contribution they have made, which fully taps their potentials.

2) Financial service companies are responding to these needs with a _____ of investment trusts designed with baby boomers in mind.

3) The large mobile phone operator is likely to exploit its scale advantage and use the knowledge of its customer base to offer _____ services such as guides to restaurants.

4) In a presentation about the London 2012 Olympic project, Mr Evans said the estimated value of the Olympic park and venues was £2.4 billion, which _____ original government figures.

5) Like most East Asian governments, Singapore's has consistently exposed its manufacturers to the forces of globalization, which has _____ throughout

the region, fostering the strong export-led growth for which Asia's tigers are known.

6) Supermarkets are now _____ to paint themselves as the ' greenest' or most responsible for the protection of the environment.

7) The BlackBerry and other portable e-mail devices are a boon to the travelling executive who needs to keep in touch with colleagues and customers, but the _____ screens and text can be hard on the eyes.

8) Some top government officials fail to realize that the low level of current investment has serious _____ for future economic growth.

9) The promotion of mass transit over automobile as an alternative mode of transportation has _____ consumer resistance.

10) The fight against inflation has been the Government's overriding economic _____ for nearly two decades.

3. **Rewrite each sentence with the word or phrase in brackets, keeping the meaning unchanged. A certain part of the sentence has been written for you.**

   1) A slip or delay can cost a firm dearly and hand the advantage to an opportunistic rival. (*pay a price*)

      _____ and hand the advantage to an opportunistic rival.

   2) The government official claimed that the profits the power plant would generate for investors dwarfed the estimated $500,000 in additional tax revenue from the plant. (*minuscule*)

      The government official claimed that _____
      _____.

   3) Member governments' financial backing for the IMF would determine any allocation that would be transferred to them, with the rich countries receiving most. (*proportion*)

      Any allocation _____
      with the rich countries receiving most.

   4) The risks stemming from a slowdown in the Chinese economy are very real and have a far-reaching impact on global markets. (*implication*)

      The risks stemming from a slowdown in the Chinese economy are very real and _____.

   5) The Fraud Advisory Panel says the Home Office and Treasury refuse to attach

primary importance to the fight against financial crime even though it costs the economy an estimated £16 billion a year or more. (*priority*)

The Fraud Advisory Panel says _____

_____ even though it costs the economy an estimated £16 billion a year or more.

6) Although the retailer's sales pitch sounds compelling, it seldom honours its commitment to be "customer-driven" and "consumer-centric" and frequently sells shoddy products. (*as*)

_____, it seldom honours its commitment to be "customer-driven" and "consumer-centric" and frequently sells shoddy products.

7) Given its poor management and lack of clear strategic vision, the chances of the company expanding its domestic business and getting out of the red are quite slim. (*likely*)

Given its poor management and lack of clear strategic vision, the company ___ _____.

8) Under Forgeard, Airbus surpassed Boeing in market share and sales volume and became No. 1 on the market, winning more orders and delivering more planes than its rival in recent years, while breaking the American firm's monopoly at the top end of the aircraft market. (*market leadership*)

Under Forgeard, _____

_____, winning more orders and delivering more planes than its rival in recent years, while breaking the American firm's monopoly at the top end of the aircraft market.

Translation

1. **Translate the following sentences into Chinese.**

   1) Consumer power has profound implications for companies, because it is changing the way the world shops.

   2) Trading on shoppers' ignorance will no longer be possible: people will know — and soon tell others, even those without the internet-that prices in the next town are lower or that certain goods are inferior.

   3) The internet is working wonders in raising standards. Good and honest firms should benefit most. But it is also intensifying competition.

4) Today, window shopping takes place online. People can compare products, prices and reputations. They can read what companies say about products in far greater detail, but also how that tallies with the opinions of others, and—most important of all-discover what previous buyers have to say.

2. Put the following sentences into English, using the words and phrases given in the brackets.

1) 从前，消费者在购买商品时，反反依靠售货员的劝告和推荐来决定是否购买。顾客往往是在了解商品的同时做出决定。(recommendation, learn about)

2) 如今，互联网的出现改变了零售业的面貌。消费者上网时只要轻点鼠标，就可以在新闻组中看到其他消费者对某种商品的评价。(change the face of, surf, review)

3) 除此之外，大家还可以通过网上交流来分享彼此的购物经历。在做出购物的决定时，消费者越来越依赖网络上了解到的商品的口碑了。(on top of)

4) 一般来说，消费者花在网上查询商品信息的时间与该商品的价值成正比。零售商再也不可能利用信息不对称（information asymmetry）来欺骗顾客了。(in proportion to, trade on)

5) 网络技术的发展不仅加剧了零售行业的竞争，而且在提高商品和服务质量方面创造了奇迹。(intensify, work wonders)

Consumer Behavior Survey

Figuring out not only *who* would buy it, but *why* they would buy it, *where* they would buy it, *how often* they would buy it, and *how* they would use it is the cornerstone of understanding consumer behavior. Marketers can benefit from an understanding of consumer behavior so that they can better predict what consumers want and how best to offer it to them. Suppose you work for a Consumer Research Institution. Now you need to conduct a general survey of consumer behavior to measure changes in consumer attitudes and expectations, to evaluate how these changes relate to consumer decisions to save, borrow, or make discretionary purchases, and to forecast changes in aggregate consumer behavior. Look at the given questions and work by the following steps.

1) Find a partner from other groups and start asking him/her the questions.

2) Change a partner every three or four questions until you have finished all the questions.

3) Come back to your own group and exchange the survey result with your group members to see which of the questions produced the impressive answers.

Survey Questions

- Do you enjoy shopping? How often do you go shopping? How much time do you spend each time you go?
- When you buy something, do you read the label? Why or why not?
- What's your favorite place to shop? Why?
- Are you a price conscious shopper? What is your opinion about discount stores?
- Have you ever been to an outlet store? If you have, what do you think of it? If not, would you like to shop at one? Why or why not?
- What store did you like best and what store did you like least? Why?
- Are thrift stores popular in your city? Do you enjoy shopping at thrift stores?
- How important is good customer service when you are shopping?
- Do you compare prices at different stores when you shop?
- How important is it for you to be up to date with the latest fashion?
- Is it important for you to own designer clothes? Why or why not?
- Do you ever buy second-hand things?
- Do you haggle when you shop?
- Do you sometimes buy things that you don't need? If so, give some examples.
- What is it that you want to buy but think you never will?
- What is the most expensive thing you've ever bought?
- What kind of things do you often shop for?
- What kinds of things are you saving your money for?
- When you buy something, what is the most important to you:

UNIT 6 Consumers

> price, quality, fashion trend, status or image?
> - What do you do if you can't get the clerk's attention at the store?
> - If you can't find an item at the store, do you find a clerk and ask for help, or do you leave and go somewhere else?
> - Your own questions ...

Language Hints

Asking questions
- Can I ask some questions?
- Can I ask a question about...?
- I'd like to ask some questions.
- There are a couple of questions I'd like to ask you...
- There's something else I'd like to know.
- ...

Responding to questions
- Yes, certainly. / Sure.
- Of course. Go ahead.
- ...

Moving on/back to the topic
- (Thank you.) Please go on.

- Good. Sorry to interrupt.
- ...

Stating problem
- (I'm) sorry. I don't quite follow you.
- I don't understand what you've just said.
- ...

Making request
- Could you go over that again?
- Sorry, could you say that again, please?
- ...

Getting time to think
- Mmm, let me see...
- Yes, that's an interesting question, well, ...
- ...

A Memo

Look at the following situations and write relevant memos. You may refer to the sample memo in Unit Five if necessary.

Situation 1

Miss Indira Purewal, senior sales officer at Calibre International Products, is worried that several customers have complained in the past few weeks of incorrect orders having been received. She asks you to write a memo under her name to Mrs Selma Pusao, a supervisor at the Packing Department. You are reminded to be tactful since Mrs Pusao is usually very efficient, but Miss Purewal wants all orders to be checked twice before they are dispatched. "All the mistakes are in Mrs Pusao's section.

We simply can't have such glaring faults in our system; our customers rightly expect quality in our service and I intend to see that they get the best." She adds, "Tell her to let you know if she is having any unusual, short-term difficulties. Something must be causing the inaccuracies! We have not had such problems previously."

Situation 2

You work at the Sneyd Public Library in the Administration Offices where you have particular responsibility for the Children's Section. The address is Sneyd Library, 19-25 Church Street, Barnstaple, Devon EX31 IBD and the telephone number is 01271 76322.

You receive a telephone complaint from a customer who had been very upset when a library assistant had told her "very rudely and loudly" to keep her children quiet. The customer explains to you that her two very young children had been happy and excited because coming to a library was a new experience for them. You apologize and reassure her that silence is not a requirement in the Children's Section and that you will send a memo to all staff reminding them of that fact.

You decide to make a few notes for possible inclusion in the memo.

- "Be quiet," ...we don't say this to children using their own Section. They are having a good time!
- Excited ...some noise...first time...telling each other about it...pictures they recognize...stories they know..., etc.
- Our Section: welcoming, NOT embarrassing to parents/children — regular customers later.
- No customer should be treated "rudely".

Business Expressions

1. Give the English equivalents of the Chinese expressions below.

UNIT **6** Consumers

Chinese expressions   English equivalents

1) 消费者权利　　　　　　　　　_____
2) 促进消费　　　　　　　　　　_____
3) 消费者利益保护委员会　　　　_____
4) 消费模式　　　　　　　　　　_____
5) 有环保意识的消费者　　　　　_____
6) 耐用消费品　　　　　　　　　_____
7) 消费大众　　　　　　　　　　_____
8) 消费者偏好　　　　　　　　　_____
9) 生活高消费化　　　　　　　　_____
10) 消费（品）价格指数　　　　　_____
11) 消费者抵制　　　　　　　　　_____
12) 家庭消费　　　　　　　　　　_____

2. **Complete the following sentences with the expressions or words in the box.**

bargaining power	consumer protection	consumption level
consumer behavior	purchasing power	consumer awareness
consumer boom	consumer watchdog	consumer tastes
consumption tax	consumer confidence	consumer education

1) Within law, the notion of consumer is primarily used in relation to _____ _____ laws.

2) In many cases, the _____ between a consumer and a business is not equal.

3) The concern over the interests of consumers has resulted in some action such as the incorporation of _____ into school curricula.

4) People's _____ is growing, which helps to boost the economy.

5) Along with the increase of _____ in China, especially in rural China, the need of beer will increase continuously.

6) In a world driven by supply and demand, product availability typically mirrors _____ and Bluetooth wireless technology is no exception.

7) Simply offering the same set of television channels and a limited number of

subscriber packages will no longer be sufficient as _____ and requirements become even more demanding.

8) In recent years, the old idea of a _____ in contrast to an income tax has been put forward by many economists, particularly by allegedly pro-free market conservatives.

9) _____ is a subcategory of marketing that blends elements from psychology, sociology, sociopsychology, anthropology and economics.

10) The high price of oil, Russia's main export, is fueling a huge _____ _____, and Russians are flocking to shopping malls as fast as developers can build them.

11) Businesses will face substantially larger penalties for misleading consumers if the government agrees to a request from _____ to beef up her powers.

12) According to the survey, conducted in the third quarter of the year, the _____ index in China stood at 106.9, while in the United States it was 82.0.

Specialized Reading

1. Read the following introductory paragraph and the given information of the sequential paragraphs. Then read another 20 sentences below and classify them under the proper paragraphs.

   Clients want to feel comfortable during a selling process. Just because you might like to be approached in a certain way, it doesn't mean that your client will. Every client wants to be sold in a way that fits them personally. There are four common personality types that customers fall into: expressive, steady, dominating, and analyzers.

   Expressive people view the world positively. They are socially comfortable and like to interact with others._____
   _____
   _____
   _____
   _____

   People who fall into the "steady" category are positive like the expressives. However, they are more comfortable being behind the scenes, not in the

UNIT 6 Consumers

"spotlight." _____
_____
_____
_____
_____

     Dominators are usually very suspicious. They feel that people are out to get them._____
_____
_____
_____
_____

     People who are considered "analyzers" are also suspicious. They, however, are very detail oriented._____
_____
_____
_____
_____

1) They don't like wasting time and are eager to get on with things.
2) They expect you to provide them with a lot of information.
3) They want you to be well-prepared and thorough.
4) Make sure that you ask clear, logical questions.
5) They would be sold by someone who is prepared and organized.
6) They are not risk-takers and are often resistant to change.
7) Don't hurry them into a decision! Let them talk while trying to direct them to a mutual agreement.
8) Make sure that your facts are straight and you provide them with references.
9) Above all, avoid pushing them, and give them time to think.
10) They are often recognition-oriented and seek out situations where they can be the center of attention.
11) They want to be sold in a way that is non-threatening.
12) They are perfectionists and love facts and details.
13) They enjoy presentations that are entertaining and fun.
14) They must feel that you are trustworthy and credible.

15) They often make decisions very quickly and hardly ever change their minds.

16) They don't show a lot of emotion, and don't like people who do.

17) They want to be sold by a sales person who shows interest in them as a person.

18) A sales person must be direct and get to the point with them.

19) They want a salesperson to respond to their ideas.

20) Make sure that you listen to them and are sincere.

2. There are many arguments over consumerism and anti-consumerism. Read the following passage and choose the correct part from A-E to fill each gap marked 1)-5)

> A. The term and concept of "conspicuous consumption" originated at the turn of the 20th century
> B. the tendency of people to identify strongly with products or services
> C. many luxuries and unnecessary consumer products are social signals
> D. this unnecessary consumption is a form of status display
> E. A culture that is permeated by consumerism

In many critical contexts, consumerism is used to describe 1) _____ they consume, especially those with commercial brand names and obvious status-enhancing appeal, e.g. an expensive automobile, expensive jewelry. 2) _____ can be referred to as a consumer culture. Impulse buyers who cannot resist spending money are commonly termed shopaholics.

Opponents of consumerism argue that 3) _____ that allow people to identify like-minded individuals through consumption and display of similar products. Some believe that relationships with a product or brand name are substitutes for the healthy human relationships lacking in dysfunctional modern societies and along with consumerism itself are part of the general process of social control and cultural hegemony in modern society.

The older term "conspicuous consumption" spread to describe consumerism in the United States in the 1960s, but was soon linked to larger debates about media theory, culture jamming, and its corollary productivism.

4) _____ in the writings of sociologist and economist Thorstein Veblen. The term describes an apparently irrational and confounding form of economic behavior. Veblen's scathing proposal that 5) _____ is made

in darkly humorous observations like the following:

"It is true of dress in even a higher degree than of most other items of consumption, that people will undergo a very considerable degree of privation in the comforts or the necessaries of life in order to afford what is considered a decent amount of wasteful consumption; so that it is by no means an uncommon occurrence, in an inclement climate, for people to go ill clad in order to appear well dressed."

3. **Discuss the following questions with your group members.**

   1) What do you think of the phenomenon that people, especially the newly rich, tend to have conspicuous consumption?

   2) What kind of consumer behavior is proper? Why do you think so?

UNIT 7
Brands

1. Look at the following brands which are famous internationally, and discuss the questions with your partner.

1) Are there any of your favorite brands on the list? If not, try to add yours to it.

2) Why do you like these brands? What qualities does each of them have?

3) What qualities are in common for the brands you like?

4) Do you often buy branded goods? If not, why not? Why might you buy a product of a less-preferred brand?

2. The following are the top 10 most valued global brands listed by a recent survey. Rank the brands yourself first, then discuss your ranking with your group members to come up with a group ranking, and discuss the following questions at the same time.

| CitiBank | Wal-Mart | IBM | Google | China Mobile |
| Marlboro | Coca-Cola | Toyota | Microsoft | GE |

1) Why are the above brands valued so highly?

2) How many of the above brands are American? What is your general impression of American brands?

3) What does a brand mean to a company and the company's consumers?

UNIT **7** Brands

Preview: In an increasingly competitive market where there are just too many products on the shelves, how does a company struggle for market domination? The answer is simple: do not underestimate the power of the brand. What exactly is a brand? Is a brand just a name, a sign, or a symbol that makes a product special and different from other similar ones? Does a brand have something else that is more important and valuable for a company? How does a company establish and maintain a brand that will sustain sales in the face of competition with other similar products? These are just the main points of the passage you are to read.

What, Exactly, Is a Brand?

*Don't believe the **mystifying, long-winded** explanations of **trendy** marketers. The answer is much simpler — and absolutely essential to grasp.*

By Christopher Kenton

[1] I have an easy solution for dramatically improving the quality of marketing. For months I've been writing on the hidden trends **underlying** business valuations, the **esoteric** debates over strategic focus, and the **minutiae** of new marketing **metrics** all in an attempt to help marketers find some solid ground in an increasingly **chaotic** environment. Yet what people really want is a simple formula. "Cut to the chase" is the **mantra** I can hear from the crowd.

[2] So here's my simple formula. I promise it will solve anything that **ails** your marketing efforts.

[3] If you have an in-house marketing team, call them into your office. If you use consultants, get them on the phone. If you're a marketer yourself, look directly into the mirror. Dispense with the small talk, and let some silence build dramatic tension in the room. Then, in a thoughtful voice, ask one question that has the power to cleanse the earth of **mushy-headed** marketing. "So tell me, what exactly is a brand?"

[4] If the answer is anything other than a clear, tangible description that can be summarized in a single sentence your crazy old aunt Alice can understand, throw the **bums** off the boat. Think of yourself as the bridgekeeper on Monty Python[1]'s Bridge of Death. If someone says a brand is a relationship, **toss** them over the side. If they say a

---

1 Monty Python / ˈmɒntɪ ˈpaɪθən / 蒙提·派森，英国六人喜剧团体，他们的电视剧系列 "Monty Python's Flying Circus" 在 70 年代风靡全球

brand is an image in the mind of the consumer, give 'em the **heave-ho**. Don't suffer any long-winded explanations. Keep a clear resolve.

[5] After the **gullies** pile up with trendy marketers, you'll eventually find your way to someone who tells you a brand is just a name, a sign, or a symbol that **distinguishes** the products and services of one company from all others. If the **loftiest metaphor** they use in their description is a burning scar on the side of a cow, hire them. Give them a raise. Hug them for heaven's sake and your budget's sake. You've just found someone who won't lead your company over the cliff with all the other marketing **lemmings**.

[6] Your brand is your name, your **logo**, your trade dress. You own it. There are clearly written laws to protect it. It is tangible enough to put a price on it. And yet, an entire generation of marketers has found a way to **obscure** the obvious, to make the brand more fantastic, and to make it hard enough to understand that you need consultants to help you figure it out.

[7] It all started decades ago, with the simple recognition that in a mass market **teeming** with **disposable** products, consumers latch on to brands they've grown to trust. No one wants to sit around reconsidering whether they'd like Coke or Fred's Cola[1] every time they're thirsty. Once you have tried Coke and like it, and it stays consistently likable every **subsequent** time you drink it, you can **relegate** that small decision to one of the 10,000 you don't have to think about every day.

[8] Not thinking about every little decision is good for you. You can save those **synapses** for something more important. It's also good for Coke, since it ensures a steady **stream** of **revenue**, as long as customers can rely on the product delivering the same experience and value. That's where all this stuff came up about your brand being a promise to the consumer of the quality of your product. Except that it's not.

[9] Your brand is your name, your logo, your burning scar on the side of your product. The expectation that consumers begin to attach to your brand is something else. It's an important something else that has value and that you should consider an important **asset** worthy of investment, but it's something else. In fact, a brand has a few something elses that are important associates of it and create value for your company.

[10] There's brand experience, the sum of all impressions consumers gain from interactions with your company. How does your receptionist answer the phone? How **courteous** are your truck drivers? Such experiences strongly influence another brand associate, brand image, which is often closely tied to brand reputation.

---

1 Fred's Cola / ˈfredzˈkəulə / 弗瑞德可乐

[11] What does your market think of your brand? How does it make your customers feel? Will they use it again? Will they recommend it to friends? If your brand image is hot, and your brand reputation strong, it can improve your "brand equity", or the **bankable** value your brand has acquired from its ability to attract and **retain** customers.

[12] All of these things are important, but they don't **constitute** brand. They're **derivatives** of brand. The more they're confused, the more **susceptible** businesses become to trendy theories that lead them over the cliff, like the one Heidi Schultz[1] **rails** against in the American Marketing Assn.[2]'s Marketing Management. The notion that customers "own" your brand.

[13] It's a **seductive** thought for companies that value their clients, but a misguided one. Your customers own their impressions, and you can influence those impressions with the quality of your product, and the experiences you **foster**. But your brand is just the symbol that **anchors** those impressions to the product you create.

[14] Don't take my formula too lightly. The definition of brand is the **canary** in the coal mine. If you're working with marketers who aren't clear-headed enough to distinguish between a tangible brand and its derivatives, how will they have the **clarity** to advise you on building a market? Get rid of them and find a marketer who can think straight. We'll all be better off.

(959 words)
From *Business Week*

New Words

mystifying /ˈmɪstɪfaɪɪŋ/
a. hard to understand; confusing 令人迷惑的

long-winded /ˈlɒŋˈwaɪndɪd/
a. talking or writing at tedious length 啰唆的，冗长的

trendy /ˈtrendɪ/
a. showing or following the latest trends of fashion 时髦的，新潮的

underlie /ˌʌndəˈlaɪ/
v. form the basis of…… 成为……的基础

esoteric /ˌesəʊˈterɪk/
a. likely to be understood only by those with special knowledge or interest 深奥的

minutiae /maɪˈnjuːʃiː/
n. very small or unimportant details 细节；琐事

metrics /ˈmetrɪks/
n. quantitative measures of performance or production used to indicate progress or achievement against strategic goals 衡量标准；衡量方法

chaotic /keɪˈɒtɪk/
a. completely disorganized 混乱的，无秩序的

mantra /ˈmʌntrə/
n. a word or sound that is repeated as prayer or to help people meditate in the Hindu and Buddhist religions 曼特罗；祷文（印

---

1 Heidi Schultz /ˈhaɪdɪ ˈʃuːlts/ 海蒂·舒尔茨，美国著名品牌专家，爱格瓦营销咨询公司执行主席
2 Assn. American Marketing Association 美国市场营销协会

度教和佛教中的符咒）

ail / eɪl /
v. trouble in body or mind 折磨；使烦恼

mushy-headed / ˈmʌʃɪ hedɪd /
a. woolly-headed, lacking in clear thinking 头脑不清的

bum / bʌm /
n. a lazy irresponsible person; an unqualified person 懒惰的人；不合格的人

toss / tɒs /
v. throw away; discard 扔掉，丢弃

heave-ho / ˈhiːv ˈhəʊ /
n. dismiss; reject 开除；拒绝

gully / ˈgʌlɪ /
n. ditch; ravine 沟壑，深沟

distinguish / dɪˈstɪŋgwɪʃ /
v. recognize the difference 辨别，区别

lofty / ˈlɒftɪ /
a. seeming to be superior 高级的；出众的

metaphor / ˈmetəfə /
n. a comparison of unlike things, often poetic 隐喻，暗喻，比喻

lemming / ˈlemɪŋ /
n. small mammal, often used to describe someone who copies other people's ideas without thinking about it 盲目仿效者

logo / ˈləʊgəʊ /
n. symbol designed for or used by a business, company 标识

obscure / əbˈskjʊə(r) /
v. make dim or indistinct 使变模糊；使变暗或不分明

teeming / ˈtiːmɪŋ /
a. full of; present in large numbers 充满……的；丰富的，大量的

disposable / dɪˈspəʊzəbl /
a. available for use 可任意使用的

subsequent / ˈsʌbsɪkwənt /
a. later; following 后来的，随后的

relegate / ˈrelɪgeɪt /
v. assign to a class or kind; give someone or something a less important position than before 把……归类；将……置于次要地位

synapse / ˈsaɪnæps, sɪˈnæps /
n. 【解剖学】神经元的神经线连接；（神经元轴突的）突触

stream / striːm /
n. a small river; a large number of things that happen one after the other 一连串；源源不断

revenue / ˈrevənjuː /
n. income 收入；税收

asset / ˈæset /
n. a valuable item that is owned; an advantage or a resource 一件有价值的所有物；优势或资财

courteous / ˈkɜːtɪəs /
a. polite; good-mannered 有礼貌的；谦恭的

bankable / ˈbæŋkəb(ə)l /
a. likely to make money for sb. 可赚钱的，可赢利的

retain / rɪˈteɪn /
v. continue to have; keep (sth.) in place or use 保留，保持

constitute / ˈkɒnstɪtjuːt /
v. make up or form 组成

derivative / dɪˈrɪvətɪv /
n. a thing that has been developed or produced from another thing 派生物，衍生物

susceptible / səˈseptəbl /
a. easily influenced 易受影响的

rail / reɪl /
v. complain, protest or reproach strongly 挑剔；抱怨；责骂

seductive / sɪˈdʌktɪv /
a. tending to charm; attractive 诱人的

foster / ˈfɒstə /
v. encourage sth. to develop 促进；培养

anchor / ˈæŋkə /
v. fasten sth. firmly so that it can not move 使稳定；固定

canary / kəˈneərɪ /
n. a small yellow bird that sings and is often kept as a pet 金丝雀

clarity / ˈklærɪtɪ /
n. the ability to think about or understand sth. clearly 清晰的思维（或理解）能力

UNIT **7** Brands

Phrases & Expressions

cut to the chase
get to the point without wasting time (比喻意义) 废话少说; 提到关键问题; 切入正题

dispense with sth. /sb.
get rid of; manage without 免除; 省却

small talk
polite friendly conversation about unimportant subjects 闲谈, 聊天

other than
different or differently from; not; except 不同, 不同于; 不; 除……以外

pile up
increase; accumulate 增多; 积累, 积聚; 堆积

trade dress
a wide range of product identifiers that can include brand name, packaging, product color, or decor 产品标识符

figure out
solve; understand 解决; 领会到; 断定

mass market
unsegmented market in which products are sold to large numbers of people through mass retailers or independent stores 大众市场; 批量销售

latch on to
become attached to sth./sb. 变得依附于……

sit around
spend time doing nothing useful 无所事事地消磨时间

come up
manifest itself; arise 显现, 出现; 产生

brand equity
the perceived assets and liabilities associated with a brand, as reflected in people's attitude towards it, that add to or detract from its value in their mind 品牌资产, 品牌价值

be better off
used to say that sb. is/would be happier or more satisfied if they were in a particular position or did a particular thing (在某种情况下)更幸福; 更满意

Exercises

Comprehension

1. Answer the following questions with your partner.

   1) What is the writer's purpose in this passage?

   2) According to the passage, what is the main problem with people's understanding of brand?

3) How important is it to make clear the definition of brand?

4) According to the writer, what metaphor can best describe what a brand is?

5) What will customers develop once they have tried a brand and like it?

6) What is the importance of a brand to a company? How should a company regard it?

7) What are "derivatives of brand" mentioned in this passage?

8) According to the passage, who own a brand, companies or customers?

9) How can companies influence their customers' impressions of a brand?

10) What is the simple solution suggested in this passage to improve the quality of marketing?

2. The text can be divided into three parts which are organized in a "problem-solution" pattern. Go through the text carefully and then complete the outline below with the missing information from the text.

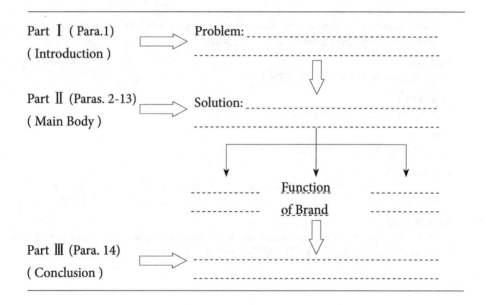

Critical Thinking

Work in group to discuss the following questions.

1) If you are loyal to one brand, will you be equally loyal to its derivatives? Give your reasons.

2) If your idol is using a certain brand, will you follow him or her? Why or why not?

3) What will influence your decision of using a brand?

UNIT 7 Brands

Vocabulary

1. **Fill in the blanks with the proper forms of the words and phrases given below.**

retain	relegate	be tied to	underlie	deliver
figure out	dramatic	disposable	subsequent	latch on to

1) In order to _____ a stable and motivated workplace, companies must be sensitive to the personal needs of their employees.

2) Estimates of world-wide electronic commerce revenues are greatly different, but there is no doubt that they will rise _____.

3) Nearly everyone _____ products they never actually use to those ones abandoned in the closet until they are forgotten.

4) More than 10 years ago, businesses were tiptoeing to the Web, trying to _____ if they could make money on it. Today, the question isn't "if"; it's "how much."

5) Undoubtedly, the notion of "a new economy" _____ the effects of technical progress on economic growth.

6) Transnational companies compete not only to offer the highest value products but also to _____ cultural myths with global appeal.

7) There are at least three fundamental factors that _____ the prosperity of one nation: faster economic growth, reductions in poverty, and more fertile soil for democracy.

8) The ability to make employees _____ strong, collaborative relationships with the company will determine whether a business evolves through time or is lost along the way.

9) The income remaining after deduction of taxes and other obligatory charges that is available to be spent or saved as one wishes is defined as _____ income.

10) Once people come to a belief that advertising is childish, dumb and a bunch of lies, they will _____ develop immunity to advertising.

2. **Rewrite each sentence with the word or phrase in brackets, keeping the meaning unchanged. The first part has been written for you.**

1) Companies' not developing the emerging local market will make people consequently take the training and technology and simply become their biggest

competitors. (*dispense with*)

If companies _____

_____

2) In order to increase their market share among competitive TV quiz shows, a popular TV show was recruiting out-of-town people. (*in an attempt to*)

A popular TV show _____

_____

3) Developing brand value by increasing the quality of interactions with customers is a strategic imperative in a market full of too many brands. (*teeming*)

A strategic imperative in a market _____

_____

4) Quality of life, on and off the job, is more important to today's workers, even to the employees without family responsibilities than ever before. (*attach...to*)

Today's workers _____

_____

5) Sports certainly produced a very high number of prima donnas and big egos, yet I was struck by how many of the winning teams were led by unpretentious people who boosted others. (*other than*)

I was struck _____

_____

6) Owning stock did make employees more loyal to the company, so they worked actively every day instead of spending time doing nothing useful and thinking about what percentage of their extra work is recoverable. (*sit around*)

Employees did not _____

_____

7) Selecting a business broker to assist you in buying or selling a business is a decision you should not make without serious thought. So we provide the information for you to help make that decision easier. (*take...lightly*)

You should not _____

_____

8) A company's attitudes toward the environmental issues can easily affect its customers' loyalty and market acceptance. (*be susceptible to*)

The loyalty of its customers _____

_____

UNIT 7 Brands

9) Understanding the preferences, shopping attitudes and price expectations of the different consumer segments is essential for marketers to succeed in the competitive consumer market in the world. (*rely on*)

The success_____

_____

10) To avoid boredom and to increase their capabilities, workers want to expand their knowledge and experience by trying different kinds of work. (*for the sake of*)

Through trying different kinds of work_____

_____

3. Choose the correct prefix for each of the words in the circle and write them into the table. Then complete the sentences below with the proper words in the table.

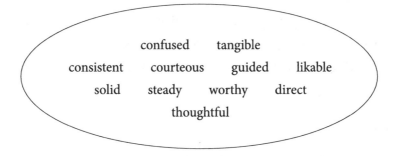

dis-	mis-	in-	un-
1)	1)	1)	1)
2)		2)	2)
		3)	3)
			4)
			5)

1) The staff's sense of belonging, initiative and creativity inspired by the corporate spirit is _____ asset of a business.

2) To create the necessary illusion of superiority, advertisers usually resort to some _____ techniques to confuse the consumers.

3) Unless the needs of the customers are constantly addressed and changed accordingly, there is the possibility that a competitor will profit from being _____ .

4) Is it a surprise that the dollar is worth next to nothing right now, leaving our banks on _____ ground?

5) When someone at Hearst Corporation does nothing _____ of recognition, flowers are sent to the employee's spouse.

6) The entire company suffers when the boss has the power to impose his selfish, _____, irrational decisions on others.

7) The company establishes not only a volunteer team, but also a set of rules to prevent their executives from _____ engagement in community service.

8) To create an _____ sense of community, management need to provide a trusting and safe environment, in which workers are free to express their ideas rather than try to "fit in" and please the managers.

9) The wide spreading of _____ practices such as bribery, cheating definitely results in disastrous chaos in a company.

10) Without better application of information technology, many service economy jobs would enjoy _____ productivity growth.

11) Accepting a business card and thrusting it immediately in your pocket is considered _____.

Translation

1. Translate the following sentences into Chinese.

    1) After the gullies pile up with trendy marketers, you'll eventually find your way to someone who tells you a brand is just a name, a sign, or a symbol that distinguishes the products and services of one company from all others.

    2) If the loftiest metaphor they use in their description is a burning scar on the side of a cow, hire them. Give them a raise. Hug them for heaven's sake and your budget's sake. You've just found someone who won't lead your company over the cliff with all the other marketing lemmings.

    3) It all started decades ago, with the simple recognition that in a mass market teeming with disposable products, consumers latch on to brands they've grown to trust.

    4) No one wants to sit around reconsidering whether they'd like Coke or Fred's Cola every time they're thirsty. Once you have tried Coke and like it, and it stays consistently likable every subsequent time you drink it, you can relegate that small decision to one of the 10,000 you don't have to think about every day.

2. Put the following sentences into English, using the words and phrases given in the brackets.

1) 长期以来，在营销领域，人们对品牌的认识不尽一致．(recognition)

2) 根据美国市场营销协会所给的定义，品牌是一种名称、术语、标记、符号或设计，或是它们的组合运用，其目的借以辨认某个销售者或销售群体的产品及服务，并使之与竞争对手的产品和服务区别开来（definition, logo, in an attempt to, distinguish）

3) 但是，美国亚马逊公司总裁杰夫·贝佐斯（Jeff Bezos）先生总结道，品牌就是指你与客户间的关系。说到底，起作用的不是你在广告或其他宣传中向他们许诺了什么，而是他们反馈了什么以及你如何做出反应。（summarize, other than, promise）

4) 口碑极其重要。正如其他专家所认为的那样，品牌就是人们私下里对某产品及其公司的评价。从这个角度来看，品牌就是企业与顾客双向互动的过程。如果没有客户的信赖和支持，品牌就会失去价值和意义。（attach, interaction）

Promotional Campaign

Nowadays, in order to arouse the consumer's interest in knowing more about their products and brands, some companies draw consumers into their promotional campaign. Work in groups. Suppose you are the customer of these companies, designing and participating in such kinds of activities for the companies' brands or products. You may refer to Unit Four for some tips if necessary.

1) Each group chooses a company on page 284 and reads the given information. Or you may choose any other company as you like.

2) Prepare a promotional campaign for the company. You may design the campaign by discussing the following points:

- *The campaign's key message;*
- *The special features of the brand or product;*
- *The unique selling points;*

- *The target audience;*
- *The proper media (TV, radio, newspaper, Internet, etc.);*
- *The special promotions;*
- *The slogan;*
- *Others...*

3) Show your campaign to the whole class, trying to answer questions they ask.

4) The class evaluate the campaign in terms of the following points:
- *Having a clear and effective message;*
- *Differentiating the brand or product;*
- *Impressing the target audience deeply;*
- *Others...*

Language Hints

Giving opinions
(*on a scale from strongly to weakly*)
- I'm convinced/ sure /positive that...
- I definitely/certainly think that...
- I really do think that...
- In my opinion...
- I think/ consider /feel that...
- As I see it, ...
- From my point of view,...
- I'm inclined to think that...
- I tend to think that...
- ...

Interrupting
- Can/May I just come in here?
- One moment, please.
- ...

Agreeing
- I totally agree with you. I fully/completely agree.
- I'm in total agreement with you there.
- I'm all in favor of that.
- ...

Partially agreeing
- Up to a point/To a certain extent I'd agree with you, but...
- Up to a point/To a certain extent I'd accept that, but...
- You could/may be right, but...
- That may/might be right, but...
- ...

Disagreeing
- (I'm afraid) I can't agree with you.
- (I'm afraid) I can't accept that.
- I don't agree.
- I don't accept that.
- ...

Press Release

A press release is a public relations announcement, written in third person, issued to the news media and other targeted publications for the purpose of letting the public know of a particular person, event, service, product or company developments.

Press releases are often sent alone, by e-mail, fax or snail mail. They can also be part of a full press kit, or may be accompanied by a pitch letter. Here are a few tips to keep in mind when writing your press release:

- Include a boldface headline that is eye-catching and will suck the press into your announcement. The title should entice the reader to continue reading, but should also clearly state the purpose of the release.
- Your first sentence should tell readers exactly what your release is about.
- The first paragraph should answer the 'who, what, when, where, why, and how' of your news. In some cases, it may take two paragraphs to accomplish this, but never more.
- Keep all sentences concise and keep paragraphs at approximately 4 sentences each if possible.
- If you are putting out a release for a product or service, be sure to include the product name, version number, where it's available, and what it costs. When describing your product, remember Feature, Function & Benefit.
- Never assume that your audience is familiar with your product. Keep your release free of industry jargon. Write in a conversational style using conversational English.
- Do not over-hype your news or use too many adjectives. Journalists see so much of this that they are immune and tend to ignore it.
- Instead of using adjectives, try using more basic, clear words. If you do need to use adjectives, use vivid and compelling ones.
- Avoid a marketing tone. Do not 'advertise' your product. Instead, stick to the facts.
- Include quotes in the release. Ideally, these should be objective opinions from long-time customers or analysts.
- The release should be free of spelling, grammatical, and punctuation errors.
- Use a legible font and ideally keep the release to one page. Legibility overrules creativity.
- Make use of bulleted points, as they are easy to scan.
- Include a brief company history section at the bottom of your release. Be sure

to include information about your products or services that will help establish your expertise. Also mention your location, years in business, and any other pertinent information. Be sure to keep it short and concise, but detailed.

- Provide a link to your website where they can find additional information.
- Always provide a contact name, telephone number, address, and email address. If your contact person is not readily available, consider providing two contacts. The contact person should be familiar with all the news in the release, and should be ready to answer questions.
- Type ### at the end of your release to indicate the end and there are no more pages.

It is highly recommended that you keep your release to one page. Most stories about new products tend to be one or two paragraphs in most trade magazines. A release longer than two pages will most likely not be read to the end.

Study the following sample, and then write a Press Release based on the given situation.

Sample

Duracell
BETHEL, Conn.

For PRNewswire
Sept.15, 2008

New Duracell Pre-Charged Rechargeable Batteries on the Market

Duracell today announced the introduction of Pre-Charged Rechargeable batteries — nickel metal

> The header should make clear who it comes from, what the subject is and which press it is aimed at.

> The subject should be put in bold.

> Lead Paragraph: who, what, when, where, why, and how

hydride (NiMH) cells that come charged and ready to use straight out of the pack. This new rechargeable technology, which retains power for up to 365 days while not in use, helps raise the bar on convenience and satisfaction as more and more consumers look for advanced battery solutions for power-hungry devices.

Available nationwide this Fall, Duracell Pre-Charged Rechargeable batteries can be recharged hundreds of times in any NiMH battery charger and can deliver hours of music and thousands of digital photos. Designed specifically for use in high-drain gadgets including digital cameras, portable gaming devices and MP3 players, Duracell Pre-Charged Rechargeable batteries eliminate the need to charge cells before using them for the first time. In addition, these new batteries stay charged longer and have to be recharged less often, packing more power for consumers' favorite gadgets.

Available at mass, drug, grocery and specialty stores nationwide beginning in September 2008, Duracell Pre-Charged Rechargeables will have a suggested retail price of $12.99 for a four-pack.

About Duracell

Part of the Procter & Gamble Company(NYSE: PG), Duracell is the world's leading manufacturer of high-performance alkaline batteries. Duracell also sells various other types of batteries including lithium and zinc air batteries, as well as rechargeable Nickel-Metal Hydride(NiMH) batteries and chargers. The company also markets general purpose flashlights. Visit www.duracell.com for more information about Duracell batteries.

Body Text:
* Be concise and to the point.
* Include name, feature, function, benefit, and price of the product.
* Write in formal style.

Brief Company History

About Procter & Gamble (NYSE: PG)

Three billion times a day, P&G brands touch the lives of people around the world. The company has one of the strongest portfolios of trusted, quality, leadership brands, including Pampers®, Tide®, Ariel®, Always®, Whisper®, Pantene®, Mach3®, Bounty®, Dawn®, Gain®, Pringles®, Folgers®, Charmin®, Downy®, Lenor®, Iams®, Crest®, Oral-B®, Actonel®, Duracell®, Olay®, Head & Shoulders®, Wella®, Gillette®, and Braun®. The P&G community consists of 138,000 employees working in over 80 countries worldwide. Please visit http://www.pg.com for the latest news and in-depth information about P&G and its brands.

SOURCE: Procter & Gamble
09/15/2008
CONTACT: Kara Salzillo of Duracell, +1-617-421-7452; salzillo.kl@pg.com
or Blayne Murphy of PainePR, +1-212-613-4924; bmurphy@painepr.com *(Contact information)*

###

Exercise:

You are working in the marketing department of P&G. Now the manager gives you some information about the newly manufactured product, Febreze To Go Fabric Refresher, and asks you to send a release to The Trade Press. Following is the relevant information about the product.

Febreze To Go Fabric Refresher is safe on virtually all fabrics including pillows, blankets, car interiors, carpet and clothing. The spray eliminates odors on fabrics including those caused by pets, cooking and musty smells, leaving a light fresh scent.

It was created for on-the-go consumers to carry in their cars, on airplanes and to their offices. The portable bottle fits perfectly in purses, suitcases or in the glove compartment, making it easy to access and use when traveling. It also complies with current airline baggage restrictions, which prohibit travelers from having liquids over 3 oz in their carry-on luggage.

Febreze, the household fabric refresher specially designed to eliminate odor on soft surfaces, now comes in a 2.8 oz travel-size bottle. Febreze To Go Fabric Refresher penetrates deeply and safely, removes odor at the source on virtually all fabrics, leaving behind a light, fresh scent anytime and anywhere.

Febreze's Brand Manager, Eric Huston said: "Febreze has resonated with consumers because of the product's unique technology that removes odors instead of covering them up." And he also said: "Fabric Refresher is one of the brand's more popular products and consumers have expressed the need to have Febreze available anytime, anywhere. Due to this interest we created a convenient package for Febreze To Go that is now the perfect size when traveling."

Three billion times a day, P&G brands touch the lives of people around the world. The company has one of the strongest portfolios of trusted, quality, leadership brands. The P&G community consists of over 135,000 employees working in over 80 countries worldwide. The company has its own website, http://www.pg.com, which publicizes the detailed information about P&G and its brand.

Contact : (Your name) of Procter & Gamble, +1-212-468-4372, marisa. abdoo @mslpr.com; or Ross Holthouse of Procter & Gamble, +1-513-983-1108, holthouse. rh@pg . com

Business Expressions

1. Match the expressions in the box with the corresponding definitions below.

brand experience	brand image	brand extension	brand tribe
brand identity	brand awareness	brand loyalty	brand management
brand attributes	brand equity	brand audit	brand personality
brand power	brand strategy		

   1) the functional and emotional associations which are assigned to a brand by its customers and prospects

   _____

   2) the value built-up in a brand, which is measured based on how much a customer is aware of the brand

   _____

   3) the outward manifestation of the essence of a corporate brand, product brand, service brand or branded environment

   _____

   4) a comprehensive and systematic examination of a brand involving activities to assess the health of the brand, uncover its sources of equity and suggest ways to improve and leverage that equity

   _____

   5) extent to which a brand or brand name is recognized by potential buyers, and correctly associated with the particular product in question

   _____

   6) the process of exposing consumers to the various attributes associated with a particular brand

   _____

   7) the application of a brand beyond its initial range of products, or outside its

UNIT 7 Brands

category

_____

8) perceived impressions of a brand by market segments

_____

9) the process by which marketers attempt to optimize the "Marketing mix" for a specific brand

_____

10) the strength of preference for a brand compared to other similar available brand options

_____

11) the brand image or brand identity expressed in terms of human characteristics

_____

12) a measure of the ability of the brand to dominate its product category

_____

13) a formal or informal group of consumers who share the same awareness, passion and loyalty for a brand or a portfolio of brands

_____

14) the "big picture" plans and tactics deployed by an organization/brand owner to create long-term brand equity and competitive advantages from branding

_____

2. **Complete the following sentences with the expressions in the above exercise. Two expressions are extra.**

1) The product that maintains the highest _____ compared to its competitors will usually get the most sales.

2) An effective _____ will create a unique identity that will differentiate you from the competition.

3) _____ or brand stretching is a marketing strategy in which a firm that markets a product with a well-developed image uses the same brand name but in a different product category.

4) The large number of visitors to the wine plant helps boost the company's ____ _____ and promote its special wine culture.

5) By creating a user experience that is appropriate to our audience, business

goals, and the competitive landscape, we can positively reinforce our customers' _____.

6) Take time and care in evaluating your _____ — it will be the key to customer and personal satisfaction for your company.

7) _____ not only means managing the brand — it also means managing the company in a total way for creating, making and keeping the brand promise.

8) _____ is the accumulated value of the brand image or identity in the consumer's mind.

9) The purpose of a _____ system is to encode a brand in people's memory and retrieve it from their memory.

10) In marketing, _____ consists of a consumer's commitment to repurchase the brand and can be demonstrated by repeated buying of a product or service or other positive behaviors such as word of mouth advocacy.

11) By taking the time to engage in a systematic _____, you might begin to see new opportunities for your brands, and new ways to make it resonate both internally and externally.

12) Our _____ represent our core beliefs, capturing the essence of our brand promise, so we should always do our best to follow these attributes in our day to day work.

3. Read the passage about some brand terms and complete the follow-up multiple-choice exercise.

A brand includes a name, logo, 1) _____, and/or design scheme associated with a product or service. Brand recognition and other 2) _____ are created by the use of the product or service and through the influence of advertising, 3) _____, and media commentary. A brand is a 4) _____ embodiment of all the information connected to the product and serves to create 5) _____ and expectations around it. A brand often includes a logo, fonts, color schemes, symbols, and 6) _____, which may be developed to represent implicit values, ideas, and even 7) _____.

Brands, " 8) _____ " and brand equity have become increasingly important components of culture and the economy, now being described as "cultural accessories and personal 9) _____."

The term brand name is often used 10) _____ with "brand," although it is more correctly used to specifically 11) _____ written or spoken linguistic elements of a brand. In this context a "brand name" constitutes a type of 12)_____, if the brand name exclusively 13)_____ the brand owner as the commercial source of products or services. A brand owner may seek to protect 14)_____ rights in relation to a brand name through trademark 15)_____.

1) A. slogan   B. language   C. theme   D. subject
2) A. productions   B. reactions   C. innovations   D. interactions
3) A. plot   B. design   C. plan   D. development
4) A. systematic   B. abstract   C. symbolic   D. vivid
5) A. combinations   B. omens   C. relationships   D. associations
6) A. noise   B. voice   C. sensation   D. sound
7) A. personality   B. temper   C. temperament   D. characteristic
8) A. branding   B. pricing   C. marketing   D. expanding
9) A. logics   B. ideals   C. philosophies   D. expanding
10) A. equally   B. similarly   C. changeably   D. interchangeably
11) A. promote   B. denote   C. declare   D. demonstrate
12) A. sign   B. feature   C. trademark   D. landmark
13) A. spots   B. identifies   C. proves   D. confirms
14) A. natural   B. civil   C. human   D. proprietary
15) A. negotiation   B. recognition   C. registration   D. affirmation

Specialized Reading

1. Read the following five paragraphs about a trademark or a brand, and write out the corresponding heading for each paragraph.

   1)_____

   A trade mark is a badge of origin, used so that customers can recognize the product of a particular trader, and it can include, for example, words, logos or pictures. Trade mark registration is the most comprehensive protection that can be obtained to protect your business name, brand name, company logo or slogan. In other words, a trademark protects words, names, symbols, sounds, or colors that distinguish goods and services. The roar of the MGM lion, the pink of the insulation made by Owens-Corning (who uses the Pink Panther in advertising by permission from its owner), and the shape of a Coca-Cola bottle are familiar trademarks. These are brand names and identities and are important in marketing a product or service.

2) _____

Naming an invention involves developing at least two names. One name is the generic name. The other name is the brand name or trademark name. For example, Pepsi® and Coke® are brand names or trademark names; cola or soda is the generic or product names. Big Mac® and Whopper® are brand names or trademark names; hamburger is the generic or product name. Nike®and Reebok® are brand names or trademark names; sneaker or athletic shoe is generic or product names.

3) _____

The marks that can be registered usually include: Trademarks that are used by their owners to identify goods, that is, physical commodities, which may be natural, manufactured, or produced, and which are sold or otherwise transported or distributed via interstate commerce. Service marks that are used by their owners to identify services, that is, intangible activities, which are performed by one person for the benefit of a person or persons other than himself, either for pay or otherwise. There are other types of marks that can be registered, however, they occur infrequently and have some different requirements for registration than the more commonly applied for trademarks and service marks. Since the benefits of registration are essentially the same for all types of marks, the term "trademark" is often used in general information that applies to service marks, certification marks, and collective marks as well as to true trademarks, the marks used on goods.

4) _____

The first person to either use a mark in commerce or file an application generally gains the right to trademark registration. Trademark registration can provide significant advantages to a party involved in a court proceeding. The USPTO(The United States Patent and Trademark Office) determines who can register. However, the right to use a mark can be more complicated to figure out. Two parties could begin using the same or similar marks without knowledge of one another and neither applied for trademark registration. Only a court could decide the right to use, with an injunction stopping one party from using the mark, and a settlement for damages caused by trademark infringement.

5) _____

When a trade mark has been registered it will remain there for several years, and it, unlike patents, can be renewed forever as long as they are being used in business. Trademark rights can last indefinitely if the owner continues to use the mark to identify goods or services. An affidavit and additional fees must be paid at certain intervals. If no affidavit is filed, the registration is canceled.

2. **The difference between own brands and generics is well-presented in the following part. Read the passage and complete the following sentences.**

With the emergence of strong retailers, the "own brand", the retailer's own branded product (or service), emerged as a major factor in the marketplace. Where the retailer has a particularly strong identity, such as, in the UK, Marks & Spencer in clothing, this "own brand" may be able to compete against even the strongest brand leaders, and may dominate those markets which are not otherwise strongly branded. There was a fear that such "own brands" might displace all other brands(as they have done in Marks & Spencer outlets), but the evidence is that — at least in supermarkets and department stores — consumers generally expect to see on display something over 50 percent (and preferably over 60 percent) of brands other than those of the retailer. Indeed, even the strongest own brands in the United Kingdom rarely achieve better than the third place in the overall market.

The strength of the retailers has, perhaps, been seen more in the pressure they have been able to exert on the owners of even the strongest brands (and in particular on the owners of the weaker third and fourth brands). Relationship marketing has been applied most often to meet the wishes of such large customers(and indeed has been demanded by them as recognition of their buying power). Some of the more active marketers have now also switched to 'category marketing'— in which they take into account all the needs of a retailer in a product category rather than more narrowly focusing on their own brand.

At the same time, generics (that is, effectively unbranded goods) have also emerged. These made a positive virtue of saving the cost of almost all marketing activities, emphasizing the lack of advertising and, especially, the plain packaging (which was, however, often simply a vehicle for a different kind of image). It would appear that the penetration of such generic products peaked in the early 1980s, and most consumers still seem to be looking for the qualities that the conventional brand provides.

1) The passage is mainly concerned with _____.

2) Own brand can also be understood as _____.

3) The fear of own brands is that _____.

4) In UK market, the strongest own brands occupy the _____

___ place.

5) Marketer's category marketing is to consider a product category instead of _____.

6) Generic products refer to _____.

7) Generic products have _____ packaging.

8) The generic products reached the peak _____.

UNIT 8
Business Leadership

1. Discuss the following questions with your partner.

   1) Have you ever admired some entrepreneurs, either at home or abroad, for their excellent business leadership? Who are they, and why are they admirable?

   2) How much do you think one's caliber as an outstanding business leader is part of his/ her personality or a result of skills he /she has learned?

   3) What skills and characteristics do you have that would work well in a leadership role?

   4) What do you think business leadership mainly consists of ?

2. The following are some of the basic traits an effective leader should have. Why do you think they are essential for an effective leader? Share your ideas with your group members.

Basic traits for effective leaders	The reasons why they are essential
Emotional stability	
Conscientiousness	
Social boldness	
Tough-mindedness	
Self-assurance	
Compulsiveness	
High energy	
Intuitiveness	
Maturity	
Team orientation	
Empathy	
Charisma	

UNIT **8** Business Leadership

Preview: As companies adapt to a changing world, one business practice remains constant — great companies require great leadership. But what does it take to ensure and sustain enduring success? This is a provocative question, one that needs critical examination as intense competition, a rapidly changing consumer base and advances in technology continue to change the way companies do business. Society also has new expectations of companies, as they learn to manage diversity and business leaders increasingly become the decision-makers who most affect the public on such issues as employment, energy, and the environment.

When It's Time to Think Again

By Alan Price

[1] A close friend of mine, Patrick, is the proud owner of a growing, albeit struggling, chocolate company in **upstate** New York. He knew his **breakeven** point, but he didn't know how to get there, and profitability remained beyond their grasp. Pouring money into the business was becoming a financial **strain** now that he had invested almost all the gains from his first business. He still had the burning drive to succeed, but Patrick was starting to doubt whether he was up to the challenge.

[2] Whether or not his business could be saved was questionable. Most "successful" chocolate companies — the small ones, at least — generate only modest profit margins. At his current growth rate, it could take another two years to become slightly profitable, and many more to recover his investment. In spite of the **odds** against him, I asked him to decide whether or not to stick with the business after he **wrestled** with the following three critical questions: What business are you in? What is your role as a manager of this company? And, what is your role as a leader of this company?

[3] Those three questions can quickly shake loose some of the critical assumptions that keep a company from being successful. Most small-business owners, pressured by daily operational details, don't make the time to **clarify** either the big picture or their role in the company. If Patrick was a typical small-business owner, his first round of answers might have been:

- I'm in the chocolate business. We sell quality chocolates.
- I have to manage **payroll**, **inventory**, manufacturing, advertising, sales, etc.
- As a leader I have to make sure that the business survives.

There may be nothing wrong with those answers, but there is nothing special about them. Patrick's chocolate business would sound like any other **generic** chocolate **outfit**, and his role would look like a cardboard **cutout** of a **stereotypical** owner. The difficult — but more **fruitful** effort — is rediscovering or creating something special about his business.

[4] Fortunately, Patrick's actual answers were far more **revealing**. After some back and forth, he realized that in his scramble for growth, he was building three different businesses. The original business was essentially a **catalogue** sales operation that sold customized chocolates as wedding favors. The orders were event-specific and repeat customers were, predictably, rare. Much of the customer traffic came through Internet search engines, but this fell off dramatically when Google changed its ranking formula. He defined this retail business as, "helping people celebrate."

[5] The second business, which was showing significant growth, sold wholesale, customized chocolates to larger chocolate shops. Margins are thin in wholesale, even if you have a specialty like customization. But his innovative operation was efficient enough to make wholesale **viable**, but only if the growth continued. He defined the wholesale business as, "providing value on which our customers can make a profit."

[6] Patrick is preparing to launch a third business: a small chocolate factory with a retail shop. Over the next four months, the current chocolate factory will **relocate** to a facility where the public can see the whole operation and take home a fresh box. He defines this business as, "a fascinating place to visit and experience the fun of chocolate."

[7] Now that he had clarified the three distinct businesses, I asked him to think about them as a single, **integrated** company. His response was almost immediate, "I'm in the business of sharing my love of **ingenuity** and fun." The side effect of this conversation was immediate: He rediscovered his passion for the business.

[8] It's always tempting to stop after the first question and analyze the business strategy. Do some parts of the business make more sense than other parts? **Arguably**. One would ask, "Is he running in too many directions at once?" Probably. But business strategy doesn't exist in a **vacuum**. Excellent management and powerful leadership can often **rescue** imperfect strategies. I pushed him on the remaining questions: What is your role as a manager of this company? What is your role as a leader of this company?

[9] Patrick's definition of effective management was, "to get out of the way and empower the team." This was **worrisome**. Empowerment is a popular idea, however it does not **absolve** a business owner of management responsibilities.

[10] His definition of leadership was, "to strategically drive the company, make choices about direction, and financially sustain it through its **infancy**." This definition made some sense, almost like a textbook definition. But there were **subtle** ways in which this definition, and the assumptions behind it, could hurt his chances for success. The simple fact that he was scrambling in three different directions indicated that he was having a hard time making choices about direction.

[11] Financially supporting a business through infancy is the role of the founder and investors, but only if there is a direction and a plan to reach profitability. Pouring money into a business doesn't sustain a business. The only thing that sustains a small business is some degree of sustainable profitability.

[12] This is the current stage of Patrick's leadership journey. Where it will end is anybody's guess. In spite of his excellent retail experience and talent, the odds may be against him. My personal belief is that Patrick will succeed, although he and his business may need to adapt along the way.

[13] What does the story of Patrick teach us about the realities of small business leadership? Plenty.

[14] First, leadership is usually **messy**. Patrick is one of many possible examples that there are no right answers. Rarely are there textbook solutions that we can copy. There are only human beings with an **abundance** of gifts, ideas, and blind spots facing situations that will present challenges in ways none of us can imagine.

[15] Second, Patrick illustrates the reality that many small-business owners have unclear and **fractured** strategies. However, with the help of good questions, assumptions can be brought to the surface and behavior **aligned** to maximize the chances for success.

[16] Finally, Patrick reminds us that leadership development is a personal journey that begins with a choice. It is a choice to reexamine what we mean by the word "leadership" and recommit to living up to our own definition.

(1042 words)
From *Business Week*

New Words

upstate / ˌʌpˈsteit /
a. belonging or relating to the parts of a state that are furthest to the north or furthest from the main city 州的北部地区（或边远地区）的

breakeven / ˌbreɪˈkiːvən /
a. having equal cost and income 得失相当的，不赢不亏的

strain / streɪn /
n. a force, influence, or factor causing excessive tension 重负；过度的要求（或指望、使用）

odds / ɒdz /
n. (pl.) the probability that one thing is so or will happen rather than another; chances〈常用作复数〉可能性，机会

wrestle / ˈresl /
v. struggle to deal with or overcome sth. 努力解决；全力对付

clarify / ˈklærɪfaɪ /
v. make sth. clearer or easier to understand 澄清，阐明，使清晰明了

payroll / ˈpeɪrəʊl /
n. an employer's list of those entitled to pay and of the amounts due to each; the sum necessary for distribution to those employees entitled to pay 工资表；在职人员名单；工薪总额

inventory / ˈɪnvəntərɪ /
n. the quantity of goods or materials on hand; stock 存货，库存

generic / dʒɪˈnerɪk /
a. having no special or unusual characteristics 一般的，普通的

outfit / ˈaʊtfɪt /
n. an organization〈口〉（工商业）公司

cutout / ˈkʌtaʊt /
n. something cut out or intended to be cut out from something else; (fig.) a person perceived as characterless or lacking in individuality 从其他东西上切割剪裁下来或要被切割剪裁下来的东西；〈喻〉没有性格特点的人

stereotypical / ˌsterɪəˈtɪpɪkl /
a. lacking spontaneity or originality or individuality; what is commonly expected 刻板的；已成陈规的，老一套的

fruitful / ˈfruːtfl /
a. producing good and useful results 富有成效的

revealing / rɪˈviːlɪŋ /
a. allowing a look at or an understanding of something inner or hidden; insightful 揭示真相的；有启迪作用的，发人深省的

catalogue / ˈkætəlɒg /
n. a complete list of items arranged systematically with descriptive details 目录

viable / ˈvaɪəbl /
a. capable of working, functioning, or developing adequately; financially sustainable 切实可行的，可实施的

relocate / ˌriːləʊˈkeɪt, riːˈləʊkeɪt /
v. move to a new location 迁移至新地点

integrated / ˈɪntɪgreɪtɪd /
a. marked by the unified control of all aspects of industrial production from raw materials through distribution of finished products 整体的；完全的；综合的

ingenuity / ˌɪndʒɪˈnjuːətɪ /
n. skill or cleverness in devising or combining; inventiveness 善于创造发明；足智多谋

arguably / ˈɑːgjʊəblɪ /
ad. able to be argued 可论证地；按理

vacuum / ˈvækjʊəm /
n. a space absolutely devoid of matter; a state of isolation from outside influences 真空

rescue / ˈreskjuː /
v. save, as from danger 营救，救援；挽救

worrisome / ˈwʌrɪsəm /
a. causing distress or worry 令人担忧的，使人发愁的

absolve / əbˈzɒlv /
v. set free from an obligation or responsibility

UNIT **8** Business Leadership

解除……的责任（或义务等）

infancy / ˈɪnfənsɪ /
n. a beginning or early period of existence 初期；幼稚阶段

subtle / ˈsʌtl /
a. not immediately obvious or noticeable; difficult to understand or perceive 微妙的，难以捉摸的；深奥难测的；隐晦的

messy / ˈmesɪ /
a. unpleasant or trying; confused or complicated 棘手的，难办的，令人为难的

abundance / əˈbʌndəns /
n. plenty; a large quantity 大量，丰富；充足

fractured / ˈfræktʃəd /
a. broken or cracked 破裂的；断裂的

align / əˈlaɪn /
v. adjust (parts of a mechanism, for example) to produce a proper relationship or orientation 调准；校正

Phrases & Expressions

be up to
  be capable of ... or fit for ... 胜任；适于

profit margin
  the amount by which revenue from sales exceeds costs in a business 利润空间

stick with
  persevere or continue with 坚持；继续

fall off
  decrease 减少

side effect
  an unexpected or unplanned result of a situation or event; a secondary and usually adverse effect 意想不到的效果；副作用

make sense
  be intelligible, justifiable, or practicable 可理解；有根据；可行

out of the way
  no longer an obstacle or hindrance to someone's plan 不再碍事，不再挡道

blind spot
  an area in which one fails to exercise judgment or discrimination （对某一领域情况的）无知，不理解；偏见

live up to
  behave in accordance with sth.; fulfil 依照某事物行事；完成；达到

Exercises

Comprehension

1. Answer the following questions with your partner.

    1) What predicament was Patrick confronted with?

2) What crucial questions did the author ask Patrick to grapple with? Why did the author put those questions to Patrick?

3) What answers would a typical small-business owner supply to the three crucial questions, according to the author?

4) How did Patrick clarify the businesses he was engaged in? How did the author comment on his reply?

5) Can you describe in your own words what Patrick's first business was like?

6) How did Patrick define his role as a manager?

7) How did Patrick describe his role as a leader of his company? How did the author evaluate his response?

8) Why does the author describe Patrick's actual answers as "far more revealing"?

9) How do you understand the sentence "Much of the customer traffic came through Internet search engines, but this fell off dramatically when Google changed its ranking formula"?

10) How do you interpret the sentence "The only thing that sustains a small business is some degree of sustainable profitability"?

2. The text can be roughly divided into two parts. Go through the text carefully. Work with your partner to complete the outline below with the missing information from the text.

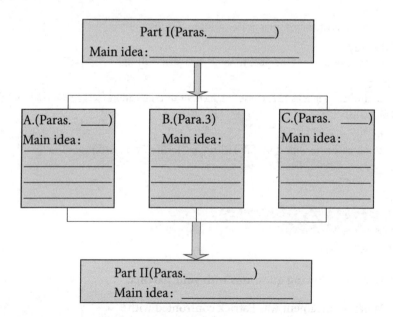

Critical Thinking

Work in group to discuss the following questions.

1) How do the author's 3 critical questions strike you? What other question might you ask if you were trying to help Patrick?

2) The following leadership quotes have been used to inspire good leaders. Which do you find is the most effective?

   - Management is doing things right; leadership is doing the right things. — Peter F. Drucker
   - A leader is a dealer in hope. — Napoleon Bonaparte
   - The leadership instinct you are born with is the backbone. You develop the funny bone and the wishbone that go with it. — Elaine Agather
   - A boss tells others what to do; a leader shows that it can be done. — Kouzes & Posner

3) If you are a leader who can be trusted, then those around you will grow to respect you. To be such a leader, there is a Leadership Framework to guide you: BE KNOW DO. It means there are certain things you must be, know, and, do. In your opinion, what do good leaders do? What are they? What do they know?

Vocabulary

1) Match each verb in Column A with a synonym in Column B. Then think of a noun or a noun phrase to follow each pair of verbs. Add a preposition if necessary.

A	B
absolve	accommodate
clarify	pose
launch	exemplify
adapt	elucidate
present	adjust
imagine	contend
illustrate	relieve
align	envisage
wrestle	initiate

2) **Rewrite the following sentences, using the noun forms of the verbs in the box without changing each sentence's original meaning.**

respond	sustain	abound	continue	assume
analyze	rescue	maximize	define	clarify

1) Social network users are not quick to respond to ads, which can be evidenced by the fact that they are often so engaged with the content on their pages and interacting with friends that they don't click on ads as frequently as users do on other kinds of sites.

    _____
    _____

2) The expert defined business leaders as people who inspire others in their organizations to lead without sacrificing teamwork, individualism or company mission.

    _____
    _____

3) The manager put some questions to him to clarify a couple of important points.

    _____
    _____

4) The famous economist perceptively analyzed the crisis in the markets.

    _____
    _____

5) In our experience, the core innovation challenge in the business world is rarely about generating more ideas; sift through any business organization and it abounds with ideas.

    _____
    _____

6) Although he insists that previous policies be continued, the new German Chancellor looks less attached to continental unity than his ardently pro-European predecessor.

    _____
    _____

7) The question the economist asks about any given contract is not whether the

UNIT **8** Business Leadership

goods to be exchanged are cheap or expensive in the abstract, but instead whether the exchange maximizes social wealth.

_____
_____

8) This policy shows the top leadership's concern as to whether China's focus on export-led, low value-added manufacturing that is reliant on trade and government investment can be sustained.

_____
_____

9) If it lowered rates to rescue the borrowers and their lenders, it would raise the risk of excessive borrowing and speculation in other sectors, possibly causing higher inflation and a stock bubble.

_____
_____

10) They can accept the contract, assuming that the rate of inflation will not increase next year.

_____
_____

3. **Explain in English the underlined words in the following sentences.**

   1) recover

      a. For an expressway to be well managed, the operator should be allowed enough time and share in the income to recover investments in SOS boxes, illumination, road marking, rescue, patrol, toll collection, rentals from service areas, etc.

      b. The recent plunge in the stock market is good because it insures a bubble does not develop in China. It would take years to recover from a bubble a la Japan.

      c. StoneRidge is likely to reduce the amount of money defrauded investors can recover in civil lawsuits.

   2) generic

      a. Ranbaxy was on the way to becoming one of the world's leading makers of generic drugs, just as the boom in such products was taking off in the mid-1990s.

      b. The firm's statisticians created customized models for each, later developing a generic one that any lender could use.

c. It is not cheap to rent even a California <u>generic</u> apartment, the kind that has white walls and was built five years ago.

3) sustain

a. Americans have had a housing bubble that <u>sustained</u> the economy for the last few years. The bubble has now burst.

b. A sharply smaller trade deficit contributed a beefy 1.4 percentage points to the second quarter's 4% growth in real GDP, which was the biggest quarterly boost in these years. Economists doubt that pace can be <u>sustained</u>.

c. Several years ago, he brought one of Japan's first product-liability lawsuits, against Mitsubishi Motors Corp, and claimed $50,000 for injuries he and three friends <u>sustained</u> in an accident involving a six-month-old Mitsubishi Pajero.

4) odds

a. Professor Smith, where do you put the <u>odds</u> of a recession?

b. The 78-year-old founder of mutual fund giant Vanguard is as legendary for pioneering index funds as he is for his blunt criticism of his industry's high fees and aggressive marketing — opinions that have put him at <u>odds</u> with his peers while endearing him to legions of investors.

c. Catharine is a remarkable young girl who has overcome great <u>odds</u> already in her young life.

5) favor

a. In the past two years, to win <u>favor</u> in China, Microsoft has pledged to spend more than $750 million on cooperative research, technology for schools, and other investments.

b. Tiffany, the jeweler, now stresses engagement rings and wedding <u>favors</u> for its Japanese clientele.

c. Some 50% of pharmacists aged 35 or under <u>favor</u> this move in health policy.

Translation

1. Translate the following sentences into Chinese.

   1) Whether or not his business could be saved was questionable.

   2) Most "successful" chocolate companies — the small ones, at least — generate only modest profit margins.

   3) At his current growth rate, it could take another two years to become slightly

profitable, and many more to recover his investment.

4) In spite of the odds against him, I asked him to decide whether or not to stick with the business after he wrestled with the following three critical questions: What business are you in? What is your role as a manager of this company? And, what is your role as a leader of this company?

2. **Put the following sentences into English, using the words and phrases given in the brackets.**

1) 新兴公司（start-up company）可以解释为刚开始运作不久的企业。这一概念如今往往和在校大学生联系在一起。(define)

2) 不少大学鼓励学生将作为课堂作业来酝酿的商业点子变为现实，从而使其在校所学的内容更加有意义。(make sense)

3) 为此，这些经验不足的年轻人们，作为新兴公司的领导者，经常要应付各种各样棘手的问题。(wrestle)

4) 他们首先要做到在销售方面至少能确保盈亏平衡。他们想要抓住眼前每一个可以将企业做大做强的机会。因为他们明白，一旦经济不景气，利润就有可能骤减。(breakeven point, fall off)

5) 当公司长时间无法获得预期利润时，这些年轻的企业家们就不得不决定是否还要继续经营这些利润空间很小的企业。(grasp, stick with, profit margin)

6) 维系一个成长着、但又在苦苦挣扎着的企业，着实需要勇气和智慧。至关重要的是，企业的领导者能否迎着挑战奋发向上。(albeit, be up to)

Selecting Leaders

A company's leaders usually determine the broad conditions under which each team operates and define and focus each team's efforts. Corporate leaders should consider critical human-capital matters in their leadership actions every day.

In the following situation, Goldman Sachs, a bank holding company, is planning to set up more subsidiaries in other areas of the United States, so they need to recruit leaders for the new branches. To select the leaders, Jack Welch, the CEO of the company, is personally interviewing some candidates, and asking many questions connected with leadership. Role-play the situation with your group members. Take turns to be the CEO and ask the candidates different questions. You may reverse your roles when you have finished at least three questions.

- What is your communication strategy as a leader? What are your communication beliefs?
- If you could teach one thing about "leadership that drives growth" to a group of new employees, what would it be?
- What are your values or beliefs about balancing work and home life? How do you integrate these into your corporate culture around the world?
- What talents or strengths do you rely on most in your daily life as a leader?

- How do you align individuals' expectations with your organizational or team strategy?
- When selecting someone to join your team, what talents or qualities will you not live without?
- Think about the individuals on your team. What is your philosophy and strategy for horizontal development (growth within a role) versus vertical development (growth out of a role and into another or to higher levels of responsibility) for these employees?
- What is your greatest personal satisfaction?

- Tell about your beliefs on "status items" at work. For example, how important are perks to you? How important are perks to other employees in our company?
- As a leader, how do you demonstrate or show that you care? What formal systems or plans are needed so that every employee in our company knows that we care?
- What development do you need to excel as a leader or manager?
- As a leader, what do you do to encourage employees to express their opinions?

- Are you seen as an open person who will listen to anyone, or are you seen as a person who has strong beliefs and is unwilling to listen to others? How open are you to the opinions of others?
- What values or beliefs are important in creating sustainability?
- Think about a situation in which two or more people disagree about something important to them. How do you help bring them together?
- What measurements do you use to track your progress and the progress of your employees?

UNIT **8** Business Leadership

Language Hints

Starting a conversation
- I say, aren't you John Henry?
- I hope you don't mind my asking, but...
- Excuse me, I hear you're a ...
- Say, don't I know you from somewhere?
- ...

Taking up a point
- About income, I think most people deserve more than what they get.
- Sorry to interrupt, but did I hear you say...
- To go back to what you were saying about...,I'm not surprised at...
- Hang on, can we stick with that point about...?
- ...

Changing the subject
- Let's change the subject.
- I think we ought to move on to the next item.
- ...

Expressing approval
- I don't think that's a bad idea at all.
- I think I would go along with you.
- It was a sensible idea, I felt.
- That sounds very sensible to me.
- That's just what I'm getting at.
- That's the way it should be.
- There is something in what you said.
- ...

Expressing disapproval
- I'm certainly not in favor of that.
- Well, I don't think much of the idea.
- Personally, I feel that might be a bit unnecessary.
- ...

Closing a conversation
- It's been nice talking to you.
- Well, I've enjoyed talking to you. Thank you!
- ...

Recruitment Advertisement

Business is thriving and you're ready to expand your enterprise by taking on extra staff. But how do you write an effective recruitment advertisement to ensure you attract the applicants of high caliber you desire? You should definitely think carefully before simply putting pen to paper or fingertip to keyboard. Just as a CV creates the first impression to a prospective employer, a recruitment advertisement is a company's marketing tool and must be written to attract the right candidate for the job. An recruitment advertisement usually includes:

- the name and address of your company with a brief description of the nature of the business;
- the job title of the position being advertised and a summary of responsibilities;
- entry qualifications;

- special requirements (including out-of-hours working or travel);
- the remuneration package;
- closing date for applications; and
- details on how to reply, and to whom.

The best techniques for writing effective recruitment advertisement are the same as those for other forms of advertising. The job is your product; the readers of the job advert are your potential customers. The aim of the job advert is to attract interest, communicate quickly and clearly the essential (appealing and relevant) points, and to provide a clear response process and mechanism. Design should concentrate on the clarity of text, layout, and on conveying a professional image. Hereis a reminder of the essential writing tips:

- Use one simple headline, and make the job advert headline relevant and clear.
- Make the advert easy to read. Use simple language, avoid complicated words unless absolutely necessary, and keep enough space around the text to attract attention to it.
- Use short sentences. More than fifteen words in a sentence reduce the clarity of the meaning.
- Get the reader involved. Refer to the reader as "you" and use the second person ("you", "your" and "yours" etc.) in the description of the requirements and expectations of the candidate and the job role.
- Try to incorporate something new, innovative, exciting, and challenging — people are attracted to new things — either in the company or the role.
- Stress what is unique. You must try to emphasize what makes your job and organization special.
- Job advert statements and descriptions must be credible. Employers or jobs that sound too good to be true will only attract the gullible and the dreamers.
- Use bullet points and short bite-sized paragraphs. A lot of words in one big paragraph is very off-putting to the reader and will probably not be read.
- Use simple type-styles: Arial, Tahoma, Times, etc., or your house-style equivalents or variations.
- Avoid italics, shadows, light colors reversed out of dark, weird and wonderful colors.

Study the following sample and do the exercises according to the directions.

HEIFER PROJECT INTERNATIONAL

Africa Program Director

$30,000–$35,000 plus benefits

Heifer Project International, a progressive, rapidly expanding, non-profit, world hunger organization with more than 50 yrs of grassroots success, based in Little Rock, AR, seeks an exp. candidate to provide leadership to our Africa Program.

What would you do?

- Develop & implement program plans in the designated areas in order to reach the goals & objectives of the org.
- Facilitate direct communication between field programs & HQ.
- Monitor & evaluate programs.
- Investigate new requests for projects.
- Make on-site visits.
- Monitor hiring & performance of direct-line field staff.
- Monitor area budget & administer grants.

What will you need to have?

- MS degree Agriculture or related field, or a BS degree, plus 5 yrs relevant exp.
- At least 3 yrs rural development or agricultural experience in Africa preferred.
- Experience w/ the NGO /PVO approach & knowledge of global sustainable development essential.
- International experience.
- Knowledge of a 2nd language.

For more info, detailed job description, & downloadable application, please visit www.heifer.org.

Send resume & cover letter by 3/2 to:

HR, Heifer Project International

1015 Louisiana St.

Little Rock, AR 72202

Fax: (501) 907-2602; email: jobs@heifer.org.

HPI IS AN EQUAL OPPORTUNITY/AFFIRMATIVE ACTION EMPLOYER BY CHOICE.

1. Look again at the situation in the section of Selecting Leaders above. As the assistant to Richard S. Fuld, the HR Manager of Lehman Brothers Holdings Incorporated, you were asked to design a recruitment advertisement to seek 3 sales managers and 2 HR managers for your company's new branches in Chicago and Los Angeles. To do the task well, you discussed with Richard about the duties of the posts, and some other information to be presented in the advert, and you noted down the important points as follows. You still need to invent anything necessary for the advert.

   Brief on Company:
   - The company's principal activity: investment banking services to institutional, corporate, government and high-net-worth individuals and customers.
   - Three business segments: Investment Banking, Securities Services and Investment Management.
   - Offices in all global financial centers.
   - Operate in the United States, Tokyo, North America, Europe and Asia Pacific.
   - ...

UNIT **8** Business Leadership

Contact info:

Richard S. Fuld

HR Manager

85 Broad Street

New York, NY 10019

Phone: (212)526-7000

Fax: (212)526-3738

www.goldmansachs.com

HR Manager : Package Circa $80K
Duties:

- recruiting activities
- employee relationship activities
- performance appraisal and goal setting
- HR policies update
- training and development, compensation, staff welfare.
- ...

Sales Manager: Package Circa $100K
Duties:

- sales performance
- technical discussions
- customer relationships
- sales forecast
- winning strategies
- internal targets
- support resources
- customer specific requirements
- market requirements
- competitive threats and other important front line information
- ...

2. Fashion Industry International, one of the United Kingdom's Fashions, is now hunting for the head of purchasing(Europe) with the responsibilities for the purchase of ladies' fashion goods from European manufacturers and optimizing purchase prices. Please design a recruitment advertisement based on the following information. You may invent anything necessary.

> **Qualifications:** 30-45 years of age, good education, competent in English and at least two European languages, experience, weighing risks against potential profit, negotiating skills, self motivation, communication skills…
>
> **Package:** £25K, travel and expense allowance, pension scheme, free sickness insurance, promotion opportunities…
>
> **Contact:** Mr. J. Cullen, Price Bowers plc, St. Michael's Court, Green Street, Stockport M62 2JF, Tel:01275 223458, Fax:01275 223444, www.pricebowers.com

Relevant Extension

Business Expressions

1. Work out the following 14 words which are about traits of business leaders. The first letters are given and the letters in the brackets need to be reorganized.

   1) J_____ (ceistu)   8) E_____ (hntsuiasm)
   2) J_____ (degmntu)   9) B_____ (aeginr)
   3) D_____ (penedbaility)   10) U_____ (enslfssihnes)
   4) I_____ (iatintiev)   11) C_____ (aegoru)
   5) D_____ (ceiesvinses)   12) K_____ (deglenow)
   6) T_____ (act)   13) L_____ (alotly)
   7) I_____ (ngtierty)   14) E_____ (ancdenru)

2. The words in the box are related to the following descriptions about what traits a good leader should have. Match each word with the corresponding description.

| Intelligent | Competent | Imaginative |
| Forward-looking | Broad-minded | Fair-minded |

UNIT **8** Business Leadership

Honest	Courageous	Inspiring

1) _____ —Display sincerity, integrity, and candor in all your actions. Deceptive behavior will not inspire trust.

2) _____ —Have enough skill or knowledge to function or develop to a satisfactory standard.

3) _____ —Set goals and have a vision of the future. The vision must be owned throughout the organization. Effective leaders envision what they want and how to get it. They habitually pick priorities stemming from their basic values.

4) _____ —Display confidence in all that you do. By showing endurance in mental, physical, and spiritual stamina, you will inspire others to reach for new heights. Take charge when necessary.

5) _____ —Use sound judgement to make a good decision at the right time.

6) _____ —Show fair treatment to all people. Prejudice is the enemy of justice. Display empathy by being sensitive to the feelings, values, interests, and well-being of others.

7) _____ —Seek out diversity.

8) _____ —Have the perseverance to accomplish a goal, regardless of the seemingly insurmountable obstacles. Display a confident calmness when under stress.

9) _____ —Make timely and appropriate changes in your thinking, plans, and methods. Show creativity by thinking of new and better goals, ideas, and solutions to problems. Be innovative!

3. **Leadership style is an approach of giving direction, motivating people and implementing plans. As there are many leaders, there are different leadership styles. Fill in the blanks with the given expressions to complete the explanations regarding some common leadership styles.**

bureaucratic leadership	participative leadership
authoritarian leadership	charismatic leadership
delegative leader	democratic leadership
multicultural leader	servant leader

1) In _____ style, a leader will clearly define what are the organizational needs and what should be done and how it should be done. He rarely allows others to help in decision making.

2) The most important and effective leadership style, also known as _____, is _____, in which the leader offers guidance to his team members, encourages group discussion and allows team members in decision making.

3) A _____ offers no guidance to the group members and allows them to take decisions on their own. This is a style in which the leader entrusts decision making to an employee of a group of employees.

4) A leader with the skills and attitudes to relate effectively to and motivate people across race, gender, age, social attitudes, and lifestyles is a _____.

5) When the leaders work by taking the help of a book containing all the rules and regulations that must be followed by an employee working in a company, this is a kind of _____ style.

6) If a leader tries to inject doses of enthusiasm into the employees in order to increase their performance level, he shows a real _____, which can also be viewed as transformational leadership.

7) One who serves constituents by working on their behalf to help them achieve their goals, not the leader's own goals can be regarded as a _____.

Specialized Reading

1. **Read the passage and finish the following multiple-choice questions.**

   To be effective as a leader, you must develop skills in strategic thinking. Strategic thinking is a process whereby you learn how to make your business vision a 1)____ by developing your abilities in team work, problem solving, and critical thinking. It is also a tool to help you confront change, plan for and make 2)____, and envision new possibilities and 3)____.

   Strategic 4)____ is like making a movie. Every movie has a context (or story) which it uses to get you to experience a certain 5)____ (an emotion, in this case) at the end of the movie. Strategic thinking is much the same in that it requires you to 6)____ what you want your ideal outcome to be for your business and then works 7)____ by focusing on the story of HOW you will be able to reach your 8)____.

   As you develop a 9)____ vision for your business, there are five different criteria (organization, observation, views, driving forces and ideal position) that you should focus on. These five criteria will help you 10)____ your ideal outcome. In addition, they will help you set up and develop the steps necessary to make your business vision a reality.

1) A. fact   B. case   C. reality   D. instance
2) A. revisions   B. transitions   C. formations   D. compositions
3) A. opportunities B. luck   C. fortune   D. interests
4) A. learning   B. cooperation   C. partnership   D. thinking
5) A. outcome   B. consequence   C. plot   D. output
6) A. shape   B. envision   C. view   D. foretell
7) A. forwards   B. backwards   C. clockwise   D. counterclockwise
8) A. destiny   B. destination   C. vision   D. prospect
9) A. prospective   B. strategic   C. picturesque   D. tactic
10) A. expand   B. enhance   C. stress   D. define

2. **Read the passage regarding differences between a manager and a leader and choose corresponding statements according to the questions.**

Are you a manager or a leader? Although these two terms are often thrown out interchangeably, they are in fact two very different animals complete with different personalities and world views.

By learning whether you are more of a leader or more of a manager, you will gain the insight and self-confidence that comes with knowing more about yourself. The result is greater impact and effectiveness when dealing with others and running your business.

Let's take a look at the different personality styles of managers versus leaders, the attitudes each have toward goals, their basic conceptions of what work entails, their relationships with others, and their sense of self (or self-identity) and how it develops. Last of all, we will examine leadership development and discover what criteria are necessary for leaders to reach their full potential.

First of all, let's take a look at the difference in personality styles between a manager and a leader. Managers emphasize rationality and control. They are problem-solvers focusing on goals, resources, organization structures, or people. They often ask questions like, "What problems have to be solved, and what are the best ways to achieve results so that people will continue to contribute to this organization?" Managers are persistent, tough-minded, hard working, intelligent, analytical, and tolerant and have goodwill toward others. Leaders are perceived as brilliant, but sometimes lonely. They achieve control of themselves before trying to control others. They can visualize a purpose, generate value in work; and they are imaginative, passionate, non-conforming risk-takers.

Managers and leaders have very different attitudes toward goals. Managers adopt impersonal, almost passive, attitudes toward goals; they decide upon goals based on necessity instead of desire and are therefore deeply tied to their organization's culture. They usually tend to be reactive since they focus on current information. Leaders, however, tend to be active since they envision and promote their ideas instead of reacting to current situations. They shape ideas instead of responding to them; they have a personal orientation toward goals and provide a vision that alters the way people think about what is desirable, possible, and necessary.

Now let's look at managers' and leaders' conceptions of work. Managers view work as an enabling process. They establish strategies and make decisions by combining people and ideas; they continually coordinate and balance opposing views and are good at reaching compromises and mediating conflicts between opposing values and perspectives. They act to limit choice and tolerate practical, mundane work because of strong survival instinct which makes them risk-averse. Leaders develop new approaches to long-standing problems and open issues to new options. They first use their vision to excite people and only then develop choices which give those images substance. They focus people on shared ideals and raise their expectations. They also work from high-risk positions because of strong dislike of mundane work.

Managers and leaders have very different relations with others. Managers prefer working with others, and report that solitary activity makes them anxious. They are collaborative; they maintain a low level of emotional involvement in relationships. They attempt to reconcile differences, seek compromises, and establish a balance of power. They relate to people according to the role they play in a sequence of events or in a decision-making process; they focus on how things get done and maintain controlled, rational, and equitable structures. They may be viewed by others as inscrutable, detached, and manipulative. Leaders maintain inner perceptiveness that they can use in their relationships with others. They relate to people in intuitive, empathetic way; they focus on what events and decisions mean to participants and attract strong feelings of identity and difference or of love and hate. They create systems where human relations may be turbulent, intense, and at times even disorganized.

The self-identity of managers versus leaders is strongly influenced by their past. Managers report that their adjustments to life have been straightforward and that their lives have been more or less peaceful since birth. They have a sense of self as a guide to conduct and attitude which is derived from a feeling of being at home and in harmony with their environment. They see themselves as conservators and regulators of an existing order of affairs with which they personally identify and from which they gain rewards. They report that their role harmonizes with their ideals of responsibility and duty. They perpetuate and strengthen existing institutions and display a life development process which focuses on socialization. This socialization process prepares them to guide institutions and to maintain the existing balance of social relations. Leaders reportedly have not had an easy time of it. Their lives are marked by a continual struggle to find some sense of order. They do not take things for granted and are not satisfied with the status quo. They report that their "sense of self" is derived from a feeling of profound separateness and is independent of work roles, memberships, or other social indicators of social identity. They may work in organizations, but they never belong to them. They seek opportunities for change (for example, technological, political, or ideological) and support change. They find their purpose is to profoundly alter human, economic, and political relationships. They display a life development process which focuses on personal mastery. This process impels them to struggle for psychological and social change.

1) Which of the following statements (A-J) is true of a manager?

___

2) Which of the following statements (A-J) is true of a leader?

___

A. They are very good at maintaining the status quo and adding stability and order to our culture.

B. They may not be good at instigating change and envisioning the future.

C. They are very good at stirring people's emotions, raising their expectations.

D. They are good at taking people's emotion and expectations in new directions(both good and bad).

E. Like artists and other gifted people, they may often suffer from neuroses and have a tendency toward self-absorption and preoccupation.

F. They ask questions such as "what problems should be resolved and what is the best solution?"

G. They shape ideas rather than respond to them.

H. They are good at reaching compromises and reconcile differences.

I. They work from high-risk positions due to their dislike of ordinary and uninteresting work.

J. They have no definite strengths and weaknesses.

3. Discuss the following questions with your group members.

   1) What do you think are the distinguished features that a business leader should possess? Why?

   2) Which position are you more fitted for in your future job, a leader or a manager? Why?

UNIT 9
Teamwork

1. **Discuss the following questions with your partner.**

    1) Team building is the process of building a good team: one that performs well together. In order to decide the best way to embark on a team building programme, you should first be able to see the difference between a **group**, a **team** and a **good team**. You can test your ability to see these differences by looking at the following expressions and words associated with team building a good team. Only one of them defines what a good team is. Find it and give your reasons.

    | a group of people | synergy | sharing one aim |
    | whole>sum | co-operation | flexibility |
    | working together | reporting to one boss | serving one customer |

    2) Below is a list of the differences that exist between an individual working as part of a group and an individual working as part of a team. Read through the list, mark G (for Group) and T (for Team) and then check with your partner by discussion.

    _____ Members work interdependently and work towards both personal and team goals, and they understand these goals are accomplished best by mutual support.

    _____ Members focus mostly on themselves because they are not involved in the planning of their group's objectives and goals.

    _____ Members are given their tasks or told what their duty/job is, and suggestions are rarely welcomed.

    _____ Members feel a sense of ownership towards their role in the group because they committed themselves to goals they helped create.

    _____ Members work independently and they often are not working towards the same goal.

    _____ Members are very cautious about what they say and are afraid to ask questions. They may not fully understand what is taking place

UNIT **9** Teamwork

          in their group.

_____ Members may have a lot to contribute but are held back because of a closed relationship with each member.

_____ Members collaborate together and use their talent and experience to contribute to the success of the team's objectives.

_____ Members are encouraged to offer their skills and knowledge, and in turn each member is able to contribute to the group's success.

_____ Members see conflict as a part of human nature and they react to it by treating it as an opportunity to hear about new ideas and opinions. Everybody wants to resolve problems constructively.

_____ Members do not trust each other's motives because they do not fully understand the role each member plays in their group.

_____ Members participate equally in decision-making, but each member understands that the leader might need to make the final decision if the team cannot come to a consensus agreement.

_____ Members may or may not participate in group decision-making, and conformity is valued more than positive results.

_____ Members are bothered by differing opinions or disagreements because they consider it a threat. There is no group support to help resolve problems.

_____ Members base their success on trust and encourage all members to express their opinions, varying views, and questions.

_____ Members make a conscious effort to be honest, respectful, and listen to every person's point of view.

   3) Do you like working with a team or individually? Why?

   4) Why do companies put so much emphasis on team building?

2. If you had an opportunity to select anyone from your organization and start a new team, who would you pick? Besides the technical skills for the work to be done, what other factors would you take into consideration in selecting your team members? Work in groups to choose the six most important from the list below. Don't forget to explain your choices, and you can also add your own points to the list.

- *communicate constructively*
- *listen actively*
- *have good taste in fashion*
- *keep up on current cultural trends*

- *make good presentations*
- *give orders*
- *share openly and willingly*
- *get along well with the boss*
- *like taking risks*
- *be attractive*
- *exhibit flexibility*
- *work as a problem-solver*
- *treat others in a respectful and supportive manner*
- *show commitment to the team*
- *have a good sense of humor*
- *...*

Preview: In the latter part of the 20th century, "Team Building" became recognized by many companies as an important factor in providing a quality service and remaining competitive. A team building success happens when a team can accomplish something much bigger and work more effectively than a group of the same individuals working on their own. There is a strong cooperation of individual contributions. Team building skills are critical for your effectiveness as a manager or entrepreneur. It is this point that drives the author of the following article to focus on the clash and disharmony between executives in businesses and the possible reasons for those problems. The author suggests that, in solving the problems, executives could learn a good lesson from the rowers in the boat race.

Executives Must Pull Together like Rowers in the Boat Race

By Stefan Stern

[1] Our lesson today is taken from the Gospel[1] according to St Mark[2], Chapter III, **verses** 24-25: "If a kingdom be divided against itself, that kingdom cannot stand. And if a house be divided against itself, that house cannot stand."

[2] It could be time for Bible[3] classes in the Sanofi[4] boardroom. According to **loose-lipped** "banking sources" who **unburdened** themselves last week, the top team at

---

1 Gospel / ˈɡɒspəl / 福音，记载于福音书中的耶稣生平及其教导
2 St Mark 约翰马可，是耶稣的十二门徒之一，教会传统认为他就是马可福音的作者
3 Bible / ˈbaɪbl / 圣经，包括旧约和新约的基督教圣书
4 Sanofi / saɪˈnɒfɪ / 法国赛诺菲圣德拉堡集团，是法国排名前列的在多项治疗领域拥有世界领先产品的专业制药企业

France's biggest drugs company is split over its **on-off** $54bn (£ 27.4bn) **merger** with Bristol-Myers Squibb[1], the US pharmaceuticals company.

[3] The deal would create one of the world's largest drugs businesses. But Sanofi's chairman, Jean-Francois Dehecq, and its chief executive, Gérard Le Fur, are apparently divided on whether the **transaction** should go ahead. In spite of repeated denials by the company, its **shareholders** will not be encouraged by **speculation** that Sanofi's most senior executives disagree about this most fundamental of strategic moves. The sums of money involved are hardly **trivial**.

[4] But, of course, this sort of **clash** is not uncommon at the highest levels in business. "The more senior you get, the more personal it can get," says Elisabeth Marx[2], author of Breaking Through Culture Shock and a partner in the leadership consulting team at the Heidrick & Struggles[3] search firm in London. At moments like these reputations are at stake.

[5] A public **row** that exposes the lack of harmony at the top is the most dramatic response to a crisis. But in practice, leadership teams reach crisis point for a number of reasons. There may be new blood at the top and an urgent need to speed up **collaboration** among colleagues who do not know each other well. In a global business, there can be difficult cultural clashes that executives struggle to **navigate**.

[6] At times of rapid change, boards may understand well that they need to start doing something differently — but what?

[7] And then there are those top teams that are simply **dysfunctional**, pulling in different directions at the same time, failing to communicate properly, in a state of war.

[8] Psychological assessment can help teams work together better. This is done by analyzing what sorts of personalities the group contains, how they are behaving towards each other and, by observing closely what is going on in the room, whether meetings are productive and so on.

[9] But the classic "career ladder" may be part of the problem here. Getting to the top in business will probably mean focusing narrowly and **ruthlessly** on your own discipline, in order to achieve the sort of results that will get you noticed. But upon

---

1 Bristol-Myers Squibb 美国百时美施贵宝公司，是一家以科研为基础的全球性的从事医药保健及个人护理产品的多元化企业，其主要业务涵盖医药产品、日用消费品、营养品及医疗器械
2 Elisabeth Marx / ɪˈlɪzəbəθ- / 伊丽莎白·马科斯博士，出生于德国的心理学家，是一家全球性的经理人猎头公司（Norman Broadbent International）的总裁
3 Heidrick & Struggles 海德思哲国际咨询公司，全球最大的提供企业领袖搜寻和企业领导咨询服务的专业公司

35　joining the senior executive team a kind of **collegiality** is required. It is no longer good enough to keep your head down while driving towards your personal goals. The top team has collective responsibility for the health and performance of the organization.

　　[10] "Your role has changed and so your behavior has to change," Dr Marx says. And that can be painful — especially when the stakes are high and the strategic
40　challenges are complicated. That is why you hear so much talk about companies seeking people who are "comfortable with **ambiguity**." At the highest level you will be asked to perform in areas that are beyond your **expertise**, outside your "comfort zone," where not all the facts can be known.

　　[11] The successful top teams of the future will display what Dr Marx calls "**cognitive**
45　**diversity**" — that is, they will have a **breadth** of outlook and approach. A team may appear to be diverse on the surface, ticking various politically correct boxes, but how will the team think and react? That rainbow **coalition** may in fact be nothing more than an army of clones.

　　[12] To witness a truly remarkable example of teamwork in action, you could do
50　a lot worse than head to the River Thames[1] in London this Saturday, where the 153rd university boat race is taking place. This year, once again, the same two teams have made it to the final. (That is a suitably **smug** Oxbridge joke: the race is, of course, always held between teams representing the universities of Oxford[2] and Cambridge[3].) Mark de Rond, a senior lecturer in strategy at the Judge Business School in Cambridge, has
55　spent the past seven months observing the Cambridge University boat club at work, conducting an "**ethnographic**" study, as it prepares its team for the race on April 7.

　　[13] While I should at this point issue the standard health warning about drawing simplistic parallels between sport and business, it turns out that rowing really does offer some interesting lessons to managers who want their teams to work better together.

60　　[14] One intriguing insight is that the strongest eight rowers on paper do not necessarily form the best team. Dr de Rond says that the team is a social entity. "The boat is so sensitive that the crew has to be perfectly **synchronized**. If they are not all working together it can be a massive brake on the boat."

　　[15] This year there has been an unusual (if limited) outbreak of democracy in the
65　Cambridge camp, with rowers being invited to share their views as to who should be selected for the first eight. "They might say: 'It feels better with X in the boat,'" Dr de

---

1　River Thames / -temz / 英国伦敦的泰晤士河
2　Oxford / ˈɒksfəd / 英国牛津大学
3　Cambridge / ˈkeɪmbrɪdʒ / 英国剑桥大学

Rond explains. Being highly skilled is not enough. The psychological factors — which combination of people **gels** best — are just as important.

[16] Old Father Thames[1] provides a highly unpredictable course for the race. The river bends and turns, its currents are mysterious, the conditions on the water are at times quite unhelpful for the precision-trained athletes.

[17] So, does the boat race offer the perfect metaphor for business? Not quite. The team that wins on Saturday will be the one that goes backwards the fastest.

(974 words)
From *Financial Times*

New Words

verse / vɜːs /
n. any one of the short numbered divisions of a chapter in the Bible (《圣经》的) 节

loose-lipped / luːs-lɪpt /
a. given to indiscreet or incessant talk 说话随便的，口无遮拦的

unburden / ʌnˈbɜːdn /
v. tell someone else problems, secrets etc. so that one feels better（通过向别人倾诉问题、秘密等以）解除自己的烦恼

on-off
a. changing, going from a certainty in one direction to a certainty in another 断断续续的；不时的

merger / ˈmɜːdʒə /
n. the act of joining together two or more companies or organizations to form a larger one（尤指两公司）合并；兼并

transaction / trænˈzækʃən /
n. a piece of business conducted or carried out 业务；交易

shareholder / ˈʃeəhəʊldə /
n. an owner of shares in a business company 股东

speculation / ˌspekjuˈleɪʃən /
n. the guesses that one makes 推断，推测

trivial / ˈtrɪvɪəl /
a. having little importance 不重要的

clash / klæʃ /
n. serious disagreement; argument 重大的分歧；争论

row / raʊ /
n. a situation in which people disagree strongly, especially when the disagreement appears in public 意见不一致，就某事看法不合

collaboration / kəˌlæbəˈreɪʃən /
n. working together with somebody 合作；协作

navigate / ˈnævɪɡeɪt /
v. maneuver, plan and control the course and position of (a ship or aircraft) 行进；经过；指引；指导

dysfunctional / dɪsˈfʌŋkʃənl /
a. not working properly or normally 功能不良的

ruthlessly / ˈruːθlɪslɪ /
ad. determinedly and firmly when taking unpleasant decisions（做出令人不快的决定时）坚决地

collegiality / kəˌliːdʒɪˈælɪtɪ /
n. shared power and authority vested among colleagues 共同掌权；同僚间分授权力

ambiguity / ˌæmbɪˈɡjuːətɪ /
n. doubtfulness or uncertainty which is difficult to understand 含糊不清，不明确，

---

1 Old Father Thames "老父亲泰晤士"，英国人对泰晤士河的习惯称呼

模棱两可

expertise / ˌekspɜːˈtiːz /
n. expert skill or knowledge, especially in a particular field 专门技能或知识（尤指在某一领域）

cognitive / ˈkɒɡnɪtɪv /
a. related to the process of knowing, understanding, and learning sth. 认知的；与认识有关的

breadth / bredθ /
n. wide extent (of knowledge); range 宽广的程度（如指知识）；范围

coalition / ˌkəʊəˈlɪʃ(ə)n /
n. a group of people who join together to achieve a particular purpose, usually a political one 结合体；联合

smug / smʌɡ /
a. self-satisfied; too pleased with or proud of oneself or one's achievements 自鸣得意的，自满的，沾沾自喜的

ethnographic / ˌeθnəˈɡræfɪk /
a. related to the scientific study of different races of people 人种研究的

synchronise / ˈsɪŋkrənaɪz /
v. arrange for two or more actions to happen at exactly the same time 使……同步，使……配合一致

gel / dʒel /
v. work well together as a group; take definite form 合为一体，形成整体；成形

Phrases & Expressions

pull together
work with combined effort in a well-organized way 同心协力；通力合作

go ahead
be carried out, take place; move forward 进行；发生

at stake
that can be won or lost, depending on the outcome of a particular action 处于危急关头；冒风险；处于未定状态中

career ladder
a metaphor used to denote vertical job promotion (In business and human resources management, the ladder typically describes the progression from entry level positions to higher levels of pay, skill, responsibility, or authority.) 职业晋升阶梯

make it
be successful in a particular activity 做某事成功了

keep one's head down
avoid danger or distraction; keep quiet 避免危险；防止分心；避免引人注意

can/could do worse than do sth.
be correct or sensible in doing sth. 做某事是正确的或可取的

UNIT 9 Teamwork

Exercises

Comprehension

1. Answer the following content questions with your partner.

   1) Why did the author say that it could be the time for Bible classes in the Sanofi boardroom?

   2) What could be inferred from "its shareholders will not be encouraged by speculation that Sanofi's most senior executives disagree about this most fundamental of strategic moves"?

   3) What are the possible reasons given by the author for a crisis point of the leadership teams?

   4) Why could "career ladder" be a problem for the harmony of a company's leadership team?

   5) What does the phrase "comfortable with ambiguity" mean?

   6) What are the most important factor mentioned by the author to be considered in forming a successful boat race team? What other factors might there be?

   7) According to the author, is it right to draw simplistic parallels between sport and business? Why or why not?

   8) What can executives learn from the rowers in the boat race?

2. The text can be divided into three parts. Put down the paragraph numbers and main idea of each part. The main idea of the last part has been done for you.

Parts	Paragraphs	Main ideas
I	Paras. _____	_____
II	Paras. _____	_____
III	Paras. _____	Though sport and business are not the same, executives can learn some interesting lessons from rowers in the boat race.

Critical Thinking

Work in group to discuss the following questions.

1) What are the characteristics of effective teams? List at least five points.

203

2) Team dynamics are the unseen forces that operate in a team between different people or groups. Team dynamics can strongly influence how a team reacts, behaves or performs, and the effects of team dynamics are often very complex.

Suppose in a small team of six people working in one office there are two people who have a particularly strong friendship. This friendship is therefore a team dynamic as it is a "natural force" that may have an influence on the rest of the team, and can be manifest in various ways, either positively or negatively. Try to identify some positive and negative effects of a strong friendship in a team.

3) The following is a small selection of classic team quotes that can be used to motivate or encourage. Try to explain the meanings of them, and add some more as possible as you can.

- *There is no "I" in "Team".*
- *Together Everyone Achieves More (an acronym for TEAM).*
- *Many hands make light work.*
- *A dwarf on a giant's shoulders sees the further of the two.*
- *It's not our preferences that cause problems; it's our attachment to them.*
- *No man is an island.*
- *...*

UNIT 9 Teamwork

Vocabulary

1. **Fill in the blanks with the proper forms of the words or phrases given below.**

pull together	on-off	speculation	collaboration	synchronize
career ladder	merger	transaction	at stake	collegiality

   1) Information technology professionals are being forced to climb a _____ with the bottom rungs missing.

   2) In view of our long-standing business relationship, we can conclude this _____.

   3) Businesses must _____ their production choices with consumer choices.

   4) Having been colleagues for 3 years, the members in this department have really got inside each other's headsets and learnt how to _____ as a team.

   5) Our work environment emphasizes _____ and the sharing of specialized knowledge and expertise both to deliver outstanding services to our clients and to foster professional growth of our attorneys.

   6) Time Warner's _____ with AOL, the deal that came to symbolize the misplaced dotcom exuberance, eventually led to a $54bn write-down.

   7) With profits _____, the company must consider all the factors to develop a new corporate strategy to turn the company around.

   8) After months of _____ negotiations, Spain's Telephonic this week became a reference shareholder in Telecom Italia.

   9) The company is building the centre in _____ with the Institute of Offshore Engineering.

   10) With all the _____ that's been going on over a tablet and the way Apple has aligned itself with partners, it's just crazy enough to be true.

2. **Rewrite the following italicized parts by using the appropriate words or expressions from the text.**

   1) Mr. Smith wanted to *relieve himself of the worry* by telling the problem to the prosecutors.

   2) The board confirmed that the company would be allowed to *move forward* with new schemes as long as the sales figures could be achieved.

   3) Now the *indiscreet* colleague is in trouble after she showed the meeting minutes to the visitor with unknown identity.

4) Many problems have stemmed from the *uncertainty and doubtfulness* of the system's specification, which has meant different manufacturers have sometimes produced incompatible equipment.

5) These adjustments may sound *unimportant* but, if they make readers feel that the company really is at home in their country, they are surely worthwhile.

6) Postbank not only has a load of retail customers but is also looking for a partner to bring it the necessary *skill and knowledge* in packaging new financial products that Deutsche Bank would clearly provide.

7) Both of us have annual leave but we can't *have the days off* at the same time.

8) UK has been much more vocal than other countries on issues like rooting out corruption and getting rid of *improper and abnormal* elements within the government itself.

9) Successfully merging two banks requires attacking costs *determinedly and firmly*.

10) He is the right candidate for the job because he has *a wide range of* experience in the business.

3. **Study the following groups of words, and then choose the proper words to fill in the blanks. Change the form where necessary.**

   1) speculate, speculation, speculator, speculative

      a. AT&T said it "did not comment on rumor or _____."

      b. Many in the industry also _____ that the CME's search for cost savings will also lead them to cull administrative jobs.

      c. Some countries are reluctant to lift interest rates further for fear of attracting _____ capital inflows and complicating further its problem in managing domestic liquidity.

   2) collaborate, collaboration, collaborative, collaborator

      a. _____ approaches involving companies, governments, inter-governmental organizations, non-governmental organizations and communities are the key to attaining "glittering rewards" for developing economies.

      b. With the joint efforts of Edward Smith and his _____ , his dream finally came true.

      c. Sergio Marchionne, Fiat chief executive, has also said that the group could look for _____ with whichever company became the new owner of

Jaguar and Land Rover.

3) navigate, navigation, navigator, navigable

   a. The _____ are considering buying six new warships.

   b. Modern, clean and easy to _____, the airport's main drawback for business travelers is the often intrusive and lengthy security check.

   c. The world's largest maker of car _____ equipment fell sharply after telling analysts that its sales were slowing.

4) cognizance, cognition, cognitive, cognizable

   a. The study also investigated _____ and motivational changes emerging from another experimental program for business juniors at the same school.

   b. The government has in the past not taken _____ of any protest unless there has been some show of violence.

   c. The present invention relates to a technique for adding _____ to business processes at any given step of a business transaction.

5) dysfunctional, functional, function, functionary

   a. The company gives the highest priority to ensuring that essential business _____ can continue under any untoward or adverse circumstances.

   b. Like a car with an engine that can't fire on all cylinders, a business that's _____ may move forward for a while. But eventually it stops running.

   c. This landmark legislation makes life for a government _____ difficult but I think that is worthwhile for the greater good of the country.

Translation

1. Translate the following sentences into Chinese.

   1) In spite of repeated denials by the company, its shareholders will not be encouraged by speculation that Sanofi's most senior executives disagree about this most fundamental of strategic moves.

   2) And then there are those top teams that are simply dysfunctional, pulling in different directions at the same time, failing to communicate properly, in a state of war.

   3) But the classic "career ladder" may be part of the problem here. Getting to the top in business will probably mean focusing narrowly and ruthlessly on your own discipline, in order to achieve the sort of results that will get you noticed.

4) But upon joining the senior executive team a kind of collegiality is required. It is no longer good enough to keep your head down while driving towards your personal goals.

5) The top team has collective responsibility for the health and performance of the organization.

2. Put the following sentences into English, using the words and phrases given in the brackets.

1) 过去，团队合作只用于某些特殊项目，而如今它已成为公司的一种准则。(norm)

2) 在充满挑战的商业社会中，企业内部往往会存在各种各样的冲突，这种内部不和会使企业的发展处于风险之中。(clash, at stake)

3) 团队精神已成为企业成功和生存不可或缺的一环。(element, survival)

4) 一个企业就如同一艘巨大的舰船，装载着整个团队。如果这个团队团结一致，同事间关系融洽，齐心协力，各部门为了企业共同的目标保持同步，通力合作，那么这个企业就能不断前进，走向胜利。(go ahead, collegiality, collaboration, pull together, synchronize)

5) 对员工个体而言，团队精神的科学运用，能使每个人的能力得到充分发挥，从而实现个人发展的目标。(expertise)

Solving Conflicts

Conflict situations are a normal part of everyday life. Routinely we hear some business people say "There is always one or two people who make it difficult for the rest of the team." It seems that in the midst of conflict there are many obstacles to overcome. Frustration and difficulties can bog down even the most successful leaders. Look at the following situation:

Richard was the Department Manager of Finance and Accounting for ABC, a prominent mid-Atlantic manufacturing company. Now he has responsibility for a large new project. Several members that don't usually work well together have

UNIT 9 Teamwork

> to collaborate for the project to succeed. The issues with the team members are as follows:
>
> **Crystal** continually leaves work early without notifying Richard or her teammates.
>
> **Betsy** is frequently absent, and just almost everyone, including one of the company's owners, accused Betsy of having extra-martial affairs.
>
> **Jane** refuses to try any new assignment and insists that she is overworked even though her in-basket is never full and her desk never has more than one stack of paper on it at any given point of time.
>
> **Rachael** refuses to do any filing, but ardently supports Richard.
>
> **Crystal** and **Jane** have formed a hardened alliance against Rachael because Rachael never says anything negative about Richard and because they suspect Rachael of "informing" on them to Richard.
>
> **Lois** is a wallflower and just stays out of the way.
>
> "They are all acting like a bunch of children. They think this is a game!" Richard growled into the phone as he related the details of the unfolding situation. "With all these antics going I'm being compelled by our Human Resources Director to have a meeting, but I feel that all I would be doing would be putting gasoline on the fire." "This is our busy time; we don't have time for this nonsense!" Richard's ten-year career with ABC has led him to become the key insider supporting the president by handling complex financial matters, but now the president is considering removing him for his lack of team building focus and poor people management skills. Richard's position looks bad, so he has called for a conflict consultant...

Work in pairs. You are Richard and the conflict consultant. Discuss the issues and consider:

- Why do you think Richard's team will not simply just do their jobs?
- Where do you think Richard should begin reconciling broken relationships?
- What steps of "progressive discipline" do you think Richard should implement? Against which team members?

When you have finished, compare your resolutions to the conflicts with those of another 2 pairs to get the relatively better ones and report to the whole class.

Language Hints

Expressing your feelings
- What I'm concerned is...
- My main concern is...
- ...

Making suggestions
- One thing you could do is...
- How about/What about...
- ...

Resolving the conflict
- How do you think we should deal with this?
- ...

Identifying the real problem
- What's really bothering you?
- ...

Expressing satisfaction
- Good/Excellent choice.
- Yes, that would be very helpful...
- ...

Expressing dissatisfaction
- I don't think that would be helpful.
- I don't think that would do much good.
- ...

Stating common goals
- We've all got the same objective/goal.
- ...

Reviewing the situation
- Let's meet next week/time and see how things are going on.
- ...

Notice

Notices are an effective means of written communication to reach a large audience. They are often used to:

- inform people of changes of plans;
- give instructions or issue warnings;
- announce social events;
- report on matters of general interests to employees;
- advertise posts for internal appointments;
- remind staff of new procedures;
- require signatures of staff of agreement or disagreement with some proposed policy of action, etc.

Notices require a clear heading at the top, followed by the main body that falls into short paragraphs. The name and position of the writer usually appear in a notice, and the date is indicated at the bottom. But if the time of the information has already been made clear in the notice itself or the readers know it clearly, the date can also be omitted.

Though often carried in newspapers or by e-mail, their style is much more formal and serious than that of memos. The heading or opening should be eye-catching and stimulating. Information must be presented in a clear and concise way, and the tone of notices is usually rather formal and impersonal.

Generally, there are four types of notices:

- A poster notice can provide information on when and where a particular activity is going to take place, commonly used inside a company, such as a meeting notice, a holiday notice, etc.
- A leaflet notice contains more information and is often used as a way of promotion.
- A mail notice may be the most efficient way to provide information to the public as it is very quick, economical, and easy to send.
- Signs make people be aware of something and it is commonly used in public places such as stations or airports. The simplicity is most appreciated for public signs.

Study the following samples and then do the exercises according to the directions.

Sample 1

Notice of the Poster Type

Basketball Match

Production Department Team

vs

Sales Department Team

    4:30 p.m., Friday, May 15, 2008

    Southern District Gymnasium

Sample 2

Notice of the Leaflet Type

Publishing Conference Proceedings

There is some possibility of publishing the papers accepted by our program committee.

If you want to have your paper considered for publication in the Proceedings, you may submit your paper read at the Conference.

If your paper is selected, you will be asked to submit the electronic version of your paper together with its hard copy.

It is noted that papers presented at the Conference are not automatically published in the Proceedings.

Program Committee

Sample 3

Notice of The Mail Type

Windows Cleaning

Dear Staff,

Please be informed that we have arranged Strong Plus Ltd. to come to clean all the glass windows of the Staff House between 9:00 a.m. to 5:00 p.m. as scheduled below:

Rooms on 9/ F-11 /F16 Dec. 08

Rooms on 6/ F-8 /F 17 Dec. 08

Rooms on 3/ F-4 /F 18 Dec. 08

Rooms on 1/ F-2 /F 19 Dec. 08

Please note that the cleaners will require access to your rooms in order to do the cleaning. To facilitate the cleaners, please remove any obstacles that are placed next to the windows. Neither the cleaners nor Staff House will be responsible for any loss or damage of personal properties if you fail to co-operate.

Thank you for your attention and we apologize for any inconvenience that may cause.

Regards,

Rocky Tang (Mr.)

Manager

UNIT **9** Teamwork

Sample 4

Notice as Public Signs

Exercises:

1. As mentioned in the section of Solving Conflicts, Richard referred to a consultant to solve the conflicts. To get the whole picture of the situation, the consultant asked Richard to notice all team members of a meeting in Meeting Room 503 at 2 o'clock Friday (July 11) afternoon. You are Richard and write this notice now.

2. The following is a notice on DUKO Christmas party which is in a letter format. Can you make it in the poster format?

> Dec. 10, 2008
>
> DUKO CHRISTMAS PARTY
>
> Dear all staff of DUKO,
>
> We wish to invite you to the DUKO Christmas party at Multi-functional Hall in Staff House starting at 7:30 p.m. on Sunday, 21st December 2008.
>
> You may bring up to one friend. Please bring a small gift (suggested price HK$20) to be swapped between others.
>
> See you at the party.
>
> Staff Relations

3. The following notice is not well done. Please revise it.

> Dear residents,
>
> We will close the Staff House Office during Chinese New Year holidays and we will open again on 4 Feb 09.
>
> Only a few staff will be on duty during the holidays; thus, we can not offer the room cleaning services. We will resume it on 4 Feb 09 also.
>
> If there is any emergency, you can call our duty staff at the Service Counter at 2249 1428 or 2249 1528 for assistance.
>
> Regards,
>
> Rocky Tang (Mr.)
>
> Manager

4. Miss Sophia Rossi has been appointed to be Personnel Manager by the board of directors. As a secretary of the Managing Director's Office, you are asked to write a notice to staff of your company and announce the news.

Business Expressions

1. Translate the following Chinese expressions into English.

   1) 优势互补 _____
   2) 团结一致 _____
   3) 优化组合 _____
   4) 人才搭配 _____
   5) 强强联手 _____
   6) 分工合作 _____
   7) 资源配置 _____
   8) 群策群力 _____
   9) 齐心协力 _____

10) 众人拾柴火焰高 _____
11) 各尽所能 _____
12) 集体观念 _____
13) 我行我素 _____
14) 个人主义 _____

2. Adjectives below could be used to describe a team player's character. Decide whether they are positive, neutral or negative. Mark √ before positive ones, × before negative ones and △ before neutral ones.

imaginative	aggressive	practical
confident	ambitious	cheerful
hard-working	crafty	naive
sociable	sensitive	curious
punctual	generous	strong-minded
broad-minded	loyal	sensible
thoughtful	self-controlled	intelligent
motivating	moody	stubborn
adventurous	trusting	reliable
charismatic	modest	tolerant

3. Each group of the following adjectives describe the features either favorable or unfavorable to teamwork. Pick out the odd one out from the choices marked with A, B, C and D.

1) A. moody　　　　B. friendly　　　　C. polite　　　　D. active
2) A. shy　　　　　B. timid　　　　　C. nervous　　　　D. courageous
3) A. easy-going　　B. ill-tempered　　C. tolerant　　　D. perseverant
4) A. outgoing　　　B. extroverted　　C. laid-back　　　D. well-coordinated
5) A. introverted　　B. changeable　　C. self-effacing　D. open-minded
6) A. cooperative　　B. collaborative　C. domineering　　D. interactive
7) A. retarded　　　B. reserved　　　C. reticent　　　D. articulate
8) A. innovative　　B. indifferent　　C. passive　　　D. impersonal

9) A. adaptable   B. hostile   C. passionate   D. enthusiastic
10) A. creative   B. farsighted   C. conservative   D. competent
11) A. haughty   B. arrogant   C. proud   D. humble
12) A. original   B. queer   C. weird   D. odd

Specialized Reading

1. **Read the first part of the passage concerning a four-stage model in team development and do the multiple-choice questions.**

   Teamwork is the concept of people working together cooperatively, such as a football team. Projects often require that people work together to accomplish a common goal; therefore, teamwork is an important factor in most organizations. Effective collaborative skills are necessary to work well in a team environment. Many businesses attempt to enhance their employees' collaborative efforts through workshops and cross-training to help people effectively work together and accomplish shared goals.

   Aside from any required technical proficiency, a wide variety of social skills are desirable for successful teamwork, including listening, discussing, questioning, persuading, respecting, helping, sharing, participating and so forth.

   The forming-storming-norming-performing model takes the team through four stages of team development. This model was first proposed by Bruce Tuckman[1] in 1965, who maintained that these phases are all necessary and inevitable in order for the team to grow, to face up to challenges, to tackle problems, to find solutions, to plan work, and to deliver results.

   In the first stages of team building, the **Forming** of the team takes place. The team meets and learns about the opportunity and challenges, and then agrees on goals and begins to tackle the tasks. Team members tend to behave quite independently. They may be motivated but are usually relatively uninformed of the issues and objectives of

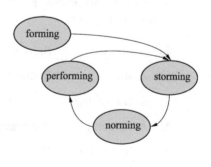

---

1 Bruce W.Tuckman is a respected American educational psychologist who first described the four stages of group development in 1965: Developmental sequence in small groups: see Forming-storming-norming-performing.

the team. Team members are usually on their best behavior but very focused on themselves. Mature team members begin to model appropriate behavior even at this early phase. Supervisors of the team tend to need to be directive during this phase.

The forming stage of any team is important because in this stage the members of the team get to know one another and make new friends. This is also a good opportunity to see how each member of the team works as an individual and how they respond to pressure.

Every group will then enter the **Storming** stage in which different ideas compete for consideration. The team addresses issues such as what problems they are really supposed to solve, how they will function independently and together and what leadership model they will accept. Team members open up to each other and confront each other's ideas and perspectives.

In some cases storming can be resolved quickly. In others, the team never leaves this stage. The maturity of some team members usually determines whether the team will ever move out of this stage. Immature team members will begin acting out to demonstrate how much they know and convince others that their ideas are correct. Some team members will focus on minutiae to evade real issues.

The storming stage is necessary to the growth of the team. It can be contentious, unpleasant and even painful to members of the team who are averse to conflict. Tolerance of each team member and their differences needs to be emphasized. Without tolerance and patience the team will fail. This phase can become destructive to the team and will lower motivation if allowed to get out of control.

Supervisors of the team during this phase may be more accessible but tend to still need to be directive in their guidance of decision-making and professional behavior.

At some point, the team may enter the **Norming** stage. Team members adjust their behavior to each other as they develop work habits that make teamwork seem more natural and fluid. Team members often work through this stage by agreeing on rules, values, professional behavior, shared methods, working tools and even taboos. During this phase, team members begin to trust each other. Motivation increases as the team gets more acquainted with the project.

Teams in this phase may lose their creativity if the norming behaviors become too strong and begin to stifle healthy dissent and the team begins to exhibit groupthink.

Supervisors of the team during this phase tend to be participative more than in the earlier stages. The team members can be expected to take more responsibility for making decisions and for their professional behavior.

Some teams will reach the **Performing** stage. These high-performing teams are able to function as a unit as they find ways to get the job done smoothly and effectively without inappropriate conflict or the need for external supervision. Team members have become interdependent. By this time they are motivated and knowledgeable. The team members are now competent, autonomous and able to handle the decision-making process without supervision. Dissent is expected and allowed as long as it is channeled through means acceptable to the team.

Supervisors of the team during this phase are almost always participative. The team will make most of the necessary decisions. Even the most high-performing teams will revert to earlier stages in certain circumstances. Many long-standing teams will go through these cycles many times as they react to changing circumstances. For example, a change in leadership may cause the team to revert to storming as the new people challenge the existing norms and dynamics of the team.

1) Which of the following is NOT mentioned as the skill necessary to work well in a team environment?

    A. Collaborative skills.   B. Technical proficiency.

    C. Social skills.   D. Collective operation.

2) According to Bruce Tuckman who put forward the model, _____.

    A. the first phase is inevitable and indispensable

    B. the second phase is the stage to face up challenges

    C. the third phase is to plan work and deliver results

    D. the fourth phase is to adjust opinions and find solution

3) In the forming stage, the team members _____.

    A. more often than not behave very independently

    B. seem to need to be directed by the supervisor

    C. usually have a high motivation

    D. are at their best and self-centered

4) During the storming stage, different ideas _____.

    A. are competing with each other for consideration

    B. bring about painful experience to most team members

UNIT 9 Teamwork

      C. can be constructive, but they will lower motivation

      D. will be on display and be evaluated in great detail

  5) The conspicuous feature of the norming stage is that _____.

      A. many team members lose their creativity at this stage

      B. motivation is fully developed with dissents tolerated

      C. supervisors become most participative of the four stages

      D. team members adjust themselves and abide by the shared norms

  6) In the performing stage, different opinions will be _____.

      A. stifled even though they are healthy and constructive

      B. tolerated as long as they do not cause confrontation

      C. expected and allowed if they are conveyed by acceptable ways

      D. acclaimed even if they challenge the existing norms and dynamics of the team

2. **Read the second part of the passage about the roles of successful teams and judge whether the following statements are True or False.**

    Meredith Belbin (1993)[1] basing on his research proposed several roles that successful teams should have:

    The **Shaper** is full of drive to make things happen and get things going. In doing this they are quite happy to push their own views forward, do not mind being challenged and are always ready to challenge others. The shaper looks for the pattern in discussions and tries to pull things together into something feasible, which the team can then get to work on.

    The **Plant** is the one who is most likely to come out with original ideas and challenge the traditional way of thinking about things. Sometimes they become so imaginative and creative that the team cannot see the relevance of what they are saying. However, without the plant to scatter the seeds of new ideas the team will often find it difficult to make any headway. The plant's strength is in providing major new insights and ideas for changes in direction and not in contributing to the detail of what needs to be done.

    The **Resource Investigator** is the group member with the strongest contacts and networks, and is excellent at bringing in information and support from the

---

1 Meredith Belbin is a British researcher and management theorist, best known for his work on management teams.

outside. This member can be very enthusiastic in pursuit of the team's goals, but cannot always sustain this enthusiasm.

The **Implementer** is well organized and effective at turning big ideas into manageable tasks and plans that can be achieved. Such individuals are both logical and disciplined in their approach. They are hardworking and methodical but may have some difficulty in being flexible.

The **Team Worker** is the one who is most aware of the others in the team, their needs and their concerns. They are sensitive and supportive of other people's efforts, and try to promote harmony and reduce conflict. Team workers are particularly important when the team is experiencing a stressful or difficult period.

The **Completer** is the one who drives the deadlines and makes sure they are achieved. The completer usually communicates a sense of urgency, which galvanizes other team members into action. They are conscientious and effective at checking the details, which is a vital contribution, but sometimes get 'bogged down' in them.

The **Monitor Evaluator** is good at seeing all the options. They have a strategic perspective and can judge situations accurately. The monitor evaluator can be overcritical and is not usually good at inspiring and encouraging others.

The **Specialist** provides specialist skills and knowledge and has a dedicated and single-minded approach. They can adopt a very narrow perspective and sometimes fail to see the whole picture.

The **Finisher** is a person who sticks to deadline and likes to get on with things. They will probably be irritated by the more relaxed members of the team.

1) _____ The shaper is to push things in a feasible direction.

2) _____ The plant usually contributes to the detail of what needs to be done.

3) _____ Compared with implementer, the resource investigator is more enthusiastic.

4) _____ The team worker is able to coordinate people's relationship within the team.

5) _____ The completer is more effective than the finisher in making team members meet the deadline.

6) _____ The monitor evaluator may fail to inspire and encourage team members.

7) _____ The specialist plays the most important role as a professional in the

UNIT 9 Teamwork

team.

8) _____ The finisher can be very impatient with the relaxed team members.

3. **Discuss the following questions with your group members.**

   1) The most important characteristic of a highly-effective team is that the members all strive to accomplish the team goals. What's the best way to communicate clear, realistic, and measurable goals, so that everyone can contribute to building plans that are supportable by all?

   2) Perhaps the most difficult part of building a winning team is building momentum, encouraging positive, informal interaction between team members when you are not present. How can you accomplish this?

   3) What are some of the problems that can rip the team-building process apart?

UNIT 10
Innovations

1. **Work with your partner on the following exercises.**

    1) Match the following names to their inventions or innovations. Then try to guess which companies are associated with them.

    | Thomas Edison | Tim Berners-Lee | Akio Morita |
    | Arthur Fry & Spencer Silver | Alexander Bell | Wright brothers |

a. airplane	b. light bulb
c. telephone	d. walkman
e. post-it notes	f. World Wide Web

    2) Jim Carroll, an expert on the topic of innovation and creativity, has put forth some words that will help a business to be innovative. Match the words with their implications.

a. observe	b. think	c. dare
d. change	e. banish	f. try
g. empower	h. question	i. do

    _____ Go forward with a different viewpoint by challenging assumptions and eliminating habit. If your approach to the future is based upon your past success, ask yourself whether that will really guarantee you similar results in the future.

    _____ In a time of rapid change, you can't expect to get by with what has worked in the past — you must be willing to do things differently. Abandon routine; adopt an open mind about the world around you. Take a look at how you do everything — and decide to do things differently.

    _____ Have you lost your ability to take risks? At the same time that you work to manage and minimize risk, your market is changing, your customers are abandoning you, and your margins are shrinking! Aren't these the biggest risks to manage? Taking risks is critical to your future success — don't throw this critical innovation baby out with the

_____ *compliance bathwater.*

_____ *Developing new skills and career capabilities is critical, given the rapid change occurring in every profession. And yet, too many people have managed to convince themselves that they can't adapt; they can't change; they can't master the new realities that surround them. They've lost their self-confidence, and they desperately need it back. Solve this problem fast.*

_____ *Take the time to look for the key trends that will impact your organization and the industry in which you compete. Far too many organizations sit back after a dramatic change and asked — what happened? Make sure that your organization is one that asks, — what's about to happen? And what should we do about it?*

_____ *Get rid of the words and phrases that steer you into inaction and indecision. Drop buzzwords: seek real solutions to real business problems rather than trying to run your business based on simplified pap. Ban complacency: shake your people up with some pretty dramatic action. Kill indecision: force your team to make decisions based on gut feel rather than over-analysis of dubious spreadsheets.*

_____ *In a world of rapid change, you can't expect that rigidly defined rules will be the appropriate response to changing circumstances. A middle manager in a remote location needs the ability to make a decision and must commit to it today — they can't afford to wait for the wheels of head office bureaucracy to churn. Destroy the hierarchy, and re-encourage a culture in which people are given the mandate and the power to do what's right, at the right time, for the right reason.*

_____ *Renew your sense of purpose, and restore your enthusiasm for the future by taking action. Too many organizations and the people who work within them go into work each day, and do the same things they did the day before, with the belief that everything today is the same as it was yesterday. It isn't.*

_____ *Analyze your observations: spend more time learning from what you see happening around you. Step back, take a deep breath, and analyze what trends are telling you. From that, do what really needs to be done.*

2. Discuss the following questions with your group members.

1) What is the difference between invention and innovation?

2) Why does a company have to innovate?

3) What happens if a company does not innovate?

4) Why is innovation becoming more important today?

5) Name some companies known for innovation. Why do you think they are good innovators?

Preview: The world is flattening because converged technological and political forces have produced a global, Web-enabled playing field that allows for multiple forms of collaboration without regard to geography or distance — or soon, even language. Historically the ability of an organization to create value was linked to its size. The new view is that value creation of a firm is determined by its links to other firms, especially when they collaborate and innovate together. Innovation is the ability to create value from inventions. Collaborative innovation begins when companies come together to solve problems and/or develop customer-centered solutions that are beyond the scope, scale or capabilities of the individual companies. How can a business succeed in collaborating with partners in a rapidly globalizing world? Four strategies have been put forward in the following article.

Businesses Must Learn to Let Go

In a rapidly globalizing world, focusing on core expertise and collaborating with partners in innovative ways are the keys to growth.

By Linda Sanford

[1] The thesis put forth by Tom Friedman[1] in *The World Is Flat* is **perceptive**, accurate and anxiety-**inducing** for many business leaders. In his current best seller, the Pulitzer Prize[2]-winning author **contends** that as we entered the new century a **confluence** of factors — the Internet, global **fiber-optic** networks, trade **deregulation**, and an explosion of software — created a platform where intellectual capital could for

---

1 Tom Friedman / tɔm'fri:dmən / 汤姆·弗里德曼，美国纽约时报的专栏作家

2 Pulitzer Prize / 'pulɪtsə- / 普利策奖，美国新闻界最高荣誉奖

the first time be delivered from anywhere. All these forces have leveled the playing field, giving companies and individuals new power to compete globally.

[2] But how should individual companies respond to globalization? How to contend with the **bewildering** pace of change brought on by globalization and convert this new reality from a threat to an opportunity?

[3] STAY FOCUSED. Companies **outperforming** their peers today and not **teetering** on the edge of the flattened globe have adopted an approach to building the 21st-century business in which they find their place not by strengthening their command and control **posture**, but by focusing on core expertise, **collaborating** with partners in innovative ways that drive value and growth for all participants, and strategically sourcing the rest. I call this philosophy: "Let go to grow."

[4] Here are a few examples: Leaders in many industries are embarking on projects involving collaborative innovation opening up their borders to work with others — in a profound shift from the past. Procter & Gamble, for example, now has an entire division devoted to collaborating with external partners on new products and technologies.

[5] That was the **genesis** of the Mr. Clean Magic **Eraser**, a household cleaning tool that has flown off the shelves since it was introduced in 2003. P&G CEO A.G. Lafley has declared that half of all new P&G products should **originate** outside P&G. Talk about letting go to grow.

[6] TAKE IT OUTSIDE. As P&G understands, no company today can corner the market on innovation. For the first time ever, we have the luxury of a global market for brainpower — largely because of the Internet — and this talent does not have to be on the payroll for a company to **leverage** it. U.S. **pharmaceutical** giant Eli Lilly[1] has set up the Web-based InnoCentive[2] to build a virtual talent pool of more than 50,000 scientists in 150 countries. Lilly posts R&D problems any scientist can tackle if he or she has the right expertise. The success rate has been far higher than in-house performance, at around one-sixth of the cost of doing it all in-house.

[7] To let go to grow, the first step a company must take is to zero in on the things it does well and that are **differentiating** — and identify functions that can be done more effectively either through process change or partnerships. This analysis is done by **componentizing** your business — breaking it down into interchangeable building blocks of functions, processes and services.

[8] The components in which a company excels should be used companywide. If

---

1 Eli Lilly 美国礼来公司，全球性的、以研发为基础的医药公司
2 InnoCentive 世界上最大的虚拟研发实验室，通过现金激励来公开回报科技创新

there's no advantage in continuing to perform an activity in-house, that component should be passed to an outside specialist or sold. This allows the company to devote its energies to enhancing its core **differentiators**, where it can **demonstrate** true innovation.

[9] THINKING AHEAD. Even BMW[1], which is built on its reputation for exceptional engineering, has found value in opening up various elements of car design and manufacturing to partners. BMW recently formed a relationship with Magna Steyr[2], an Austrian company, to handle all aspects of manufacturing for the BMW X3[3] sports utility vehicle, including a pioneering four-wheel-drive system.

[10] This move freed up BMW engineers to work on designing new vehicle models. The relationship has allowed BMW to add a new model every three months; five years ago, BMW experienced gaps of three years between models.

[11] It's a mistake to think "letting go" is just another way of saying "outsourcing." Collaboration takes many forms. Not only can it lead to new innovation in product design but it can create entirely new business models that drive organic, sustained growth for leaders willing to let go.

[12] THE RIGHT RELATIONSHIPS. Take Li & Fung[4], a Hong Kong company that supplies **apparel** to retailers in the U.S. and Europe. It's interesting to note that it doesn't make anything. Instead, it draws on a web of 7,500 suppliers to **orchestrate** the manufacture and delivery of apparel to meet quickly the **specifications** of its 350 customers around the world. In a low-margin trading business, Li & Fung has **parlayed** its role as master collaborator into remarkable business performance, doubling revenue and **tripling** profits over the past three years in an industry with a 2% growth rate.

[13] The common denominator in all these examples is **enlightened** leadership. The leaders who understand the implications of a flat world are changing their business models and their company cultures to let go of some control, opening up their organizations to work with external partners in new, deeper ways than traditional supplier relationships.

[14] In our collaborative age, this is the right formula for creating **breakthrough** innovation, which will ultimately drive growth for all successful companies in the flat world.

(865words)
From *Business Week*

1　BMW 德国宝马公司，驰名世界的汽车企业，也被认为是高档汽车生产业的先导
2　Magna Steyr / mɑgnə-staɪr /　马格纳·斯泰尔公司，奥地利汽车零部件供应商
3　BMW X3 宝马车型系列新的延伸，也是汽车细分市场的一个全新车型种类
4　Li & Fung 香港利丰贸易有限公司

UNIT 10 Innovations

New Words

perceptive / pə'septɪv /
a. having or showing insight, discerning; keen in discernment 有洞察力的；富有见地的；极端敏锐的

induce / ɪn'djuːs /
v. bring about; cause 引起或诱发（某事）

contend / kən'tend /
v. put forward (sth.) as one's opinion; argue; assert 主张（某事物）；争辩；认为

confluence / 'kɒnfluəns /
n. coming together 汇合，汇集，聚合

fiber-optic / 'faɪbə-ɒptɪk /
a. of, relating to, or using fiber optics 光导纤维的

deregulation / diː,regjʊ'leɪʃən /
n. removing the regulations from (sth.) 撤销对（某事物）的规定、管制

bewildering / bɪ'wɪldərɪŋ /
a. confusing, puzzling 令人困惑的；费解的

outperform / aʊtpə'fɔːm /
v. perform better than sb. or sth. else 做得比……好，胜过……

teeter / 'tiːtə /
v. stand or move unsteadily 摇晃地站立或移动

posture / 'pɒstʃə /
n. the way you behave or think; attitude 看法，立场，态度

collaborate / kə'læbəreɪt /
v. work together (with sb.), especially to create or produce sth.（与某人）合作，协作（尤指创造或生产某事物）

genesis / 'dʒenəsɪs /
n. beginning; starting-point; origin 起源；开端；创始

eraser / ɪ'reɪzə /
n. a thing used for cleaning or removing marks and traces 清除、清洁用具

originate / ə'rɪdʒɪneɪt /
v. start to develop in a particular place or from a particular situation 发源于；来自于；产生于

leverage / 'liːv(ə)rɪdʒ /
v. use for gain, exploit 利用

pharmaceutical / ,fɑːmə'sjuːtɪkl /
a. of or connected with the making and distribution of drugs and medicines 制药的；配药的

differentiate / ,dɪfə'renʃɪeɪt /
v. recognize or express the difference between things or people 辨别，区别，区分

componentize / kəm'pəʊnəntaɪz /
v. divide sth. into smaller, more manageable, or more flexible parts 将……分成小部分

differentiator / ,dɪfə'renʃɪ,eɪtə /
n. the expertise or characteristic which differentiates one company from others 使某公司区别于其他公司的知识技能

demonstrate / 'demənstreɪt /
v. show or prove sth. clearly 表明；表示；证明

apparel / ə'pærəl /
n. clothing; dress 衣服；服装

orchestrate / 'ɔːkɪstreɪt /
v. carefully arrange sth. in order to bring about a desired result 精心安排

specification / ,spesɪfɪ'keɪʃən /
n. details and instructions describing the design, materials, etc. of sth. to be made or done 规格；规格说明

parlay / 'pɑːlɪ, 'pɑːleɪ /
v. increase the value of sth. that you have by using all your opportunities well; maneuver to great advantage 充分利用某事物使其增值

triple / 'trɪpl /
v. become three times as much or as many 增至三倍；成三倍

enlightened / ɪn'laɪt(ə)nd /
a. showing a good understanding of sth.; free from prejudice, ignorance, etc. 开明的；有见识的

breakthrough / 'breɪkθruː /
n. important development or discovery 重大的发展、发现、突破

229

Phrases & Expressions

let go
stop holding sth.; give up control 松开或释放某人/某事物；放弃

put forth
suggest or propose sth. for discussion 提出

best seller
product, especially a book, that sells in very large numbers 畅销的产品（尤指书）

playing field
environment for all companies to compete 竞争环境

contend with
deal with sth. difficult or unpleasant （与困难等）搏斗，斗争

bring on
make sth. bad or unpleasant happen 导致、造成或引起某（不好或令人不快的）事物

embark on
start or engage in (especially sth. new or difficult) 开始或从事（尤指新的或难的事）

corner the market
gain control of market 垄断市场

zero in on
fix attention on sb./sth.; focus on sb./sth. 将注意力集中于某人/某事物

building blocks
the pieces or parts which together make it possible for sth. big or important to exist 事物的基本成分或基础部分

sport utility vehicle
SUV, a type of vehicle that is bigger than a car and is made for travelling over rough ground 运动型多功能车

free sb. (up) to do sth./for sth.
give someone time to do sth. by taking away other jobs that they have to do 使某人可用于（某一目的或活动）

common denominator
an attitude or quality that all the different members of a group have 共同点，共同特色

Exercises

Comprehension

1. Mark the following statements with T (true) or F (false) according to the text. Discuss with your partner about the supporting points for each statement.

   1) _____ Tom Friedman's book *The World Is Flat* won the Pulitzer Prize.

   2) _____ "Let go to grow" implies focusing on core expertise and collaborating with partners in innovative ways that drive value and growth only for

UNIT 10 Innovations

your own company.

3) _____ The author uses the term "Take it outside" to mean that a company relies on outside specialists to provide goods or services that it cannot do well itself.

4) _____ The flat world refers to the leveled playing field for companies and individuals to compete globally.

5) _____ With the help from the Web-based InnoCentive, Eli Lilly can have much higher R&D success rate at 6-fold of the cost of doing it all inside the company.

6) _____ The collaboration between BMW and Magna Steyr makes it possible for BMW engineers to speed up the process of designing new vehicle models.

7) _____ The relationship between Li & Fung and its 7,500 suppliers is the traditional buyer-supplier relationship.

8) _____ According to the author, in this collaborative age, the right formula for creating breakthrough innovation consists of 3 factors.

2. The text can be divided into three parts. Put down the paragraph numbers and main idea of each part. The last one has been done for you. In Part II the author uses some examples to support the subheadings, which make the text very clear. Please write down the subheadings and the corresponding examples.

Parts	Paragraphs	Main ideas
I	Paras. _____	_____
II	Paras. _____	_____
III	Paras. 13-14	Draw a conclusion about the right formula: crucial role of enlightened leadership.

Part II

Subheadings	Examples

Critical Thinking

Work in group to discuss the following questions.

1) What personal experience in your life can support Tom Friedman's view that "the world is flat"?

2) Innovation is usually considered difficult to manage due to some barriers to it. What barriers do you think are there in terms of the organization itself, environment, resources, group behavior and individual behavior?

Organization	Environment	Resources	Group behavior	Individual behavior

3) People tend to need some creative inspiration on their work. The following are some simple ways to be more creative on one's work. Which of them are your favorites? Why?

a. Find the most creative people at work and ask for their ideas.

b. Play music in your office.

c. Reward yourself, in specific ways, for small successes.

d. Take regular daydreaming breaks.

e. Take a shower in the middle of the day.

f. Keep an idea notebook at your desk or in your briefcase.

g. Recall a time in your life when you were very creative. Feel it.

h. Wander around a bookstore while thinking about a challenge.

i. Open a magazine and free associate off of a word or image.

j. Write down your ideas when you first wake up in the morning.

k. Get fast feedback from people you trust.

l. Pilot your idea, even if it's not completely ready.

m. Challenge everything you do.

n. Make connections between seemingly disconnected things.

o. Laugh more, worry less.

p. Do whatever is necessary to create a sense of urgency.

q. Go for a walk anytime you're stuck.

UNIT 10 Innovations

Vocabulary

1. Find the synonyms for the following words from the text. The first letter has been given to you.

puzzling	b_____	attitude	p_____
junction	c_____	beginning	g_____
cooperate	c_____	stagger	t_____
clothing	a_____	deep	p_____

2. Match the words in Column A with the words in Column B to make collocations as they appear in the text, and then translate them into Chinese.

A	B
external	growth
collaborative	design
intellectual	deregulation
trade	seller
best	capital
sustained	innovation
product	partner
core	rate
process	market
success	performance
global	change
in-house	differentiator

3. Choose the word or phrase that is closest in meaning to the underlined one.

   1) The rapid growth of the company's business proves that the decision made by the CEO is a <u>discerning</u> one.

      a. satisfactory   b. careful   c. perceptive   d. impressive

   2) The Complex Product System (CoPS), which has been enabling the European economy to <u>contend with</u> the mass production of U.S.A, has a great impact on the National Competition.

      a. struggle with   b. fight for   c. come up with   d. manage with

   3) China and Russia <u>embark</u> on cooperation in Deep-sea Manned Robot.

a. continue   b. set out   c. think about   d. decide

4) From a business perspective, the benefits of good service are many, as it <u>brings on</u> greater revenue from customers, reduces operation costs and in turn provides for a healthier business.

a. exaggerates   b. commences   c. leads to   d. creates

5) A large number of such organizations have government connections, and <u>monopolize</u> the market in their respective sectors.

a. own   b. occupy   c. enter   d. corner

6) This <u>enlightened</u> approach includes employing senior level manufacturing staff who are involved in the business of the plant and are not just employed for their technical expertise.

a. open-minded   b. confused   c. illuminated   d. illustrated

7) There have been several rules which define "European" products as goods having a certain proportion of parts, or certain key components, <u>originating</u> within the EEC.

a. producing   b. stemming   c. selling   d. inspecting

8) The automation of these processes has made two full-time employees <u>available</u> for more customer-centric activities such as promotions and pricing.

a. put up   b. discharge   c. freed up   d. released

4. Choose 10 out of the 12 words in the box to replace the underlined parts in the following sentences. Change the words into their phrases or derivatives if necessary.

embark	put	enlighten	differ	break	perform
induce	leverage	componentize	orchestrate	regulate	specify

1) <u>The removal of government controls</u> in electricity is giving Texas's businesses the power to choose their retail electricity provider in much the same way Texans can now choose phone service.

2) As to the <u>detailed and exact description</u> of our products, please refer to the latest catalogue we sent to you last week.

3) This company expects to <u>do better than</u> its competitors by using Customer Management Systems.

4) The experience from the Danish market indicates that low interconnection rates <u>stimulate</u> the occurrence of the competition in most segments.

5) China Wednesday <u>suggested</u> a four-point proposal on attaining the common goal of promotion and protection of human rights at a meeting on the issue of human rights of the Third Committee of the 56th Session of the UN General Assembly.

6) This restaurant wants to <u>show the difference between</u> weekend hours and weekday hours and then estimate the average consumption per person.

7) <u>Breaking</u> business <u>down into units</u> is a nice shortcut for companies to create sales forecasts.

8) With more than 25 years of experience in managing change throughout the IT environment, Serena Software provides Change Governance software to help global 2000 organizations visualize, <u>carefully arrange</u> and enforce effective business processes throughout the IT lifecycle.

9) A recent survey has taken the view that firms should <u>make full use of</u> resources on the basis of an assumed scarcity as opposed to actual abundance.

10) The company has made <u>a great achievement</u> in the development of overseas market for its latest product.

Translation

1. **Translate the following sentences into Chinese.**

    1) "Let go to grow" is a philosophy.

    2) Companies outperforming their peers today and not teetering on the edge of the flattened globe have adopted this "Let go to grow" philosophy to build the 21st-century business in which they find their place not by strengthening their command and control posture, but by focusing on core expertise, collaborating with partners in innovative ways that drive value and growth for all participants, and strategically sourcing the rest.

    3) To let go to grow, the first step a company must take is to zero in on the things it does well and that are differentiating — and identify functions that can be done more effectively either through process change or partnerships.

    4) This analysis is done by componentizing your business — breaking it down into interchangeable building blocks of functions, processes and services.

2. Put the following sentences into English, using the words and phrases given in the brackets.

1) 进入 21 世纪以来，在互联网、全球光纤网络、贸易管制撤销等诸多因素的集中作用下，越来越多的各国企业和个人能在公平的环境下进行全球性竞争。（confluence, deregulation, level, playing field.）

2) 在迅速全球化的世界里，如何保持增长，击败对手是每个企业都面临的现实问题。（globalize, rival）

3) 针对这一问题，IBM 随需迁移部门的高级副总裁琳达·桑福德提出以退为进的创新战略。（put forth, let go）

4) 所谓以退为进，是指企业将力量集中在其擅长且易与竞争对手相区分的核心技能上，同时以开放的姿态和创新性的方式与别的企业进行双赢合作。（core expertise, differentiate, collaboration, posture）

Innovation Design

Many companies have growth ambitions that cannot be achieved through "business as usual." In many industries, opportunities for mergers and acquisitions are drying up, which leaves innovation as the main source for creating company growth. Design thinking and design approaches such as ethnographic research and consumer intimacy are essential for successful innovation. Designers see it as their role to challenge, experiment, expand boundaries and explore new and different ways of doing things.

Now you work in a design company, facing the clients who are in different situations as follows. Work with your group members and figure out the solutions to the problems in the situations. Each of you is responsible for one situation and design an innovation scheme for it. Then make a presentation in your group.

1) Little Trekkers is based near Sheffield and specializes in children's outdoor and active lifestyle clothing. In the highly competitive world of online commerce a strong brand is essential if an internet retailer is to stand out from the crowd. How do you think the company can increase brand differentiation?

2) National Savings, the government backed savings provider, is struggling.

UNIT 10 Innovations

Consumer research shows that many feel it is old-fashioned and no longer relevant to mainstream savers and investors. It is perceived as a savings scheme for grannies and children. How to change this situation?

3) *Nicola Massey is supplying her range of homemade chutneys and sauces to school fetes and local markets. Now her close friend Adrian Collins suggests it is time to take the business to the next level. How do you think a local homemade product can be turned into an instantly recognizable and appealing brand?*

4) *Mobile phone retailer Oskar has a good share of the Czech market because of its reputation for high quality at low prices. However, the company is keen to move away from its low-cost positioning and drive more business through its high street retail outlets. Oskar grew very quickly, initially on a low price positioning, but as its business has evolved, they need to attract higher value customers. And it has soon become evident that their retail outlets aren't living up to the brand's promise. How to solve this problem?*

Language Hints

Expressing curiosity
- Can someone tell me about...?
- I wish someone would tell me the secret.
- What's in your mind?
- I hope you don't mind my asking, but...
- I'm rather curious to know...
- ...

Believing
- It seems credible.
- I have complete faith in what he said.
- I think it's believable.
- ...

Disbelieving
- How is that possible?
- I know better than that!
- It's too good to be true.

- There you are! You just imagine it.
- ...

Expressing certainty
- I don't think there can be any doubt.
- I'm quite convinced of her experience in it.
- That's my conviction.
- There is no room for doubt about it.
- ...

Expressing uncertainty
- I'm in two minds about which to choose.
- I feel in such a muddle.
- I can't say for certain what to do.
- Let's leave it to chance.
- I can't have a clue about...
- I wouldn't be too sure about that.
- ...

Questionnaires

Questionnaires are a simple, productive tool to aid you in obtaining constructive feedback from both existing and potential customers or to ask staff for their opinions/comments on points already given, or to make suggestions of their own. Questionnaires are designed to gather information from a large number of people. And the results of questionnaires will be analyzed carefully to form the basis of a report or decision-making for management of innovations.

A questionnaire usually includes five parts: title, introduction, question, close and footnote.

The most effective questionnaires are those that have been carefully thought out in which questions are easy to understand and answer. The following are some golden rules:

- Keep the survey as short as possible, asking only those questions that will provide the information you need.
- Use a casual, conversational style, making the questions easy for almost anyone to understand.
- Structure the survey so that the questions follow a logical order.
- Use multiple-choice questions whenever possible. This helps the respondent to better understand the purpose of your question and will reduce the time to complete the questionnaire.
- Avoid leading questions that might generate false positive responses.
- Don't use jargon or pompous language.
- Leave enough space for the answers and leave space between the lines.
- Underline or use bold for emphasis.

The following are the commonly used types of questions:

Multiple choices

Where do you live?

___ north   ___ south   ___ east   ___ west

Numeric open end

How much did you spend on food this week?

_____

Text open end

How can our company improve working conditions?

_____

Rating scales

How would you rate this product?

___ excellent   ___ good   ___ fair   ___ poor

Agreement scale

How much do you agree with each of the following statements?

___strongly agree   ___agree   ___disagree   ___strongly disagree

My manager provides constructive criticism ___ ___ ___ ___

Our medical plan provides adequate coverage ___ ___ ___ ___

I would prefer to work longer hours on fewer days ___ ___ ___ ___

Study the following samples and then design questionnaires according to the directions. Add anything necessary.

Sample 1

Staff Questionnaire: Flexible Working Hours Pilot Scheme

You have just discussed the company's pilot scheme on flexible working hours. Now we need to decide whether it is feasible to implement the scheme across the whole company. Please fill in the required information and tick the appropriate boxes below.

1. Has the system helped you in meeting your personal needs?

    Yes ☐   To a certain extent ☐   No ☐   N/A ☐

Title/heading

Introduction

Questions

2. Do you want the system to continue?

   Most definitely ☐   Quite ☐   Neutral ☐   No ☐

3. What time did you opt to start work during the pilot scheme?

   8:00 am ☐   8:30 am ☐   9:15 am ☐

4. Was your choice of start time free or directed?

   Free/ Directed (delete as appropriate)

5. Please give any other comments on the flexitime scheme for our company.

   _____
   _____
   _____
   _____

Thank you for spending time completing the survey. Please turn this questionnaire in to the Personnel Department before 23 July 2008.

Name: _____
Staff No.: _____
Dept.: _____

Close

Footnote

Sample 2

Website Usability Questionnaire

Please provide the following information so we can further develop this website to make it more usable.

1. How easy was it to understand each of the links on the home page?

| Very Easy | Easy | Average |
| Difficult | Very Difficult | |

2. On the home page, how easy was it to find the appropriate link for information you wanted?

| Very Easy | Easy | Average |
| Difficult | Very Difficult | |

3. How easy was it to understand the titles on each page you accessed?

| Very Easy | Easy | Average |
| Difficult | Very Difficult | |

4. How easy was it to scan the titles in text to find the information you wanted?

| Very Easy | Easy | Average |
| Difficult | Very Difficult | |

5. How easy was it to understand links to other websites?

| Very Easy | Easy | Average |
| Difficult | Very Difficult | |

Exercises:

1. Peter works at the Personnel Department of a company. Many employees often complain to the company about their health problems and the stress they are feeling, so Peter was asked to design a questionnaire to do some related investigations. The following is the questionnaire he drew up, but is not properly designed. Please revise it and add anything necessary.

Questionnaire

1. Do you feel fatigue during or after work?

   | Everyday | Frequently | Sometimes | Rarely | Never |

2. Do you have headaches or any respiratory problems during or after work?

   | Everyday | Frequently | Sometimes | Rarely | Never |

3. Have you often had disagreements with your bosses?

   Everyday   Frequently   Sometimes   Rarely   Never

4. Do you find your job stressful?

   Yes   No

5. On a scale of 1 (worst) to 10 (best), how well do you perform your job?

   1) 2) 3) 4) 5) 6) 7) 8) 9) 10)

   a. What could be done to help you do your job better? _____

   b. What are your suggestions? _____

   c. Has your job become more or less demanding over time?_____

   More   Less

6. Are you given opportunities to voice your opinions to management?

   Everyday   Frequently   Sometimes   Rarely   Never

7. Have you often had disagreements with your co-workers?

   Everyday   Frequently   Sometimes   Rarely   Never

8. Do you have any eye problems during or after work?

   Everyday   Frequently   Sometimes   Rarely   Never

2. **Employees at a firm have a shared responsibility (along with their managers) to help ensure that everyone is as productive and motivated as possible. Your company has recruited new hires. Design a questionnaire to find out what motivates and frustrates the new hires most so you can personalize your management and improve motivation for new hires to help enable them to be more productive. The questionnaire should include the following points:**

   - *the reason why he accepted this job*
   - *the reason why he quitted his last job(s)*
   - *his initial concerns about this new job*
   - *the things that normally frustrate him on a job*
   - *the things to motivate him to do great work*
   - *the way he likes to be managed*

   And you should give brief explanations to each question so as to help the new hires who are to reply to the questionnaire understand the purposes of the questions and answer them more effectively.

UNIT **10** Innovations

Business Expressions

1. Scholars have identified a variety of classifications for types of innovations. The following is an unordered ad-hoc list of examples. Match the expressions in column A with their explanations in column B.

A	B
1) radical innovation	a. It involves the implementation of a new or significantly improved production or delivery method.
2) breakthrough innovation	b. It is a market-oriented approach to innovation policy which addresses not only the suppliers and immediate users of new knowledge but also indirect beneficiaries, end-users and intermediaries.
3) systemic innovation	c. It is where an agent (person or company) develops an innovation for their own (personal or in-house) use because existing products do not meet their needs.
4) incremental innovation	d. It involves considerable change in basic technologies and methods, created by those working outside mainstream industry.
5) entrepreneurial innovation	e. It occurs in the sourcing of input products from suppliers and the delivery of output products to customers.
6) process innovation	f. It involves the creation or alteration of business structures, practices, and models, and may therefore include process, marketing and business model innovation.
7) supply chain innovation	g. It is a step forward with little uncertainty about outcomes and success and is generally

243

minor improvements made by those working day to day with existing methods and technology (both process and product), responding to short term goals.

8) substantial innovation h. It involves launching an entirely novel product or service rather than providing improved products & services along the same lines as currently.

9) end-user innovation i. It may give rise to new industrial sectors, and induce major change across several branches of the economy.

10) organizational innovation j. It introduces a different product or service within the same line, such as the movement of a candle company into marketing the electric light bulb.

2. **Match the expressions in the box with the phrases below.**

innovation ambition	innovation climate	peer review
design awareness	empathic design	innovation journey
lifelong learning	idea generation	technology transfer
technology foresight	innovation performance	diffusion of innovation

1) the degree to which people within an organization are aware of the value of the contribution design can make

2) one approach that goes beyond asking the customer what they want, which involves observation and the immersion of the designer in the customer's situation and daily activity

3) the process by which businesses and other organizations seek product ideas that will help them achieve their objectives

4) the degree to which managers in any one organization seek to drive company performance through innovation, and what kind of innovation they are seeking to generate

UNIT **10** Innovations

5) the conditions within an organization that either support or hinder innovation

6) a process of moving an idea from phase to phase with all the uncertainties, twists and turns, dead ends, and surprises of traveling through unexplored territory to a new destination

7) an organization's ability to innovate and deliver value through such innovation

8) the process, by which new ideas are communicated to members of a particular target audience

9) the process of assessing the future needs and opportunities for the economy of a region or country, in the light of technological and market trends

10) the conveyance of know-how between organizations through licensing or marketing agreements, co-development arrangements, training or the exchange of personnel

11) the exchange of tools, methods and experience between policy-makers on the basis of information about relative performance

12) the continuing development of knowledge and skills that people experience after formal education and throughout their lives, an essential means of accelerating assimilation of new technologies

3. **Complete the sentences with the appropriate expressions from the above exercise.**

   1) As the companies progressed along the _____, they became less dependent on government funding sources and more dependent on private investors (angels), venture capital, strategic partnerships and public markets.

   2) Key drivers of an organization's _____ are clarity and pervasiveness of

strategy and vision, the leadership style, the company's culture and the physical work environment.

3) To improve _____, companies need to establish a range of measures covering inputs, throughputs and outputs.

4) More and more countries are engaging in activities of _____ and observation prompted by an interest in not falling behind in the international technology competition and losing their ability to compete internationally.

5) Organizations that have a high level of _____, either in order to grow or to survive, will need to develop a culture that is tolerant to the risks associated with step-change.

6) The goal of _____ is to ensure that the product or service designed meets end-users' needs and is usable.

7) They rated the computer as an important tool for _____ and the computer brainstorming process as "Much Better" than manual brainstorming.

8) Acquiring foreign technologies through _____ can help developing countries progress both economically and socially.

9) Since reviewers are normally selected from experts in the related fields, the process of _____ is considered critical to establishing a reliable body of research and knowledge.

10) One of the reasons why _____ has become so important is the acceleration of scientific and technological progress.

11) This innovation programme has the objective to raise the level of _____ within your company and to identify the potentials for your company.

12) The study of the _____ is the study of how, why, and at what rate new ideas and technology spread through cultures.

Specialized Reading

1. Read the passage concerning the degree of innovation and classify the following 7 examples marked with A-G into two categories.

   How new or different does something have to be before it can be called an innovation at all? If a paint company that currently offers 12 shades of white adds a thirteenth, is this an innovation? If a store that is presently open from 8 a.m. to 6 p.m. adopts a policy of staying open around the clock, this would seem to be an innovation. But what if it changes its opening time from 8 a.m. to 7:45 — is this innovation? If an airline that now offers ten flights a day from New York to Chicago adds an eleventh flight, is this innovative?

At the other extreme, if a flower shop owner decides there is no hope for her business, and so closes up her shop and reopens it a month later as a used book store, is this an innovation? How about when U.S. Steel decided to branch out into oil and natural gas and change its name to USX? Was that an innovation? These issues may appear to be so trivial as to involve only word games, but in all the writings on innovation we have found no clear definition of the concept. To think clearly about an issue, it is helpful to define its limits.

There are some innovations that are so minor and are barely perceived as changes. Clearly they have no impact on a firm's basic strategies. At the other extreme, some innovations are so great that they result in a fundamental change in the very nature of a business, leaving behind nothing of the old business. Both these extremes are beyond the scope of our discussion; instead, we are concerned with the vast middle ground.

Some innovations are dramatic in their scope and impact and clearly fall into the category of radical. For example, the introduction of automatic teller machines made a fundamental change in the availability of some retail banking services. The personal computer, though still a computer, is a radically different way of providing computing power to many people who previously had access to it only through the medium of mainframes or minicomputers and the intervention of information systems professionals.

Innovations that are radical when first introduced appear less so after they have become popular and their adoption is widespread. Apple's introduction of the personal computer was a radical innovation. When IBM introduced its first PC several years later, the innovation was less radical. When Dell and Gateway 2000 began retailing personal computers, the product was commonplace, but the method of distribution (direct mail) was seen by some as a radical departure from previous sales methods.

The slightest of incremental innovations begins at whatever point we decide there is an innovation at all. Because they build on existing products, services, or routines and modify them to some degree, incremental innovations are generally easier to plan and implement, and involve less change than radical innovations. This is not to say that they do not have strategic value, or that the total result of a series of incremental innovations cannot be quite impressive when compared to the starting point.

The single lens reflex 35mm camera has been on the market for a number of years. Many small improvements have been made since its first introduction. And although each would qualify as an incremental innovation, today's 35mm SLR camera is nonetheless quite different from the first one introduced.

Inventions are, by definition, only introduced by one firm, or at most by a small handful of firms that bring a new product or service to market simultaneously. Companies that attempt to introduce an invention should logically stand to gain some substantial advantage, because there is a real risk of coming late to the finish line and gaining no prize. Companies that succeed in commercializing an invention are sometimes known as first movers.

1) The incremental innovations are _____.
2) The radical innovations are _____.

   A. A store that is presently open from 8 a.m. to 6 p.m. adopts a policy of staying open around the clock.
   B. An airline that now offers ten flights a day from New York to Chicago adds an eleventh flight.
   C. If a flower shop owner decides there is no hope for her business, and so closes up her shop and reopens it a month later as a used book store.
   D. The introduction of automatic teller machines made a fundamental change in the avail-ability of some retail banking services.
   E. Apple's introduction of the personal computer into the market.
   F. Dell and Gateway 2000 began retailing personal computers by a new method of distribution.
   G. The single lens reflex 35mm camera has been on the market for a number of years.

2. **Read the following passage concerning the quality of innovators and do the multiple-choice exercises.**

   Life constantly throws choices at us, and expediency trains us to think that decisions must always be made. The tiramisu tastes good but has too many calories. Pleasing our boss means spending less time with our family. Or, to use an IT analogy, adding features to the software means delaying the project by a month.

UNIT 10 Innovations

Humans accept trade-offs because, frankly, it's the easy thing to do. But breakthrough innovation often comes from challenging the "either/or" status quo and seeking solutions that harmonize seemingly conflicting choices. The engineers at Palm Computing, for example, were famous for refusing to accept the "fact" that a useful computer couldn't fit in the palm of a hand.

In an engaging new book, The Opposable Mind, Roger Martin argues that this ability to craft solutions out of two opposing ideas is a core skill of innovative thinkers. Martin, who is dean of the Rotman School of Management at the University of Toronto, came to this epiphany while interviewing more than 50 successful leaders in his consulting and academic work, including some of the most successful executives and entrepreneurs in North America.

The book cites examples of opposable thinking that anyone can relate to. Isadore Sharp founded the Four Seasons hotel chain by challenging the assumption that successful hotels had to be either functional and impersonal or friendly but lacking in amenities.

Sharp came up with the idea for a midsize hotel chain that offers the attentive customer service of boutique lodges along with the high-end resources that business travelers expect. He made a successful bet that business travelers would pay a premium for that distinctive combination, and today the Four Seasons is one of the great brands in travel.

Robert Young, the cofounder of Red Hat Software, entered a market that assumed customers needed to pay high license fees to get the support they needed. His radical notion was to give software away in order to build a huge customer base and then swoop in with the best support available — at a price. At the time, many people thought the Red Hat business model was crazy, but today Red Hat has a $4 billion market capitalization and an unquestioned leadership position in its market.

1) The first paragraph mainly tells us that _____.

   A. we are living in a world full of contradiction

   B. tiramisu does more good than harm to our health

   C. IT industry can be used to draw an analogy

   D. people can hardly balance career and family

2) The word "trade-off" in the first line of the second paragraph, most probably means _____.

A. bargain   B. purchase   C. compromise   D. interaction

3) Breakthrough innovation, more often than not, is derived from _____.

A. seeking opportunities that harmonize contradictory choices

B. challenging the current situation and coming up with solutions

C. refusal of "either/or" status quo and seeking solutions

D. a group of innovation thinkers and successful leaders

4) Four Season hotel chain is different from others in its _____.

A. customer-tailored service   B. various functions

C. friendly and luxurious atmosphere   D. pleasant and grand scale

5) The passage primarily proposes that innovators should _____.

A. be considerate to take the initiative in the market

B. learn from the founders of those great brands

C. be able to harmonize seemingly conflicting ideas

D. have an unquestionable leadership position

6) The cofounder of Red Hat software, Robert young, became successful due to _____.

A. charging high license fees

B. producing high-end products

C. giving away his software unconditionally

D. utilizing a huge customer base

3. **Discuss the following question with your group members.**

1) The causes of innovation failure have been widely researched and can vary considerably. Some causes will be external to the organization and outside its influence of control. Others will be internal and ultimately within the control of the organization. What are the internal and external causes of failure of innovation in your eyes?

2) According to some experts, innovation can be conceptualized as a process. Looking at innovation as a process is helpful, as it enables us to identify clearly specific skills associated with innovating successfully. There are five phases in the process of innovation, including Searching, Exploring, Committing, Realizing and Optimizing. Look at the happenings of the process given in the box and discuss to make clear what should be done during each phase.

UNIT 10 Innovations

Framing the inquiry	Facilitating creativity
Investigating ideas	Validating ideas
Influencing stakeholders	Selecting promising ideas
Experimenting to narrow the field	Assessing value created
Identifying opportunities	Hunting and gathering ideas
Creating/Sustaining high-performing team	Allocating resources
	Preparing a business case
Improving the innovation process	Driving for timely results
Making decisions	Preparing a business case
Managing political issues	Making decisions
Realizing maximum value	Managing process
Celebrating achievements	Influencing stakeholders

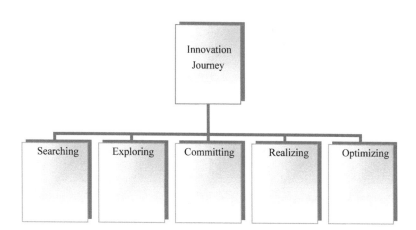

GLOSSARY

Words	Units		Definitions
absolve	8	v.	解除……的责任（或义务等）
abundance	8	n.	大量，丰富；充足
abundantly	5	ad.	大量地
acutely	6	ad.	剧烈地
ail	7	v.	折磨；使烦恼
aisle	6	n.	（商店、超市等的）过道
align	8	v.	调准；校正
amber	2	a.	琥珀色，黄褐色
ambiguity	9	n.	含糊不清；不明确；模棱两可
anchor	7	v.	使稳定；固定
apparel	10	n.	衣服；服装
arguably	8	ad.	可论证地；按理
associate	1	n.	共同经商者，合伙人
assortment	1	n.	属于一类或数类的各色物品之集合
autobiography	1	n.	自传
bandit	5	n.	土匪；强盗
bankable	7	a.	可赚钱的，可赢利的
beaten-up	1		年久失修的；残破的，破旧的
beset	5	v.	围绕（某人／某事物）；困扰
besiege	5	v.	围住（某人／某事物）；团团围住
bewildering	10	a.	令人困惑的；费解的
billboard	4	n.	大幅广告牌
binary	4	a.	二进制的
biotech	4	n.	生物科技
blend	3	v.	混合；掺杂
blog	4	v.	在网络上写日志或发表评论
boost	1	n.	上升，提高 v. 增加；增强；激起……的热情；强有力地宣传

Words	Units		Definitions
breadth	9	n.	宽广的程度（如指知识）；范围
breakeven	8	a.	得失相当的，不赢不亏的
breakthrough	10	n.	重大的发展、发现、突破
brew	2	n.	（尤指某地酿造的）啤酒
brick(s)-and-mortar	6	a.	（相对网络公司而言的）传统公司的；实体的；（企业）按传统模式（而非通过因特网）运营的
bubble	6	n.	〈喻〉泡沫
bum	7	n.	懒惰的人；不合格的人
buzz	4	n.	兴奋之感；喜悦心情；成就感；好奇或兴奋的谈论或关注
by-pass	6	v.	越过；避开
cabin	3	n.	木橱，木柜
cajole	4	vt.	劝诱；哄骗；诈骗
calculating	6	a.	审慎的；精明的
canary	7	n.	金丝雀
capacity	5	n.	能力；本领；能量
catalogue	8	n.	目录
category	2	n.	种类，类别
chaotic	7	a.	混乱的，无秩序的
clarify	8	v.	澄清，阐明，使清晰明了
clarity	7	n.	清晰的思维（或理解）能力
clash	9	n.	重大的分歧；争论
client	3	n.	顾客，客户或主顾
coalition	9	n.	结合体；联合
cognitive	9	a.	认知的；与认识有关的
collaborate	10	v.	（与某人）合作；协作（尤指创造或生产某事物）
collaboration	9	n.	合作；协作
collectible	6	n.	收藏品
collegiality	9	n.	共同掌权；同僚间分授权力
compelling	6	a.	激发兴趣的；引人注目的；强制性的
component	5	n.	成分；系统的组成要素
componentize	10	v.	将……分成小部分
confine	6	v.	限制；使局限

附录 1 Glossary

Words	Units		Definitions
confluence	10	n.	汇合，汇集，聚合
conservative	2	a.	保守的；谨慎的
constitute	7	v.	组成
consumer-centric	6	a.	以消费者为中心的
contend	10	v.	主张（某事物）；争辩；认为
cornerstone	5	n.	最重要的部分；基础；柱石
cornucopia	6	n.	丰富；充裕
co-star	4	v.	与其他明星联合主演
coupon	3	n.	优待券
courteous	7	a.	有礼貌的；谦恭的
cover	2	v.	包括；涉及
crash	4	v.	不请自来；不经邀请进入（如宴会）；闯入
curmudgeon	5	n.	脾气坏的人（尤指老人）；难取悦的人
customer-driven	6	a.	以顾客为本的
customize	4	v.	定做；按照客户具体要求制作或改制；用户化
cutout	8	n.	从其他东西上切割剪裁下来或要被切割剪裁下来的东西；〈喻〉没有性格特点的人
dealership	6	n.	商品特许经销商
dearly	6	a.	昂贵地；惨重地
decree	6	v.	命令；规定
decry	4	v.	公开谴责
democratization	4	n.	民主化
demonstrate	10	v.	表明；表示；证明
depot	6	n.	仓库
deregulation	10	n.	撤销对（某事物）的规定、管制
derivative	7	n.	派生物，衍生物
differentiate	10	v.	辨别，区别，区分
differentiator	10	n.	使某公司区别于其他公司的知识技能
discreet	2	a.	（言行）谨慎的，慎重的
disposable	7	a.	可任意使用的
distinguish	7	v.	辨别，区别
distributor	3	n.	经销商；分销商
dogged	5	a.	顽强的，不屈不挠的

Words	Units		Definitions
down-slide	2	n.	下跌，下降
draft	4	v.	选派；抽调
drawing	3	n.	抽签
drop	2	n.	下降；下跌；减少
dysfunctional	9	a.	功能不良的
eccentric	1	a.	（人、行为等）古怪的；偏执的
embrace	1	v.	抓住（机会）；欣然接受
empower	6	v.	授权于；增强（人）的力量和信心（尤指使能够掌握自身命运及维护自身权利）
enchant	5	v.	对……施行妖法，用妖术迷惑；使心醉；迷住
encounter	6	v.	与……邂逅，与……偶遇
encrypted	4	a.	设成密码或暗码的
enlightened	10	a.	开明的；有见识的
enlist	4	v.	争取，谋取（帮助、支持或参与）
entrepreneurship	3	n.	创办企业
epitomize	1	v.	成为……的缩影；集中体现
eraser	10	n.	清除、清洁用具
esoteric	7	a.	深奥的
ethnographic	9	a.	人种研究的
exceed	1	v.	超出，超越
excess	5	a.	过量的；超额的；多余的
execution	5	n.	实行；执行；实施
expertise	9	n.	专门技能或知识（尤指在某一领域）
explode	6	v.	激增；迅速扩大
family	2	n.	由同一生产商生产的具有共同性质和特征的一组东西
famished	5	a.	非常饥饿的
fiber-optic	10	a.	光导纤维的
fickle	2	a.	反复无常的
fizz	2	n.	充气饮料的气泡或其嘶嘶声
flavor	3	n.	味；味道
formula	5	n.	公式；准则
formulate	3	v.	设计；规划
foster	7	v.	促进；培养

附录 1 Glossary

Words	Units		Definitions
fractured	8	a.	破裂的；断裂的
fruitful	8	a.	富有成效的
function	2	v.	行使职责；工作；运转
fundamental	3	a.	基本的；根本的 n. 基本规律；根本法则；基本原理
gaunt	5	a.	（指人因饥饿或疾病）憔悴的；骨瘦如柴的
gel	9	v.	合为一体，形成整体；成形
generic	8	a.	一般的，普通的
genesis	10	n.	起源；开端；创始
grim	5	a.	坚定无畏的
gully	7	n.	沟壑，深沟
hatchback	4	n.	舱盖式汽车
haul	1	v.	用力拖或拉
heave-ho	7	n.	开除；拒绝
hedge	1	v.	做两面买卖以防损失
heist	4	n.	抢劫；盗窃
hone	5	v.	磨炼；训练；使……完美
hucksterism	4	n.	大吹大擂（或强行）推销商品的言论或做法
implement	5	v.	履行；落实；实施；执行
implication	6	n.	可能的影响（或作用、结果）
inclusive	4	a.	包罗万象的；综合性的
inconvenience	1	v.	使感到不便；感到困难
indefatigable	1	a.	不倦的；不屈不挠的
induce	10	v.	引起或诱发（某事）
infancy	8	n.	初期；幼稚阶段
ingenuity	8	n.	善于创造发明；足智多谋
ingredient	5	n.	（混合物的）组成部分；成分，要素
innovation	2	n.	新思想；新方法
innovative	4	a.	革新的，创新的
insanity	5	n.	十分愚蠢的行为；荒唐的行为
integrated	8	a.	整体的；完全的；综合的
intense	5	a.	（指感情等）强烈的，热烈的
intensify	6	v.	加强；增强
intriguing	4	a.	引起兴趣的；有诱惑力的

Words	Units		Definitions
inventory	8	n.	存货，库存
invigorate	2	v.	使蒸蒸日上；使兴旺发达
languish	2	v.	变得衰弱无力，失去活力；凋萎
laptop	4	n.	便携式电脑
lemming	7	n.	盲目仿效者
lemonade	3	n.	柠檬汁
leverage	10	v.	利用
localise	6	v.	使本土化；使具有地方特色
lofty	7	a.	高级的；出众的
logo	7	n.	标识
long-standing	2	a.	存在已久的，悠久的
long-winded	7	a.	啰唆的，冗长的
loose-lipped	9	a.	说话随便的，口无遮拦的
loyalty	6	n.	忠诚，忠心
maintenance	3	n.	养护；维修
maneuver	3	v.	移动
mantra	7	n.	曼特罗；祷文（印度教和佛教中的符咒）
marvel	4	v.	感到惊奇；大为赞叹
maturity	2	n.	成熟；成熟期
mentality	5	n.	思想；心理；心态
merchandise	1	n.	商品；货品
merger	9	n.	（尤指两公司）合并；兼并
messy	8	a.	棘手的，难办的，令人为难的
metaphor	7	n.	隐喻，暗喻，比喻
metrics	7	n.	衡量标准；衡量方法
middleman	1	n.	中间商
mindset	5	n.	观念模式；思想倾向或习惯
minuscule	6	a.	非常小的；微不足道的
minutiae	7	n.	细节，琐事
mix-up	2		混乱，杂乱
modification	5	n.	变更；修正；改进
mom-and-pop	6	a.	（小店）夫妻经营的
monarch	6	n.	君主；国王；皇帝
mushy-headed	7	a.	头脑不清的

附录 1 Glossary

Words	Units		Definitions
mystifying	7	a.	令人迷惑的
naive	4	a.	天真的；幼稚的
navigate	9	v.	行进；经过；指引；指导
notoriously	2	ad.	著名地，众所周知地
obscure	7	v.	使变模糊；使变暗或不分明
odds	8	n.	〈常用作复数〉可能性，机会
offering	2	n.	提供；用品；供消遣的产品
onlooker	4	n.	旁观者；观众
on-off	9	a.	断断续续的；不时的
opportunistic	6	a.	机会主义的
option	3	n.	可选择之物；选择
orchestrate	10	v.	精心安排
originate	10	v.	发源于；来自于；产生于
outfit	8	n.	〈口〉（工商业）公司
outlet	6	n.	商店，门店
outperform	10	v.	做得比……好，胜过……
outsource	4	v.	交外办理；外购
overindulgence	5	n.	过度放纵
parlay	10	v.	充分利用某事物使其增值
payroll	8	n.	工资表；在职人员名单；工薪总额
perceptive	10	a.	有洞察力的；富有见地的；极端敏锐的
pertinacity	5	n.	坚持；顽强，不屈不挠
pharmaceutical	10	a.	制药的；配药的
phase	2	n.	阶段；时期
phenomenally	1	ad.	非凡地；非常地
photocopier	3	n.	影印机
pitch	4	v.	推销；争取支持（或生意等）
placement	3	n.	布置；定位；销售渠道
plagued	5	a.	受麻烦困扰的
plot	4	n.	故事情节；布局
posture	10	n.	看法，立场，态度
potion	5	n.	（含药物、毒物或有魔力的）饮料
prescription	5	n.	计划；建议；秘诀
pretension	1	n.	自负，自命不凡

Words	Units		Definitions
price	3	v.	定价；标价
prime	5	a.	最重要的；主要的；基本的
priority	6	n.	优先考虑的事
profile	5	n.	印象；形象
profit	3	v.	获益，得到好处
profound	6	a.	（状态、品质或情感）深刻的
promote	3	v.	宣传；推销；促销
promotion	3	n.	促销
prospect	3	n.	可能的顾客、委托人或购买者
prospective	5	a.	预期的；未来的
punch	4	n.	力量；有效（影响）
radical	1	a.	激进的
rail	7	v.	挑剔；抱怨；责骂
referral	5	n.	被推荐的人；销售线索
refine	5	v.	（去粗取精、一丝不苟）改良（某事物）
refreshments	3	n.	点心；快餐，方便饮食
relegate	7	v.	把……归类；将……置于次要地位
relocate	8	v.	迁移至新地点
rescue	8	v.	营救，救援；挽救
retain	7	v.	保留，保持
revealing	8	a.	揭示真相的；有启迪作用的，发人深省的
revenue	7	n.	收入；税收
rival	6	n.	竞争对手；敌手
row	9	n.	意见不一致，就某事看法不合
ruthlessly	9	ad.	（做出令人不快的决定时）坚决地
sagacity	5	n.	睿智；精明；精确的判断
scrub	4	v.	擦掉；消除
seductive	7	a.	诱人的
shareholder	9	n.	股东
sibling	2	n.	兄弟；姐妹；同胞；同属
silhouette	5	n.	（人的）体形；（事物的）形状
silverware	3	n.	刀具；餐刀
single-mindedly	1	ad.	专心致志地
skeptical	6	a.	表示怀疑的

附录 1 Glossary

Words	Units		Definitions
skip	6	v.	略过；跳过
slip	2	v.	下降；下跌；变差，变坏
slip	6	n.	疏忽；差错
smug	9	a.	自鸣得意的，自满的，沾沾自喜的
snatch	6	v.	一把抓起（某物）；夺得
sneaker	4	n.	帆布胶底运动鞋
solicit	4	v.	索求；请求……给予（援助、钱或信息）；征求；筹集
sophisticated	3	a.	通世故的；老练的
spark	4	v.	引发；触发
specification	10	n.	规格；规格说明
speculation	9	n.	推断，推测
splinter	6	v.	分裂
stand	3	n.	摊子，摊位
stereotypical	8	a.	刻板的；已成陈规的，老一套的
stern	5	a.	严格的；苛刻的；坚定的
strain	8	n.	重负；过度的要求（或指望、使用）
strategy	2	n.	策略，计策
stream	7	n.	一连串；源源不断
stride	1	v.	大步跨过
subsequent	7	a.	后来的，随后的
subtle	8	a.	微妙的，难以捉摸的；深奥难测的；隐晦的
supercenter	1	n.	超级中心；集规模较大的商场和小副食品商店为一体的、为顾客提供一站式消费服务的商场
susceptible	7	a.	易受影响的
swallow	3	v.	接受，毫无疑问地接受；吞，咽
swollen	5	a.	肿起的；膨胀的
synapse	7	n.	【解剖学】神经元的神经线连接；（神经元轴突的）突触
synchronise	9	v.	使……同步，使……配合一致
tackle	5	v.	着手处理
tally	6	v.	符合；吻合
tangible	2	a.	有形的；实际的；可触摸的

Words	Units		Definitions
teeming	7	a.	充满……的；丰富的，大量的
teeter	10	v.	摇晃地站立或移动
tenfold	1	n.	十倍
toll-free	4	a.	免费的
top-notch	5	a.	顶级的
toss	7	v.	扔掉，丢弃
tow	3	v.	拖，拉
transaction	9	n.	业务；交易
transform	6	v.	彻底改变，使发生巨变，使改观，变革
trendy	7	a.	时髦的，新潮的
triple	10	v.	增至三倍；成三倍
trivial	9	a.	不重要的
tsunami	4	n.	海啸
unburden	9	v.	（通过向别人倾诉问题、秘密等以）解除自己的烦恼
underdog	1	n.	竞争失败者；处于劣势者
underlie	7	v.	成为……的基础
undermine	1	v.	逐渐削弱；破坏，损坏
uneven	2	a.	无规律的；不规则的
unfurl	3	v.	展开；拉开
ungainly	3	a.	难看的；笨手笨脚的
unprecedented	1	a.	前所未有的；空前的
upstate	8	a.	州的北部地区（或边远地区）的
vacuum	8	n.	真空
verse	9	n.	（《圣经》的）节
viable	8	a.	切实可行的；可实施的
virtual	6	a.	【计算机】虚拟的
wares	3	n.	货品；商品
weave	4	v.	（把……）编成，编造（故事等）
webcast	4	v.	网络广播
worrisome	8	a.	令人担忧的，使人发愁的
wrestle	8	v.	努力解决；全力对付

Phrases & Expressions

Phrases & Expressions	Units	Definitions
a crop of	5	（同时涌现的）一批；一群；一系列
a ton of	4	大量的
anti-corporate warriors	1	反公司强硬派
arrive at	3	作出（决议等）；得出（结论等）
at stake	9	处于危急关头；冒风险；处于未定状态中
at the ready	3	随时可用，即刻使用
be better off	7	（在某情况下）更幸福；更满意
be engaged in	3	从事；忙于……
be in order	5	妥当，适宜
be up to	8	胜任；适于
best seller	10	畅销的产品（尤指书）
blind spot	8	（对某一领域情况的）无知，不理解；偏见
branch out	1	（指公司、业务等方面）向新的方向发展，扩充范围
brand equity	7	品牌资产，品牌价值
break down ...into	3	分门别类；划分
bring on	10	导致、造成或引起某（不好或令人不快的）事物
bring up	3	提出；引出
building blocks	10	事物的基本成分或基础部分
buy into sth.	2	〈口〉相信；接受
by all means	5	当然
can/could do worse than do sth.	9	做某事是正确的或可取的
capital infusion	1	资金注入
career ladder	9	职业晋升阶梯
carry out	3	实行；完成；进行
cheat sb. (out) of sth.	6	（尤指用不诚实或不正当的手段）阻止某人得到某物

Phrases & Expressions	Units	Definitions
closed shop	1	（根据工会与资方协议）只雇用某一工会会员的商店
come on the scene	2	出场，上场
come up	7	显现，出现；产生
common denominator	10	共同点，共同特色
contend with	10	（与困难等）搏斗，斗争
corner the market	10	垄断市场
corporate monster	1	企业巨头
cut out	1	（在竞争中）击败对手；排挤对方
cut to the chase	7	（比喻意义）废话少说；提到关键问题；切入正题
death knell	2	丧钟；事物完结的信号
deep pocket	2	富裕，殷实；财力雄厚
dispense with sth./sb.	7	免除；省却
distribution channel	2	分配或分销渠道
draw on/upon sth.	2	利用；凭借
embark on	10	开始或从事（尤指新的或难的事）
face time	5	实时沟通时间
fall off	8	减少
fall over each other	6	互相竞争；争先恐后
figure out	7	解决；领会到；断定
flash in the pan	2	转瞬即逝且很难再现的成功
folk hero	1	民间英雄
for all intents and front line	1	最重要的、最前面的或责任最大的位置
free sb. (up) to do sth./for sth.	10	使某人可用于（某一目的或活动）
get/buy sth. on the cheap	4	便宜地得到或买到某物
get/have a handle on	3	弄懂，理解，搞明白
give away	4	免费送出某物；赠送
go after	5	追求；设法得到
go ahead	9	进行；发生
go for sth./sb.	5	适用于某事物（某人）
go through	2	经受；经历

附录2 Phrases & Expressions

Phrases & Expressions	Units	Definitions
gun dog	1	猎犬
in proportion to	6	与……成比例
in the pipeline	2	(口)在进行中；在生产中；在处理中；在运输中；在讨论(或规划、准备)中；在酝酿中
keep one's head down	9	避免危险；防止分心；避免引人注意
latch on to	7	变得依附于……
let go	10	松开或释放某人/某事物；放弃
lie in	1	在于
life cycle	2	盛衰周期；生命周期
live up to	8	依照某事物行事；完成；达到
look at	6	考虑或研究某事物
lose sight of	1	忽略或未考虑某事
make it	9	做某事成功了
make sense	8	可理解；有根据；可行
market segment	3	市场细分
marketing campaign	4	营销活动
mass market	7	大众市场；批量销售
melt away	5	融化；消失；消散
no less	5	(表示惊讶或钦佩)竟，居然
on hand	3	现有；在手头
on top of	6	除……之外
open up	6	开发；开辟
other than	7	不同，不同于；不；除……以外
out of the way	8	不再碍事，不再挡道
participate in	4	参加某事
pass... on to	1	将某物传、交给(某人)
pile up	7	增多；积累，积聚；堆积
place the call	4	打电话
playing field	10	竞争环境
pop-up ad-blocker	6	弹出广告拦截器
predilcated on	1	使基于
profit margin	8	利润空间
pull together	9	同心协力；通力合作

Phrases & Expressions	Units	Definitions
put ... up	4	显示，展示
put forth	10	提出
put on	3	增加，添加
put up	1	提供（资金）
put... into action	5	实行；实施
rock bottom price	1	最低价格
run short of	5	用尽；使供给缺乏或不足
sales agent	3	销售代理
sales pitch	4	推销员的游说；商品宣传
see to it that	3	务必做到；保证
serialized mystery	4	连载广告（故事）
set out	4	开始；打算；规划
side effect	8	意想不到的效果；副作用
sit around	7	无所事事地消磨时间
small talk	7	闲谈，聊天
sport utility vehicle	10	运动型多功能车
stick with	8	坚持；继续
target market	3	目标市场
thanks to	6	幸亏；由于
trade dress	7	产品标识符
trade on sth.	6	利用某事物谋取私利
turn away from	5	拒绝帮助某人；对……不再感兴趣
turn to	3	开始工作；着手
turn ... off	4	不注意
variety stores	1	小百货商店；杂货店
warehouse club	1	仓储式零售商店，大型零售商店
wash over	4	涌进（某人的）脑子里；突然袭来
wholesale club	1	批发式会员店
window shopping	6	浏览商店橱窗
wine cooler	2	由葡萄酒、果汁、冰和苏打水调制成的冰镇果酒饮料
zero in on	10	将注意力集中于某人/某事物

 Activity File

Unit One

Role A

VERIZON

COMPANY

Verizon Communications Inc.. A leader in delivering broadband and other wireline and wireless communication innovations to mass market, business, government and wholesale customers. Began trading on the New York Stock Exchange (NYSE) under the VZ symbol on Monday, July 3, 2000.

HEADQUARTERS

Based in New York, the United States.

FOUNDATION

Incorporated in Delaware, formed on June 30, 2000, with the merger of Bell Atlantic Corp. and GTE Corp.

SERVICES

Operates America's most reliable wireless network, serving 59 million customers nationwide.

Deploying the nation's most advanced fiber-optic network to deliver the benefits of converged communications, information and entertainment services to customers.

Role B

ECOLAB

COMPANY

With $5 billion in global sales, the world's leading provider of cleaning, food safety and health protection products and services for the hospitality, foodservice, healthcare and industrial markets.

HEADQUARTERS

St. Paul, Minnesota, USA

FOUNDATION

Founded by St. Paul native Merritt J. Osborn in 1923 as Economics Laboratory. Changed its name to Ecolab in 1986.

EMPLOYEES

More than 23,000 associates worldwide.

GLOBAL REACH

Direct operations in nearly 70 countries. 100 other countries are reached through distributors, licensees and export operations.

PATENTS

Issued more than 4,000 patents worldwide, including the industry's first patents for solid warewashing detergent, clean-in-place technology for beverage and food processing, and a no-rinse enzyme-based floor cleaner for grease removal in foodservice operations.

Role C

GM

COMPANY

General Motors Corp. (NYSE: GM), the world's largest automaker, the global industry sales leader for 76 years.

FOUNDATION

Founded in 1908, with global headquarters in Detroit, the United States.

EMPLOYEES

About 284,000 employees around the world.

GLOBAL REACH

- GM manufactures its cars and trucks in 33 countries.
- Millions of GM cars and trucks were sold globally under the following

brands: Buick, Cadillac, Chevrolet, GMC, GM Daewoo, Holden, HUMMER, Opel, Pontiac, Saab, Saturn and Vauxhall.

• Has product, powertrain and purchasing collaborations with Suzuki Motor Corp. and Isuzu Motors Ltd. of Japan.

• Has advanced technology collaborations with DaimlerChrysler AG and BMW AG of Germany and Toyota Motor Corp. of Japan, and vehicle manufacturing ventures with several automakers around the world, including Toyota, Suzuki, Shanghai Automotive Industry Corp. of China, AVTOVAZ of Russia and Renault SA of France.

Role D

IBM

COMPANY

The International Business Machines Corporation

The world's largest information technology services and consulting provider with early 100 years of history.

HEADQUARTERS

Based in New York, United States

EMPLOYEES

Some 190,000 professionals in more than 160 countries.

SERVICES

Help clients integrate information technology with business value—from the business transformation and industry expertise of IBM Business Consulting Services to hosting, infrastructure, technology design and training services.

DIVISIONS

Main divisions including hardware, software, financing management service, comprehensive IT services, innovative technologies etc.

MISSION

- Strive to lead in the invention, development and manufacture of the industry's most advanced information technologies.
- Delivers integrated, flexible and resilient processes across companies and

through business partners, enabling clients to save money and transform their businesses to be more competitive.

Unit Two

Product A: Swatch Mise & Cow Watch

Product Features

- Swatch-ORIGINAL (series)
- Complete Watch, New in box with 2 years of Swatch guarantee
- Super-cute, big-eyed cartoon animals float in a pale blue sky on the plastic strap of this original Gent.
- The birds, worm, chicken, sheep and cow are complemented by a toothy cartoon mouse on the blue and white dial within a clear plastic case.
- Blue-rimmed white Arabic numerals appear at hours 1 and 7 through 12.
- Black hour and minute hands and blue seconds hand mark the time.

Product Details

- Crystal Material: Plastic
- Case Material: Plastic
- Case Diameter: 34 millimetres
- Case Thickness: 10 millimetres
- Band Material: Plastic
- Band Width: 17 millimetres
- Movement: Swiss Quartz
- Water Resistant Depth: 30 metres
- Boxed-product Weight: 96g
- Price: $ 34.88

Product B: EcoPure Reverse Osmosis Drinking Water System

Product Features

- This drinking water system uses reverse osmosis technology to reject up to 99% of the impurities in your tap water, so you can enjoy fresh, clean water for drinking or cooking.
- Improves the quality of water used for cooking and beverages.
- System easily integrates with the rest of your sink assembly.
- Reduces lead, nitrates, cysts (Cryptosporidium and Giardia), arsenic, sodium and other contaminants in your tap water.
- 3-gallon storage tank ensures you'll have clean, great-tasting water when you need it.
- Faucet filter change reminder lets you know when the filter needs replacement; twist-and-pull design provides fast, sanitary filter changes; uses EcoPure replacement filter ECOROF and EcoPure replacement filter membrane ECOROM.
- Reverse osmosis process rejects impurities in your water, flushing them down the drain.
- For best system performance, sediment/carbon filter cartridges should be replaced every 6 months.
- NSF certified, ensuring strict health and safety standards.

Product Details

- Product Height: 15cm
- Product Width: 14cm
- Product Weight: 8kg
- Product Depth: 18cm
- Price: $159.99

Product C: Freeplay Energy Kito LED Self-Powered Flashlight—Yellow

Product Features

- Wind-up technology eliminates the need for replacing batteries and

recharging from the wall.
- LED bulb provides bright, consistent light.
- Quick 60-second wind provides an hour of illumination.
- Stylish, compact and rugged design.

Product Details

- Product Height: 5cm
- Product Width: 3cm
- Product Weight: 500g
- Product Depth: 8cm
- Price: $19.99

Product D: Omron HEM-650 Wrist Blood Pressure Monitor with APS (Advanced Positioning Sensor)

Product Features

- Advanced positioning sensor
- IntelliSence Sigma Cuff Technology for accurate reading
- Irregular heartbeat detector
- Date and Time feature
- 90 Memory with averaging last three readings

Product Details

- Product Height: 8cm
- Product Width: 5cm
- Product Weight: 200g
- Product Depth: 6cm
- Price: $ 25.88

Unit Three

Product A: Adventure Vacations Travel Agency–Adventure Travel International(ATI)

Card 1 Executive Summary

Adventure Travel International(ATI) will begin operations in September, 2008 and provide adventure, sport/travel packages to people in the Pacific Northwest, specifically the greater Woodville area. The founders and employees of ATI are experienced travel-industry professionals and passionate about the activities ATI will promote and offer.

An opportunity for ATI's success exists because the national tourism and travel industry is growing 4% and adventure travel 10% annually. Further, the Woodville adventure travel market is growing at least 12% annually and has no providers who specialize solely in adventure travel. ATI is poised to take advantage of this growth and lack of competition with an experienced staff, excellent location, and effective management and marketing. The Woodville area, like much of the Pacific Northwest, has a large concentration of outdoor recreation enthusiasts. These health-conscious individuals, couples, and groups interested in popular adventure sports, such as skiing, kayaking, trekking, etc., are ATI's primary customers. ATI's target market is an exploitable niche and ATI will provide a specialized and thus differentiated service. Prices will be competitive with the remainder of the market. The company's estimated sales for the first year of operations is $534,607, increasing 10% annually for the next two years.

Card 2 SWOT Analysis—Strengths

• MANAGEMENT: ATI's manager has a successful record in this industry. His experience and the network of valuable connections he has developed will contribute greatly to ATI's success.

• LOCATION: ATI will be ideally located. The Pacific Northwest is a mecca for people who meet ATI's target audience profile. In addition, Woodville is located 45 miles from the coast and less than two hours from the mountains. Five rivers are within a two-hour drive. These geographic features will continue to attract potential customers.

• EXPERIENCED STAFF: The ATI team is experienced in the travel business and in adventure sports. All members have over five years experience. Moreover, they are willing to sacrifice extra time and effort to build a successful business. Along with the intangible benefits derived from succeeding in an independent endeavor, ATI will offer profit sharing and potential partnership opportunities to its ground-floor members.

• POPULARITY OF ADVENTURE TRAVEL: Adventure activities are very popular, and ATI is betting that the popularity will continue to grow. Many of the adventure sports, such as kayaking, mountainbiking, alpine and rock climbing, have had a kind of cult following for many years. However, in the last five years, these sports have started to go mainstream.

Card 3 SWOT Analysis—Weaknesses

• START-UP STATUS: ATI is a start-up and the odds are stacked against small start-up companies.

• LIMITED PERSONNEL: Though ATI's staff is exceptional, they will be faced with long hours for little pay during the first two years of operation.

• FINANCING: Preliminary estimates of sales and expenditures suggest that ATI will remain financially stable. However, unforeseen expenditures or poor sales will threaten ATI's cash position, which will be particularly vulnerable in year one.

Card 4 SWOT Analysis—Opportunities

• GROWTH MARKET: The national adventure travel market is growing 10% annually, and preliminary estimates suggest that the Woodville market exceeds that growth rate.

• POTENTIAL TO ACHIEVE SALES FROM THE NATIONAL MARKET: As ATI establishes itself and gains financial stability, it can begin to market its services nationally. ATI plans to begin this effort via a World Wide Web campaign in the first year of operation and diversify its communications efforts in years two and three.

• POTENTIAL TO BECOME A PREMIER PROVIDER: ATI has the management and staff to produce a top-quality service.

• VERTICAL INTEGRATION: The potential to integrate services and add branches exists.

Card 5 SWOT Analysis—Threats

• INTERNET AND PRICE COMPETITION: When the airlines were deregulated, price competition increased. Further, the Internet has provided a sales medium for consolidators who compete on price and has also given consumers the ability to plan and arrange trips for themselves. Thus, the traditional agency faces greater competition.

• LOCAL COMPETITION (EXISTING AND POTENTIAL): There are no agencies in the Woodville area that specialize solely in adventure travel. However, any one of the approximately 30 can book an adventure trip. Moreover, additional adventure travel specialists may follow ATI's lead.

• ECONOMIC DOWNTURN: The strong domestic economy has been good for the travel and tourism industry. Continued growth is anticipated. However, unforeseen or unanticipated economic recession would reduce disposable income and threaten ATI's sales.

Product B: Health Fitness Program—Corporate Fitness (CF)

Card 1 Executive Summary

Corporate Fitness will serve Seattle-area businesses, helping them to become more productive, while lowering their overall costs with innovative wellness programs and strategies.

Our business is based on two simple facts:

1. Healthy employees are more productive than chronically ill employees.

2. It costs less to prevent injuries or illnesses than to treat them after they occur.

At Corporate Fitness (CF), we tie worker productivity directly to the health care issue. We believe that traditional approaches to the current health care crisis are misdirected. These traditional efforts are what we call reactive — that is, they wait until after the worker has been stricken with illness or injury, and then pay for the necessary treatments. Our approach, which emphasizes prevention and good health promotion, is much more proactive.

By helping employees change their behavior patterns and choose more healthy lifestyles, CF will lower companies' health care expenditures, while raising worker productivity. Health care expenditures will decrease due to reduced medical insurance premiums, reduced absenteeism, reduced turnover rates, reduced worker's compensation claims, reduced tardiness, shorter hospital stays, etc.

The state of America's health care crisis, coupled with current demographic changes, threaten to not only exacerbate the crisis, but further erode worker productivity as well. These environmental factors coupled with the local competitive situation signal a favorable opportunity in this market. We feel the time is right for Corporate Fitness.

Card 2 SWOT Analysis —Strengths

• Results-orientated approach to attracting and maintaining customers.

• A well-researched, detailed health wellness program that is long-term in focus.

• Intensively trained staff.

Card 3 SWOT Analysis—Weaknesses

• High costs associated with customized, personal service.

• The inability to work on a high volume business model.

• The costs of attracting a large corporate client.

Card 4 SWOT Analysis—Opportunities

• Participation within a growing market.

• The large increase in clients that follows with the acceptance of CF's program by a single company.

• The ability to leverage future quantitative analysis that supports the contention that long-term wellness programs have a significant, positive impact on a company's bottom line.

Card 5 SWOT Analysis—Threats

• Lack of immunity to an economic downturn.

• Potential competition from larger, well established competitors.

- A change in society where the individual begins to take far more responsibility for his/her health maintenance.

Product C: Car Wash—Soapy Rides (SR)

Card 1 Executive Summary

Soapy Rides Car Wash will be the prominent car wash for luxury vehicles in East Meadow, Long Island. It is owned by Mark Deshpande, a young entrepreneur who has worked in the family car repair business for over 10 years. Having owned a car repair shop in East Meadow for over 30 years, the Deshpande family is well-known and respected in the neighborhood.

The differentiator for Soapy Rides (SR) will be Mark and the Deshpande name. It is believed that people will come to the car wash not only to have their cars cleaned and detailed, but also as a social outing to meet up with and chat with Mark and his father Barry. Additionally, the car wash will provide excellent service, efficiently and expertly cleaning customer's cars so that they will be repeat users of the service.

The car wash will be based in East Meadow, New York. This area has a number of benefits in terms of the market that it will provide for the business. Over 40% of households in the immediate neighborhood earn over $70,000 annually. John is a family friend and has worked with the Deshpande family for 23 years. He has worked with hundreds of small-and medium-sized businesses during his career.

Soapy Rides will have 20% market share of the hand car wash business in the East Meadow neighborhood by the end of year three, and it aims to convert a larger percentage of people away from machine car washes, which damage a car's finish. Soapy Rides will maintain a 95% gross profit margin and make 11% net profit margin after 12 months of operation.

Card 2 SWOT Analysis — Strengths

- Good relationships with many perspective customers in the target market.
- Strong family name recognition and equity in the community.
- Well trained employees.

Card 3 SWOT Analysis—Weaknesses

• The need for reliance on outside investors.

• The learning curve associated with entering an industry without direct prior experience.

• The need to have a fairly constant volume of business to support the necessary service staff.

Card 4 SWOT Analysis—Opportunities

• Participation within a steadily growing industry.

• A high likelihood of repeat business.

• The ability to decrease the fixed costs as a percentage of an individual sale as volume increases.

Card 5 SWOT Analysis—Threats

• Future/ potential competition from a franchised firm.

• A slump in the economy, reducing discretionary spending.

• The perception that there is not a difference in quality between a hand and machine wash.

Product D: Video Store-Independent Choice Flicks (ICF)

Card 1 Executive Summary

Independent Choice Flicks(ICF) is an alternative video rental store located in Ann Arbor, MI. ICF will rent movies not often available from the larger chains: film festival movies, independent releases, foreign films and other "arts" films.

Ann Arbor clearly has the market for these types of films, as evidenced by the general demographics (liberal, educated, college town) and the popularity of the Monarch Arts Cinema, a first run movie theatre concentrating on this same genre of movies.

This market has been ignored by the dominant stores in Ann Arbor. They may have a few films that fit these descriptions, but in general they are far and few between. It is too difficult for the large corporations to market to this specific segment, particularly with their current business model which is putting a store in all cities that are very similar in feel and library, with a concentration on large scale commercial releases.

Through the use of ICF's competitive advantage, attention to customers, it will grow steadily to profitability. This will be manifested in two ways, 1) providing outstanding customer service and knowledgeable help, and 2) supplying movies that have a demand in Ann Arbor but have been previously ignored. The demand has yet to be addressed by the other players who leave it off their radar, assuming it is only for the fringe of the general population. Fortunately, the fringe in Ann Arbor make up a large part of the general population here.

ICF will begin profitability by month nine and will have projected profits of almost $32,000 by year three.

Card 2 SWOT Analysis—Strengths

- Strong relationships with distributors.
- Excellent staff who are well informed and customer attentive.
- A centrally-located store front.
- An unmatched selection.

Card 3 SWOT Analysis —Weaknesses

- The struggle to raise brand awareness.
- A limited budget to acquire customers.
- Not having the buying power that the giants have, increasing acquisition costs.

Card 4 SWOT Analysis—Opportunities

- A growing rift in the market between artsy and commercial films and the corresponding viewers.
- The opportunity to decrease customer acquisition costs over time as more customers are acquired through referrals.
- The ability to leverage the fact that the "giants" ignore the majority of the

alternative/intellectual population segment.

> **Card 5 SWOT Analysis—Threats**
>
> • Competition from the giants if they decide to change their course and address the alternative crowd.
>
> • A significant increase in movie theatre technology that makes the in-the-movie experience more difficult to replicate at home.
>
> • Increased popularity of independent and foreign films, ensuring that the giants carry these titles.

Unit Four

Product A

> ### Lyons Coffee
>
> **Product features:**
>
> ◇ Roasted in a different way, under pressure.
>
> ◇ The very essence of the bean is preserved.
>
> ◇ Not let the aromas, the flavour and other coffee goodness escape.
>
> ◇ More of the aromas and flavor.
>
> ◇ More of the goodness.

Product B

> ### Cold Prevention Dental Cream
>
> **Product features:**
>
> ◇ Being skillfully concocted with selected raw material of superb quality comprises the chlorophyll and extracts from the Chinese traditional medicine herbs.
>
> ◇ Make your teeth clean and white, your breath fresh.
>
> ◇ Prevent you from catching cold.
>
> ◇ Prolonging the duration of brushing and gargling will turn out to be more

effective.

◇ Clinical trials of this dental cream observed by New York Medical Society, City Hygiene and Epidemical Prevention Station and relevant Hospital on 2239 persons showed a total efficiency of 99.69%.

Product C

AVON the Smartest Shop in Town

Product features:

◇ Sale lipstick, night cream, eyeshadow, fragrances, gifts, etc.

◇ Everything can be returned — call 1-800-858-8000 or your Avon Representative.

◇ Everything you buy from Avon is uncoditionally guaranteed.

◇ You'll be given an exchange or a refund.

◇ Have got unbeatable products, like Color Release Long Wearing Lipstick.

◇ With Avon, you really can't go wrong.

Product D

Petal-Drops

Product features:

◇ For the girl who wants a petal-soft skin.

◇ Give your skin a petal-fresh softness and fragrance.

◇ A special blend of mild soapless oils, delicately perfumed herbal essences and the gentlest of toning agents—all combined with loving care to give that oh-so-good-to-be-alive feeling.

Unit Five

Card A

China Highlights

China Highlights is a full service China travel agency providing popular China tours and Yangtze River cruises. We specialize in "Tailor-Made" and "Customized" individual, family and group tours throughout China including Yangtze River Cruises.

Service details:

◇ Help you find the right China experience.

◇ Offer over <u>100 existing</u> China tour packages which showcase the best that China has to offer.

Service features:

◇ We have a website for you to search the engine to find a China tour that suits you.

◇ We can easily customize an existing China tour to meet your needs. All tours are flexible and tailor-made to your needs.

◇ We offer the best value for your money travelling in China.

◇ All of our travel advisors and guides are experienced and professional.

<u>8 day Essence of China Tour from</u> $1,350 USD (Tourist Class, 2~5 persons)

Destination: Beijing → Xi'an → Shanghai

Attraction: Great Wall at Mutianyu, The Forbidden City, Temple of Heaven, Summer Palace, Terracotta Warriors (include golf carts), Oriental Pearl TV Tower

<u>China Dreams Tour</u>   from $2006 USD (Tourist Class, 2~5 persons)

Destination: Beijing → Xi'an → Guilin → Yangshuo → Guilin → Shanghai

Attraction: The Forbidden City, The Tian'anmen Square, Terracotta Warriors (include golf carts), Forest of Stone

Tablets Museum, Li River Cruise, Oriental Pearl TV Tower plus History Museum

12 day China Highlights Signature Tour   from $4,391 USD (Superior Class, 2~5 persons)

Destination: Beijing → Xi'an → Chongqing → Yangtze → Yichang → Shanghai

Attraction: The Forbidden City, Temple of Heaven, Terracotta Warriors (include golf carts), City Wall, Shanghai Museum

For more information, please visit our website (www.chinahighlights.com).

Card B

China Ticket Online

China Ticket Online is the largest English Ticket Website in China. We are the No. 1 visited Chinese ticketing website and are selected as "Top 10 Shopping Websites Recommended by Chinese Netizens." We Established brand name with top growth rate on Chinese live events ticketing market. Lenovo invested into PIAO.COM.CN due to its leading position and rapid development.

Ticket Booking Hotline: 86-10-64177845

Service details:

◇ Help you book Chinese live events tickets online or by telephone.

◇ Provide professional and safe delivery service.

Service features:

◇ A leading platform for you to book the tickets to that attracts you.

◇ In China the first and unique ticketing company to provide integrated online/offline tech: E-ticket, print at home, 0-delivery bank online sales, feature of "choosing preferred seats online, and on mobile", etc.

◇ National platform coverage: Beijing, Shanghai, Guangzhou, Nanjing. Remarkable sales performances nationwide and other 2nd-tier cities, such as Xi'an, Ji'nan, Nanchang, Changsha, Nanning, Suzhou, Xuzhou, etc.

◇ Management team has continuous innovation capability of creating and implementing new business in the context of industry evolution.

◇ The largest in-city-scope express company Pony Express (ponyex.com.cn) provides professional and safe delivery service.

Hot events:

Events	Venue	Time	Price
China Philharmonic Orchestra 2008—2009 Musical Festival	Forbidden City Music Hall	2009/ 4 /19	80, 180, 380, 480, 680, 880
Broadway Musical Cats	Beijing Exhibition Theater	2009/ 1/19—2009/1 /27	80, 180, 280, 480, 680, 880, 1280, 1680
Swan Lake By Russia Ballet Troupe	Poly Theatre	2009/ 1/31—2009/2 /1	50, 100, 200, 300, 500, 800, 1000
Traditional Chinese Acrobatics Show	Chaoyang Theater	Everyday 7:15 pm—20:30 pm	180, 280, 380, 580

For more information, please visit our website (www.piao.com.cn).

Unit Seven

Company A

AVON
the company for women

Company overview

Avon, the company for women, is a leading global beauty company. As the world's largest direct seller, Avon markets to women in well over 100 countries through over five million independent Avon Sales Representatives. Avon's product line includes beauty products, fashion jewelry and apparel, and features such well-recognized brand names as *Avon Color*, *Anew*, *Skin-So-Soft*, *Avon Solutions*, *Advance Techniques*, *Avon Naturals*, *Mark*, and *Avon Wellness*. Its dedication to supporting women touches not only beauty, but health, fitness, self-empowerment and financial independence. World-class scientists and technicians are masterminding Avon's latest product innovations. The Company for Women is staying at the forefront of the beauty marketplace by bringing leading-edge, technology-based products to women around the world.

Company's Products (e.g.)

AVON Color

Avon Color is Avon's flagship global color cosmetics brand which offers a variety of color cosmetics products, including foundations, powders, lip, eye and nail products. Avon Color's palettes contain shades that suit the skin tones of women of all ethnicities. Avon Color's product portfolio includes:

• Avon Instant Manicure self-adhesive dry nail enamel strips which can be applied to the nail and then formed to fit.

• Super FULL mascara, a volumizing mascara that makes lashes up to five times fuller.

• Daring Definition Mousse Mascara, which contains exclusive Aerosphere Technology to create a light mousse mascara that expands lashes for extreme definition and coats every lash for the deepest, darkest color.

• Shine Supreme Lip Color features Avon's first-to-market, patent-pending Rejuvi-Shine Technology, an exclusive blend of emollients, which adhere to the lips to deliver long-lasting color, and clear shine polymers which rise to the surface creating high, volume shine.

• My Lip Miracle, features breakthrough intuitive color technology, including new films that build exceptional shine and hydrophobic pigments that provide long wear with comfort. Liquiwax esters and gelled jojoba also add a cushioned and ultra-moisturizing feel.

Beyond Color

Beyond Color is a leading anti-aging color cosmetics brand enriched with sophisticated ingredients and Avon's patented technology to improve and enhance skin's texture around the eyes, cheeks and lips. Beyond Color's product portfolio includes:

• Avon Beyond Color Plumping Lip Color SPF with Double the Retinol, a lipstick formulated with a double dose of Retinol to help stimulate collagen renewal for lips that are firmer, youthful and more supple in appearance.

• Avon Beyond Color Lip Recovery Cream, an Avon innovation, a full color lip balm that instantly reduces the appearance of chapped lips.

• Avon Beyond Color Radiant Lifting Foundation SPF 12, a foundation with exclusive skin-lifting ingredients works to tone, firm and lift while liquid vitamin-enriched color blends seamlessly with your skin for a naturally flawless, radiant look.

Fragrance

Several of Avon fragrances for both men and women extend to a line of ancillary products such as body creams and lotions. Avon fragrance portfolio includes:

• Crystal Aura, Avon's latest fragrance which combines star fruit and amethyst rose with a radiant blend of musk and woods packaged beautifully with a crystal motif.

• Derek Jeter Driven, the new fragrance for men.

• Extraordinary which combines the richness of chocolate truffles and the sparkling effervescence of champagne.

Company B

Company overview

Founded in 1959, Amway is a global leader in direct selling, with over three million Independent Business Owners (IBOs) in over 80 countries and territories around the world. Amway products are sold directly to consumers by IBOs or sales representatives through one-on-one, in-person selling or via the internet. Our global vision is to help people live better lives and we share a commitment with our Business Owners to succeed in building better businesses that support better lives.

Company's Products (e.g.)

We are proud of our products, which generally fit into the health and beauty categories. Amway offers a range of exclusive, competitive brands that meet proven customer needs around the world. From nutritional supplements to water treatment, cosmetics to cleaning products, these brands are the solid foundation for a successful, independent retail business.

NUTRILITE Nutritional Supplements

NUTRILITE is the world's leading brand of vitamins, minerals and dietary supplements. We are proud to be the only source of NUTRILITE nutritional products, a respected name in supplementation around the world. Our vitamin, mineral, and herbal supplements are made from plants grown on our own certified organic farms in California, Washington, Mexico, and Brazil and manufactured under the strictest of standards to ensure consistency, quality and safety. Our best known multivitamin, DOUBLE X (TRIPLE X in Japan) Multivitamin/Multimineral Supplement, provides the nutrients that might be missing from your diet.

Amway Home Care Products

If it is cleaner laundry, easier dishwashing, and immaculate household surfaces you seek, the SA8™, DISH DROPS™, L.O.C.™ and PURSUE™ brands will do the job quickly and thoroughly, with stunning results. Amway's Home Care brands provide complete cleaning systems that fit with everyone's needs. Their versatile, effective product systems offer the features and benefits consumers want.

The eSpring Water Purifier is the first in-home system to combine ultraviolet light technology with a patented multi-stage carbon-block filter to provide the quality drinking water your family deserves.The eSpring Water Purifier destroys more than 99.99% of waterbourne disease-causing bacteria and effectively removes more than 140 contaminants. Other systems treat water eSpring purifies it.

The iCook Cookware is the healthiest way to cook anywhere in the world. The iCook Cookware brand delivers on its promise of quality and nutrition.